PRAISE FOR

MW01034143

"The current Classical Education revival has, for the most part, been operating on the 'grammar' level, recovering basic concepts and foundational truths. This book, literally, takes Classical Education to the next level, that of logic or dialectic. Not only does it show how to turn middle-school-aged children into excellent thinkers; it also recovers the teaching method of the great classical educators, the art of Socratic questioning, in which students are guided into discovering truth for themselves."

—Gene Edward Veith, Provost & Professor of Literature at Patrick Henry College; Author of *Classical Education*, with Andrew Kern

"Leigh Bortins has followed her wonderful book, *The Core*, with another sensational and inspirational work. *The Question* is for teachers and parents (who may be one and the same) who wish to see their students (and themselves) better prepared to be leaders rather than followers in our world. What training can best prepare a pupil in all matters in life? What can advance that training? This book offers richness and reward—tactics and tools—to all seeking knowledge and understanding."

—Becky Norton Dunlop, Vice President, The Heritage Foundation

"In *The Question*, Leigh Bortins reminds us that we must first seek if we are to find, and that often what we find are more questions that stretch and shape us into wiser people. Following the style of *The Core*, she gives clear and practical direction to educators who wish to learn the art of dialectic—asking wise questions that lead students to do the same.

Taking her point of departure from the common topics (definition, comparison, relationship, circumstance, testimony) of Aristotle, Leigh Bortins shows us how we can craft thoughtful questions of any art, study, and discipline and so cultivate students who engage, reflect, think, and gradually grow wise. In an age that privileges the *what*, Bortins helps us recover the more profound *why* that is at the heart of a classical education."

—Christopher Perrin, Co-chair, Society for Classical Learning Publisher, Classical Academic Press

"My next writing project is a book tentatively titled *How To Win An Argument*, and as I think about it and contemplate its design, I will have the advantage of Leigh Bortins' *The Question* as a guide and a model."

—Stanley Fish, Davidson-Kahn Distinguished University Professor of Humanities, Florida International University, Author of *How to Write a Sentence: And How to Read One*

"Leigh has furthered the cause of classical Christian education with this clear and insightful book. Her description of the arts includes both principles and practical applications, and her description of the Socratic method would be helpful to anyone aspiring to teach classically."

—John Mason Hodges, Founder and Director of the Center for Western Studies

Also by Leigh A. Bortins:

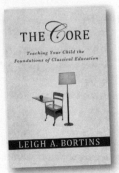

"*The Core* provides an altogether practical curriculum, a handy reference work for busy parents who want their children to enter adulthood fully equipped with the knowledge and skills possessed by responsible citizens, discerning consumers, and ethical selves."

—Mark Bauerlein, author of *The Dumbest Generation*

Available from
CLASSICALCONVERSATIONSBOOKS.COM

THE QUESTION

Teaching Your Child the
Essentials of Classical Education

LEIGH A. BORTINS

THE QUESTION
©2013 Classical Conversations® MultiMedia

All Scripture quotations, unless otherwise indicated, are taken from the King James Version of the Bible.

Printed in the United States of America

ISBN: 978-0-9851701-2-7

To Sarah Ellison, who asks many questions.

CONTENTS

ACKNOWLEDGMENTS

I want to thank Jen Greenholt, who has helped me write books ever since she edited my Doctorate of Ministry project and thesis. She has been instrumental in ensuring I meet deadlines, writing portions of my books, and reorganizing my sloppy thought processes. Cyndi Widman is the best final editor. She knows my mind so well that she can correct most of my grammatical errors without even asking me what I meant.

I am grateful to the Classical Conversations MultiMedia writing team as well as some guest writers. This book was definitely a team effort, and it includes contributions from Jennifer Courtney, Kate Deddens, Tucker Teague, Heather Shirley, Denise Moore, and Lisa Bailey. Matt Bianco and Courtney Sanford repeatedly met with Jen and me as we went through later revisions. And the book is beautifully formatted, thanks to Kathi James. Both Kathi and Courtney worked on the cover graphics. Thank you to Patty Bianco for providing meals during writing weeks; her delicious meals fed our souls as well as our bodies.

The appendices provide additional resources for your journey through the dialectic stage.

PREFACE

My husband, Rob, and I are in the midst of raising two sons who, at fifteen and seventeen years old, have managed to follow in their older two brothers' footsteps and now tower over me. I like that our sons have all grown past me in stature, as it reminds me that I want them to grow past me in many arenas of life. Their height forces me to look up to them. As I do, I pray that the people they encounter will also look up to them, not just physically but as men who are worthy of respect. I hope they become men who are careful and weigh the cost of their choices in light of more than personal ambition. I hope that they become kinder, more gracious adults than I am. I expect them to be better educated and more aware of the world they live in. More than I want my children to be wealthy or athletic or famous, I want them to be men of honor and integrity. As a classical educator, I know that we become what we mimic, so I want my young sons to spend time with men of honor and integrity, like their father and older brothers, their pastor, their employers, as well as the neighbor who spends his retirement years finding affordable housing for those struggling financially in our county.

I want many of the same things all loving parents want for their children. Yet, it seems that we live in a culture in which youth are expected to behave as juvenilely as possible so they can relate to movies called *Jackass* and reality shows called *16 and Pregnant*. When I first moved to our county, I asked other local employers where they found their summer help since I needed to hire some students for our shipping department. I was stunned when the first two men I asked said they would never hire anyone under thirty years old. My experience with young people has always been positive. I recently asked a thirty-year-old if he had a friend I could hire to do some major moving of dirt in our garden, and he said he would not hire any of his friends. He told me he knew a guy in his sixties that he would recommend.

It seems that today's youth are often criticized for their poor work ethic, and logically, the only one to blame is my generation—after all, we raised them. They copy us. I know the older generation has always looked down on the younger with some disdain, but somehow it seems especially disheartening when, during an economic downturn, a young man cannot recommend a single friend to work, although he can tell me what computer game they are playing as they sit at home.

What are we doing to teach our children to be employable, respectful, hardworking initiators who work because it is pleasurable to serve others? Are we looking up to our youth as they grow past us, or are we crippling them with low expectations? When I analyze the cultural and academic attitudes toward our youth, it seems as though we are content to put them in a holding pattern until they are "grown up"—but then later we wonder why they never grew up!

For example, in the past, a youth could babysit, usher viewers into movie theaters, deliver papers, or mow lawns without Red Cross certifications, child labor laws, or minimum wages hindering their opportunities. Now they are told they cannot clean floors at the local warehouse until they are fourteen and if any heavy equipment is used in the building, they have to wait until they are sixteen. Many states have increased the age to obtain driving licenses to seventeen or eighteen, when it used to be fifteen or sixteen. We cannot tell our youth that they are immature and then be surprised when they act like it. Some will argue that these actions are taken in the interest of safety. But, have we stopped to consider that there may be worse things than the risk of being physically injured? The invisible injuries to the souls of our youth might arguably be worse.

I believe the same attitude is pervasive in academics. Middle-school students are considered too old to memorize multiplication tables (which they still need to do) and too young to think abstractly (which they can be trained to do), so we do not give them particularly meaningful schoolwork right at the time they are ready to be challenged. A negative cycle begins. Our students recognize that the work they have been given to do is inconsequential, so they do not give it their best effort, and as a result, few adults are willing to trust them with work that **is** consequential. I think we're not quite sure what to do with them, as they are neither small children nor young adults. In earlier times, the same model of education that prepared thirteen-year-olds to apprentice to businessmen and tradesmen also prepared fourteen- and fifteen-year-olds to enter Harvard and Yale. Adults knew how to teach this age group. They taught their youth to look outward to give them a vision of how their world could expand while their minds and bodies grew. I know today's students can be resourceful and responsible. They can be trusted and respected. If we return to the classical model of education, I know that today's students can be just as resourceful and innovative. As they gain dialectical skills, we will be able to trust them with important responsibilities and look up to them with respect once again.

Through my work with Classical Conversations, I have the privilege of hiring lots of competent students to help with camps, ship from our warehouse, and manage social media. How do I find such trustworthy students? They are the same ones who work hard at Latin, logic, mock trial, and science fairs; they labor over their writing essays and argue over the decisions of Hamlet and Achilles. They are students who have been asked to give up the constant buzz of social activity to contemplate, wrestle, grapple, and struggle with hard things. They know that working in an air-conditioned warehouse with plenty of food and water is easy compared to picking tobacco leaves or bundling hay because they read about the lives of children in the past. They actually know things and are engaged by the adults with whom they work. These are today's students who study the classical model of education. No matter their physical stature, these are students my generation looks up to because these students are formed by respect—respect for those who have struggled with the great classical conversations of the past and respect for the adults who teach them how to question the relationship of mankind's past conversations with today's concerns. This book is about restoring a model of education that teaches adolescents to embrace the tension between the relative safety and ease of youth and the struggles and responsibilities of adulthood. Just as healthy nutrition, activity, and rest are necessary for growing the body, asking questions is essential (and natural) for nourishing the mind and spirit of our soon-to-be young adults.

Leigh A. Bortins

FOREWORD

More than twenty years ago, I was introduced to the idea of classical education when a friend gave me a copy of Dorothy Sayers' essay "The Lost Tools of Learning." I was so inspired by her ideas that I wrote an essay predicting that classical education would be one of the top new trends in homeschooling.

However, the more I learned about classical education, the more I wondered how accessible this form of teaching would be for real-life moms and dads. Then I met Leigh Bortins. Leigh created Classical Conversations, which has, for thousands of families, answered the question "How do I deliver this kind of excellent education to my children while retaining my sanity?"

Leigh's new book takes the reader a step further along the path of becoming a classical mentor—which requires the teaching parent to also model lifelong learning. As a lawyer, I relate to the methodology that Leigh promotes in this book. In a trial, the lawyer's job is not to tell the whole story and give all of the facts himself. He gives the jury an overview, but the vast majority of the information the jury must receive requires the lawyer to ask questions of the witnesses. By the lawyer's skillful posing of the right series of questions, the story of what really happened begins to unfold. The lawyer is not supposed to give the jurors a single fact; he is instead supposed to ask questions.

At the end of the trial, the lawyer's job is to sum up the story into a logical and cohesive whole. This requires getting the facts straight and utilizing a high level of analysis. The lawyer has to explain what the law is, suggest how the facts apply to the law, and encourage the jury to make the necessary synthesis of facts and law and reach a conclusion.

A good trial lawyer resembles a good teacher. It is essential for the skillful practitioner of both disciplines to be able to help jurors or students discover both facts and big truths through the process of asking good questions.

Leigh would make a great lawyer because she is a great teacher. And I am confident that anyone who reads this book will become a better teacher by learning to ask better questions.

> ***Michael P. Farris***, *founder and chancellor of Patrick Henry College*
> *and founder and chairman of the Home School Legal Defense Association*

INTRODUCTION

When I began teaching my own children classically, few were teaching in this mode beyond the grammar school stage. Middle-school students were generally leaving classical private or home schools to re-enter the public school arena. The need for information about the foundations of a classical education was overwhelming, but no one seemed to care much about the dialectic or rhetorical arts of learning. Well, the restoration of classical education is advancing, and now the general population is curious about the dialectic arts. So, I am delighted to continue the conversation that began with *The Core: Teaching Your Child the Foundations of Classical Education*. The subtitle for this book is *Teaching Your Child the Essentials of Classical Education* in keeping with the notion that the essential skill needed to transition from the proverbial sponge of childhood to the mature rhetorician of adulthood is learning to ask questions.

In part 1, I provide an overview of classical education, focusing on the dialectic. Chapter 1 touches on the reasons to consider the classical model of education and why this model protects our humanity in a world increasingly dependent on machines. Chapter 2 is a discussion about the dialectic arts in detail. In chapter 3, I answer some frequently asked questions and look ahead to the changes that will result from a culture that embraces the classical model.

In part 2, I describe the art of the dialectic within specific subjects. Chapters 4 through 11 will concentrate on the following individual fields: reading, writing, math, geography and current events, logic, history, science, and the fine arts. The epilogue looks ahead to the rhetoric stage of the classical model as I reflect on the process of writing a book, because a book is the ultimate form of rhetoric.

Part 3 is made up of the appendices, wherein I will provide additional resources for your journey through the dialectic stage. Specifically, appendix 1 presents a list of model questions to jump-start dialectic learning. Appendix 2 provides a list of resources for further reading.

PART ONE

————

THE CLASSICAL MODEL

CHAPTER ONE

WHY WE STILL NEED CLASSICAL EDUCATION

"A child kicks his legs rhythmically through excess, not absence, of life. Because children have abounding vitality, because they are in spirit fierce and free, therefore they want things repeated and unchanged. They always say, 'Do it again'; and the grown-up person does it again until he is nearly dead. For grown-up people are not strong enough to exult in monotony. But perhaps God is strong enough to exult in monotony. It is possible that God says every morning, 'Do it again' to the sun; and every evening, 'Do it again' to the moon. It may not be automatic necessity that makes all daisies alike; it may be that God makes every daisy separately, but has never got tired of making them. It may be that He has the eternal appetite of infancy; for we have sinned and grown old, and our Father is younger than we."

—G. K. Chesterton, *Orthodoxy*

THE PURPOSE OF CLASSICAL EDUCATION

The purpose of a classical education is two-fold: to know who you are and to know where you are. As a Christian, I would restate those purposes: to know whose you are and to know where you are going. Education teaches us to rightly assess mankind and the world in which he lives. Classical education consists of teaching seven liberal arts that have been instrumental in the formation of Western civilization. The trivium arts—grammar, dialectic, and rhetoric—allow us to grapple with words. The trivium engages us in the realm of ideas and abstractions. The quadrivium arts—algebra, geometry, harmonics, and astronomy—give us a deeper, numerical understanding of what we began in the trivium and allow us to subdue the universe. The quadrivium enables us to engage in concrete reality. Together, the trivium and quadrivium form the humanities, the arts that make us human.

We exchange knowledge, information, and ideas through words, spoken or symbolic. Words are processed, weighed, and analyzed through other words, even if they originated in a picture or image or experience. Words are used to share concrete and abstract ideas. Words allow us to build great cities, negotiate peace between countries, and share a pleasant meal with friends and family. The goal of education is to teach children to become adults who can handle complex ideas, in uncertain situations, with confidence. We feel confident when we can competently manage words and ideas. Moreover, those particular skills enable us to assess mankind and the world around us.

My previous book, *The Core: Teaching your Child the Foundations of Classical Education*, focused on the art of grammar. This book focuses on the second art of the trivium, the dialectic. As students learn to ask questions, they learn to ask follow-up questions, which lend the mind to the formation of logical processes. I often think of the word *dialogue* when I think of the dialectic because students practice thinking best when thinking aloud with an interested adult who asks and answers many questions. The dialectic arts can be practiced in all arenas of life as students become more abstract thinkers with broader experiences and vocabularies.

Beginning with chapter 2, the rest of this book provides copious examples of the dialectic to be practiced at home, in the classroom, and in the car. First, as a reminder to readers of *The Core* (and for the benefit of those who have stumbled upon *The Question* first), I want to review some basic concepts concerning the trivium. As a personal indulgence, I've included an epilogue on rhetoric at the end of this book to whet my readers' appetites for more of the seven liberal arts.

In *The Rhetoric Companion*, by N. D. and Douglas Wilson, there is a chapter called "Basic Copiousness." The authors make the point that a copious vocabulary supported by voluminous reading allows one to pull thoughts into any context. A mark of being educated is the ability to use lots of words well. Developing the art of memorization adds to the ease of developing a copious vocabulary. Memorization is a lost art that should be fairly easy to recover, since every human, from Shakespearean actors to three-year-olds, memorizes his mother tongue. We have not lost the ability to memorize. Every infant memorizes. What we have lost is the intentionality of learning the art of memorizing.

Technology has contributed to the recent rejection of repetition as a good educational tool when it comes to mastering the multiplication tables, identifying geographic locations, or learning the correct spelling of words. After all, you can look it up. In the popular *Everyday Math* text series used in public schools across the country, the editors state this prevalent theme in the *Teacher's Reference Manual*:

> The authors of *Everyday Math* do not believe it is worth the time and effort to develop highly efficient paper-and-pencil algorithms for all possible whole number, fractions and decimal division problems. . . . It is simply counterproductive to invest hours of precious class time on such algorithms. The math payoff is not worth the cost, particularly because quotients can be found quickly and accurately with a calculator. (Garelick, 34)

Can you imagine if the NFL commissioner said something equally as silly? Every athlete and musician knows that they must overpractice before new skills become easy and natural. And so our modern educational system inculcates weak study habits. Think of how this weakening applies to our culture. Do congressmen have the Constitution memorized? Do our congregants have Scriptures memorized? Do students have quotes from classical literature memorized? Yet, we'd be disgruntled if our car mechanic had to look up the names of parts on our car before he repaired it. A possible counterargument says that we already experience this, as today's cars are so computerized. But, our family has two cars with computerized parts that our dealer's mechanics just can't get right. Are we really satisfied with a society that has to look up everything?

The purpose of a classical education is to ensure that one is never excluded from any realm of human endeavor. This requires consistent discipleship or mentoring by a concerned adult over a long period of time with very specific academic goals, for eventually, the child wants to know why she must learn so much terminology and what to do with what she has learned. These natural questions lead children into dialectic and rhetorical studies, which give them the keys to make wise judgments, unlock complex ideas, and access every realm of human endeavor. In this way, classical education gives our children the tools to know God and to make Him known, no matter what career path they choose to tread.

THE CLASSICAL MODEL IS THE METHOD

The classical model works. It is intimately linked to the humanities because it is the educational model that makes us human. Although Dorothy Sayers, a novelist and friend of C. S. Lewis and J. R. R. Tolkien, described a classical model of academics in her seminal lecture on the classical model, "The Lost Tools of Learning," her thoughts are applicable to every endeavor. The novice must first behave like a parrot, repeating the basic vocabulary, ideas, and concepts of the master craftsman. Every student must learn to speak the language of the subject.

For instance, when I laid sod for the first time, I had to learn the language of sodding. When I called the sod company, they me asked what kind of grass I wanted. I did not know. "Grass" grass? So I asked what kind they sold. They told me I could have Patriot Bermuda that day, or if I waited they would have hardier varieties of Bermuda in one week, and they would also begin cutting Centipede. I did not know this grass grammar, so I hung up and called my husband. He was happy with the Patriot. (He plays golf and knows a lot about grasses.) So I prepared the ground and rolled out the sod and kept it watered until it took root. Meanwhile, the lawn maintenance guy showed up and told me that I had Centipede, various Bermudas, and Bahia. He wanted to know if I considered the Bahia a weed or if I wanted to keep it. How did I know? I wanted him to ask me about the Centipede and Bermuda because I knew they were grasses I had paid for, so I was pretty sure I did not want to pay to kill those! I told him to keep them all. Three weeks later, when all was so beautiful, we decided to kill the Bahia. It grew too fast compared to the others, and the yard never looked mowed. So, even though I am middle-aged, I still had to learn new grammar. And I learned it by

Lifelong learners are always in grammar school.

listening to the saleslady, repeating back to the saleslady the words she said, calling my husband and telling him the words, calling the saleslady back and telling her the words, and then talking to the lawn guy, who had added one new word to the conversation.

Now, if you visit me, I can show you the various grasses in my yard and tell you their growth patterns. I am not a grass expert. I'm only in grass grammar school, but I am on my way to understanding my lawn better. Lifelong learners are always in grammar school. If I can share new ideas with others using the specific language of a subject, then I am becoming educated in that field.

Classical education is analogous to brain training. When encountering new information, the brain must know how to store data, retrieve and process data, and express data. You already have the skill to learn anything if you know how to perform these elementary steps:

- Memorize vocabulary and rules (also called *grammar*)
- Process new concepts logically (also called *dialectic*)
- Clearly explain the grammar and dialectic to others (also called *rhetoric*)

GRAMMAR RESTORES MEMORIZATION SKILLS

Grammar, the first skill set to practice, roughly corresponds to the stage of elementary school, or to students up to about age eleven or twelve. *Webster's Universal Unabridged Dictionary* defines *grammar* as, "general systems and principles of speech and writing" (1936, p. 738, def. 1–4). Definition 5 explains *grammar* as, "an outline of the principles of any subject; as, a grammar of logic." A more contemporary dictionary, the *Oxford English Dictionary*, defines *grammar* as, "the fundamental principles or rules of an art or science" (def. 6), citing an example from *The Times* of London (1963): "The *grammar* of the film was established."

The foundation of a classical education begins with parents teaching children the art of memorization and grammar studies. Whether or not adults and professional educators believe it, children love rote memorization. They cannot wait to say, "Do it again." All is mysterious, new, and wonderful to them. Go ahead and repeat whatever it is, for all of creation is delightful. Robert Farrar Capon, in *The Supper of the Lamb*, tells us that our response to "loveliness is not always delight: It is, far more often than it should be, boredom. And that is not only odd, it is tragic; for boredom is not neutral—it is the fertilizing principle of unloveliness" (3). We adults often feel bored by repetition because our business does not afford us time to find the loveliness. I do not want my children's education to be so fast-paced and so abstract that there is no time to meditate on the fantastical. I do not want them to treat glorious facts as mundane.

Grammar studies assume there is basic information all humans should know and aim to ensure that students learn this information. I think geographical terms fall in this category. It is odd that we all live on only one planet yet few of us spend a concentrated amount of time naming its parts. In Genesis, Adam's first job was to name the animals. So that is the first thing we teach our youngest children to do: to name animals, people, and all the things they see. We can extend that example to the place we live. *North, south*, *Africa*, *Rwanda*, *mountain*, and *current* are good geography terms that most of us know. Yet when I ask groups of adults to sketch the globe, its five great circles of latitude, and the seven continents, they mostly look at me rather than their paper. Earth is the only place they have lived, and they really know so little about its general structure.

Grammar studies also assume there are words that we are delighted to know and should spend much time saying. For a long time, as children, my boys would say, "'Me, too,' said Amanda" whenever they wanted to be included in an activity because we had read a delightful picture book where a silly little girl named Amanda would say that phrase all the time. Every family should have idioms, phrases, and quotations that are definitive to the thought life of that family. Sayings like "Haste makes waste" and poems like "The Pirate Don Dirk of Dowdee" provide funny memories for our family. Calling one "a wicked sinner" or "o, best beloved" has special meaning to our family. We dwell on words because they bring us closer together and link one context to another. When I told my seventeen-year-old son that he was "a strong and delicious word never before seen, never to be repeated," he immediately posted it on his Facebook wall and has asked me to repeat this thought from Michael D. O'Brien to his friends. I have met a two-year-old who named her cat Amenhotep after hearing her older siblings say the pharaoh's name over and over in a timeline they were memorizing. And what child does not laugh the first time she hears the word *onomatopoeia*?

In summary, rote memorization is attractive because

- it strengthens the student's brain by straining it a little more each day,
- the student takes in quality content that informs an educated person, and
- and it tickles our senses with delightful and meaningful words.

Modern educators often want their children to like learning. In contrast, classical educators want to prepare children to work hard at learning until the skills *become* enjoyable. Consider this important difference: classical teachers prefer to teach children to *like* memorizing quality content (such as a rhyme or sonnet) so that one day they can *enjoy* difficult assignments. We want their self-esteem to be based on actual accomplishments.

LOGIC RESTORES ANALYTICAL SKILLS

Once the brain has gathered and stored information, questions are the logical next step. We will discuss this step in more detail in the next chapter, but at its most basic, the logic or dialectic stage teaches us to ask questions and seek answers. Abstract thought allows us to compare the more concrete ideas learned in the grammar stage. Dialectic-age students naturally debate the merits of anything. So, the classical model complements and exercises their natural tendencies to "talk back" by teaching young teenagers to argue effectively by using formal logic. It takes a wise parent to trust that it is appropriate to teach her young child to argue well, to ask questions, to make new comparisons, to examine true relationships, and to discover false premises. After all, we may have to correct our own dogma if we engage in deep discussion with the next generation.

As students become conversant in a subject, they learn to apply their new vocabulary in a logical context. For example, a student progresses from memorizing math facts and math laws to their logical application—algebra. Algebra forces the student to ask questions. There are so many ways to approach an algebra problem that students are stymied when they don't know which questions to ask. Teachers often think their students do not know what to do next because they have not memorized the next step, when, really, they do not know the next question to ask. Modern math students are shown how to cross multiply to solve for an unknown in a fraction, but classically trained students would be expected to recognize that the identity law is the rule that allows them to cross multiply. Classically trained math students consistently ask, "How do I use the identity law to solve this equation?" The grammar of math problem-solving is specifically identified and studied so that students begin to learn that algebra is the logical application of only a few simple questions answered by the laws and operations already learned in arithmetic.

A good historian will have learned historical grammar, such as a basic timeline of events, which provides her with mental pegs on which to hang new information (the Renaissance followed the Middle Ages, for example). She also memorizes maps so she can see in her mind's eye where events happened. This data is learned so she can question the information. For example, why did Italy switch sides in World War I? What events made the Italians realign their allegiance? We can analyze Italy's decisions only if we know how geography, economics, faith, and politics were influential to the power struggle. The historian wants to logically analyze pertinent facts related to Italy in order to form coherent conclusions.

The blank piece of paper and a well-inked pen become the main tools of the dialectic in academics, while conversations and questions are the main tools used spontaneously in everyday life. The dialectic develops through lots of questions and answers recreated in well-written paragraphs. During the dialectic or logic stage, proficient readers learn the skills of decoding, comprehending, and analyzing increasingly complicated literature while simultaneously developing writing skills, particularly paragraph development. Excerpts, worksheets, and handouts are replaced with blank sheets of paper on which children transcribe their own knowledge. This develops a culture or "habit of mind" that enables the student to think on paper. The child who has mastered grammar has learned the basic structure of words and sentences. Now it is time to teach the child to put correctly written sentences into logical order within a topical paragraph. And so the learner asks questions: "Is my point clear?" "Did I use related examples?" "Did I clinch my opening sentence?" "Has communication occurred, or did I just vent?"

In summary, we love the dialectic because

- it fosters conversations,
- it utilizes people rather than machines, and
- it tickles our senses with curiosities.

RHETORIC RESTORES COMMUNICATION SKILLS

Today, the word *rhetoric* is often defined as "venting, or meaningless words, or sound bites." Aristotle, however, formalized it as a course of study to train people in public speaking. To classical educators, *rhetoric* refers to the practice of very specific skills in order to be the most persuasive in expressing truth, goodness, and beauty. Rhetoric students are able to recognize how the particulars of one specialization relate to the particulars of another. As Christians, we practice rhetorical skills in light of our desire to woo others to love Christ. You can be absolutely right in an argument, but if your opponent does not feel respected, he is less likely to be persuaded in the argument. Rhetoric skills should help us defend our point of view in light of a true understanding of our audience's beliefs. In rhetoric school, students learn to speak and write persuasively and eloquently about a particular topic while integrating allusions and examples from other fields of study. Rhetorical skills are the final tools practiced in a trivium education. Once grammar, logic, and rhetoric are overpracticed, a student is prepared to tackle any field of study.

If students have really mastered the language of a field of study, we want them to be able to express the conclusions of their questions. This is often referred to as having strong communication skills because expressing yourself can be practiced. The term *rhetoric* is closely tied to the idea of oral, documented, or physical evidence explained to the appropriate audience. For example, a student might be asked to write an essay comparing Harper Lee's *To Kill a Mockingbird* to E. M. Forster's *A Passage to India*. Both stories are about a court case concerning an assault on a woman that never happened. The point of both books is to discuss racial oppression. The white woman in *A Passage to India* confesses her lie, contrary to the woman in *To Kill a Mockingbird*, yet both novels end on a note of hope. Both books have loveable characters and despicable actions. A student of rhetoric needs to know the vocabulary of the countries, cultures, and court systems involved. She needs to ask comparative questions about the plots, the characters' motives, and the authors' intentions before she will be able to articulate any thoughtful written analysis. I will cover this concept in more detail in the chapter on writing.

It often helps to talk aloud about a topic before writing a paper because it takes interaction and reflection to investigate an idea. The student discovers the flaws in her thinking by presenting it to someone else, and furthermore, the listener provides another perspective to refine or clarify the original idea. In this way, the dialectic forms the rhetorical expression. As a child learns to engage with other voices during the writing process, she loses the fear of presenting her final product. After all, she has already played tug-of-war over the idea with another thinker.

The classical rhetorician also learns that ideas have consequences. Even if the ideas have been imparted to her by "dead authors," they still have current applications. She needs to not only judge the characters and their actions in their historical context but also address similar situations in current events. Have we improved race relations since the author's time? Is race really the issue, or is it our inability to love our neighbor as ourselves? We may hate the discrimination in the book, but are there cultures we currently discriminate against? The student who can calmly, simply, logically, and eloquently express thoughts through words or actions is a rhetorician. A classically trained student will have the skills needed to read the original text, ask and find answers to her own questions, and clearly present her findings to her audience in a meaningful manner. By contrast, modern high schools emphasize a survey of textbooks in which the authors trivialize history and literature, first, by teaching through excerpts and summaries rather than original documents, and second, by reducing their ideas to multiple-choice answers on a test.

In summary, we love rhetorical skills because
- they are practiced by leading discussions,
- they allow group discussions to remain focused, and

• they succeed when applied to a reasoned argument.

Almost any skilled person you encounter must have rhetorical tools to be successful in his or her field. For example, a good surgeon who owns a successful practice is usually a great rhetorician. First, he learned the grammar of anatomy. He knows the names of all the parts of the body. He knows the vocabulary of his field of expertise. He is trusted because he can explain the purpose of a heart valve or an enzyme. Second, he has learned to compare, analyze, and process the facts he knows about anatomy. He understands how the parts of the body work together. He can diagnose a hip problem by watching how a person walks. The experienced surgeon learned this by spending a lot of time around bodies and talking to other surgeons. He is trusted because his experience of repeatedly examining many people under the supervision of another has enabled him to easily diagnose medical issues. Lastly, he learned how to express his knowledge clearly. He knows how to explain to patients their medical condition, and he can even impart his surgical knowledge to others. His honestly earned reputation means that his patients will recommend his services to their friends. Trust comes from more than knowledge; we have trouble trusting a surgeon with a bad bedside manner. A good rhetorician knows how to share his knowledge confidently and wisely in order to benefit the greater community.

Excellence in any realm of study requires perseverance, sweat, wrestling, time, tears, and just plain labor over the fundamentals. I know it is a cliché, but you only live one day at a time. Your children are not given to you fully grown. Look for the grammar, dialectic, and rhetoric as you go about your day. Your brain is always thinking. Notice what it is thinking and how you learn so that you can share your "ah-ha" moments with your own children. Your children may not care about what you learned at that moment, but they will begin to realize that reflection and thinking and learning are normal parts of life. When parents model the trivium arts of memorizing, questioning, and conversing, even difficult subjects will become accessible to the entire family. The classically trained student will rise to meet the challenge of a rigorous education.

Mastering the *skill* of the dialectic is essential. In addition, the *content* mastered is significant because it provides timeless material to study. The classical model is just commonsense education, and it applies equally to vocational trades and scholarly endeavors. The classical arts of grammar, dialectic, and rhetoric were the norm for earlier generations of Americans. Anyone can study these arts. Our job as parents is to restore our own education as we translate our vision of quality academics into small, daily deeds. In this way, education is transformed from an endeavor rewarded by grades for short-term memory into the gift of a lifestyle of learning. This book naturally divides the dialectic into small, attainable steps so that all families can restore this model to their students, no matter what their situation in life may be.

CHAPTER TWO

———

HOW THE DIALECTIC TEACHES FAMILIES TO WRESTLE

"Some things I have said of which I am not altogether confident. But that we shall be better and braver and less helpless if we think that we ought to enquire, than we should have been if we indulged in the idle fancy that there was no knowing and no use in seeking to know what we do not know;—that is a theme upon which I am ready to fight, in word and deed, to the utmost of my power."

—Socrates, Plato's *Meno*

Transforming your child's education in terms of the classical model, the human soul, and the demands of the global economy may seem to be less of a priority when you come face-to-face with your twelve-year-old offspring. He is in the process of becoming an abstract thinker, but you might not know it by the kinds of exchanges that take place at the dinner table. At this age, youth excel at asking the kinds of questions designed specifically to aggravate and exasperate anyone in a position of authority. "Who says?", "Why not?", "Who cares?", and "How should I know?" are just a few of the many possibilities. Then, too often, when it is time to talk about current events, math, or classic literature, the rapid-fire questions are replaced by a mumbled, "I dunno." As a parent, it is easy to become frustrated, but if you can learn to channel your child's inquisitive and argumentative nature into constructive questions, you will be well on your way to finding delight in the dialectic stage of classical education.

A DEFINITION OF DIALECTIC

Definitions are an essential first step in any pursuit of understanding. Let's begin with a discussion of what is meant by the words "logic" and "dialectic," two words I will be using interchangeably. Travel back in time with me to the Middle Ages, when scholars in Europe made a concerted effort to revive the classical model of education. One of the most determined advocates for classical education was a bishop called John of Salisbury, whose professional career included serving under several archbishops of Canterbury and walking a delicate line between the Catholic Church and Henry II, a king of lax ethics. Talk about a man who needed to be able to speak with diplomacy and delicacy! For John, mastery of the dialectic was literally a matter of life or death. It is no wonder that John believed so staunchly in the importance of studying logic and argumentation. His treatise on the subject, *Metalogicon*, became a classic of educational philosophy.

John turned to theologian and philosopher Saint Augustine for a definition of logic. In his *De Dialectica*, Augustine called logic "the science of effective argumentation" that seeks "to investigate the truth and meaning of what is said" (*Metalogicon* 80–81). Whereas "grammar chiefly examines the *words* that express meanings, dialectic investigates the *meanings* expressed by words" (81, emphasis added). Okay, but what does *that* mean? Good question! In asking it, you are illustrating the point at hand. Augustine's definition is made up of words. A grammar student might simply memorize the definition of logic, but a dialectic student would want to understand what it means. By nature, children progress from wanting to absorb knowledge to wanting to question, challenge, and argue with the basic facts and parroted ideas they have learned during the grammar stage.

In writing this book, I have in mind the eleven- to fourteen-year-old age range, but every child reaches the dialectic stage at a different time, and all of us are grammarians as well as logicians any time we study a new subject. If your child has not yet mastered the basic grammar of a subject, or if he has not yet begun to see the tension between ideas, I recommend that you rest in the grammar stage until he is ready to move ahead. I suggest that you begin with my earlier book *The Core: Teaching Your Child the Foundations of Classical Education*. When your child begins to argue with the most basic set of instructions and loses patience with your reserve weapon of choice—"Because I said so"—you will know that it is time to turn to the art of logic.

Dorothy Sayers says in "The Lost Tools of Learning" that the basic objective of the logic stage of education should be to prepare both teacher and student "to detect fallacy, slipshod reasoning, ambiguity, irrelevance, and redundancy, and to pounce upon them like rats." Too often, classical educators limit the dialectic stage by simply adding formal logic to an existing curriculum and calling the project finished. Formal logic is an excellent way to train your brain to think in an organized fashion, and we will discuss it in more depth in the chapter on logic, but dialectic learning is so much more than a subject. When you begin to think dialectically, you begin to ask questions about all subject areas. You begin to define terms, compare ideas, and recognize patterns and rules. In science, men like Aristotle and Linnaeus recognized that our brains naturally group similar things together as a way of making sense of what we see. Out of that natural way of thinking, they used a series of questions to develop scientific systems of classification. In the sixteenth century, international merchants knew that they needed good

When you begin to think dialectically, you begin to ask questions about all subject areas. You begin to define terms, compare ideas, and recognize patterns and rules.

translators to accompany them because they had to speak a common language in order to negotiate trades. Now, when students practice argumentation and debate, they begin by defining the terms of their topic so that both opponents and audience will know what the debaters mean by "policy" or "democracy" or "justice."

One of the criticisms modern educators raise against the classical model is that it focuses excessively on rote memorization (a pejorative term) at the risk of brainwashing the child rather than teaching him critical thinking (a desirable outcome). I would say to them that you cannot obtain critical thinking without memorization. Let me give you an example. Imagine that you want to learn more about rocks, but you do not have access to books or the Internet. How would you begin? Well, you would need to collect a variety of rocks. Then you could figure out what all of the rocks had in common. "What makes them rocks?" "What is their essence, or 'rock-ness'?" You could compare them to other objects such as pieces of wood and empty turtle shells. You could compare them to one another. "How do they differ?" None of this would be possible if you had not first collected a pile of rocks.

In other words, we must collect knowledge before we seek understanding. In the same way, the grammar stage is not the end of education. A pile of rocks that sits in your closet serves no purpose, but if you gather understanding about rocks, you might be able to use your knowledge to build a structure that can withstand earthquakes, or to identify an ancient artifact, or to carve a monument like Mount Rushmore. Understanding, honed in the logic or dialectic stage, is the necessary middle step between acquiring knowledge and practicing wisdom through rhetoric.

Ultimately, dialectical thinkers learn to integrate individual subjects into a comprehensive vision of the world. This is the true meaning of the term *critical thinking*. Unfortunately, the phrase has become a buzzword in education, on a level with "creative problem-solving" and "career readiness." We are told that these are desirable traits, but no one is certain how best to foster them within the family, let alone on a national level. Our goal must be to reclaim the idea of critical thinking and give it fresh meaning. Socratic discussion, which I cover in detail in this chapter, will help your children ask insightful questions about every subject they study, in order to hone their thinking about that subject and pursue truth through it.

A WALK WITH SOCRATES

Historians don't know much about the actual life of the Greek philosopher and teacher named Socrates; most of what they do know comes from a series of dialogues written after his death by his student Plato, around the turn of the fourth century BC. In these dialogues, the most famous of which is *The Republic*, Socrates uses a series of leading questions to point his students toward knowledge and away from faulty thinking. The dialogues portray Socrates sitting down with students who demand that he answer difficult questions about ethics, politics, and society. The type of teaching he models in his responses is known as the Socratic method, but the Greeks were not the only ones to employ this technique. Similar approaches can be found in Hebrew schools. In Eastern Europe from the fifteenth and sixteenth centuries onward, the Hebrew word *pilpul*, meaning "sharp analysis," was used to describe the vigorous questioning and debate surrounding interpretation of the *Talmud*, the text that forms the basis of rabbinical law. American author Chaim Potok's novel *The Chosen* gives a vivid contemporary example, telling the story of two Jewish boys who learn in this way.

The common factor between these historical methods is that a mentoring teacher uses questions to push his students toward greater knowledge and a better understanding of truth. As Tracy Lee Simmons explains in *Climbing Parnassus*, "The novice is thereby led through the bracken of his assumptions and biases to the clear light of knowledge. The teacher holds him responsible for all words and ideas he utters, pressing him to define them with greater exactitude. Just what do we mean by Justice, Freedom, Courage, Virtue? Are they achievable in this life? Or are they beyond the grasp of even the most righteous? And this method remains a cardinal means of testing intellectual mettle" (52).

Let's look at an example from *The Republic*. Don't worry so much about understanding the argument at this point; focus on the kinds of questions that Socrates asks.

Excerpts from *The Republic*, Book I

SOCRATES And what is that which justice gives, and to whom?

POLEMARCHUS If, Socrates, we are to be guided at all by the analogy of the preceding instances, then justice is the art which gives good to friends and evil to enemies.

SOC. That is his meaning then?

POL. I think so.

. . .

SOC. But see the consequence:—Many a man who is ignorant of human nature has friends who are bad friends, and in that case he ought to do harm to them; and he has good enemies whom he ought to benefit; but, if so, we shall be saying the very opposite of that which we affirmed to be the meaning of Simonides [who said justice is giving good to friends and evil to enemies].

POL. Very true, he said: and I think that we had better correct an error into which we seem to have fallen in the use of the words "friend" and "enemy."

SOC. What was the error, Polemarchus? I asked.

POL. We assumed that he is a friend who seems to be or who is thought good.

SOC. And how is the error to be corrected?

POL. We should rather say that he is a friend who is, as well as seems, good; and that he who seems only, and is not good, only seems to be and is not a friend; and of an enemy the same may be said.

SOC. You would argue that the good are our friends and the bad our enemies?

POL. Yes.

SOC. And instead of saying simply as we did at first, that it is just to do good to our friends and harm to our enemies, we should further say: It is just to do good to our friends when they are good and harm to our enemies when they are evil?

POL. Yes, that appears to me to be the truth.

SOC. But ought the just to injure any one at all?

POL. Undoubtedly he ought to injure those who are both wicked and his enemies.

SOC. When horses are injured, are they improved or deteriorated?

POL. The latter.

SOC. Deteriorated, that is to say, in the good qualities of horses, not of dogs?

POL. Yes, of horses.

SOC. And dogs are deteriorated in the good qualities of dogs, and not of horses?

POL. Of course.

SOC. And will not men who are injured be deteriorated in that which is the proper virtue of man?

POL. Certainly.

SOC. And that human virtue is justice?

POL. To be sure.

SOC. Then men who are injured are of necessity made unjust?

POL. That is the result.

SOC. But can the musician by his art make men unmusical?

POL. Certainly not.

SOC. Or the horseman by his art make them bad horsemen?

POL. Impossible.

SOC. And can the just by justice make men unjust, or speaking generally, can the good by virtue make them bad?

POL. Assuredly not.

SOC. Any more than heat can produce cold?

POL. It cannot.

SOC. Or drought moisture?

POL. Clearly not.

SOC. Nor can the good harm any one?

POL. Impossible.

SOC. And the just is the good?

POL. Certainly.

SOC. Then to injure a friend or any one else is not the act of a just man, but of the opposite, who is the unjust?

POL. I think that what you say is quite true, Socrates.

> Soc. Then if a man says that justice consists in the repayment of debts, and that good is the debt which a just man owes to his friends, and evil the debt which he owes to his enemies,—to say this is not wise; for it is not true, if, as has been clearly shown, the injuring of another can be in no case just.
>
> Pol. I agree with you.

Notice a key point about this exchange: Socrates allows Polemarchus to do most of the work. Rather than lecturing or handing out a list of facts to be memorized (as might be done during the grammar stage), Socrates speaks almost exclusively in questions. He allows Polemarchus to make statements, and then he shows his pupil where those statements are flawed. How does Socrates do that? He shows Polemarchus what will happen if they agree to take Polemarchus's argument to its logical conclusion. Socrates gives multiple, seemingly simple examples, thus permitting Polemarchus to become confident in his faulty belief, and then he leads Polemarchus to a statement with which Polemarchus cannot agree.

Notably, Polemarchus is the one who identifies the error in thought and then explains how to correct it. Parents know that if they tell their young daughter not to look in the box under the bed in the guest room, her first instinct is to sprint for the guest room. Now take this principle to the level of ideas. What if your now-teenage daughter begins to ask questions about ideas with which you disagree? The topic might be evolution or a form of religion or a political position. If you tell her that the idea is just plain bad and that she should stay away from it, what is her first instinct? To sprint toward it at full speed. But what if you encourage her to study it with you? By asking good questions, you can help her to reach an informed conclusion about the subject. You can point her toward trustworthy authorities on the subject. You can help her to consider both sides as she forms her own opinion about it.

What is more, she will be able to claim the opinion she reaches as her own because she walked toward it step by step; she will know the route you traveled to get there, not just the destination. In a very real way, you are teaching your child to be the driver, no longer just a passenger. Like those early driving lessons, it is a little scary. Sometimes you may need to scream, "Brake! Brake!" Sometimes you may have to grab the wheel. But your goal is to relinquish more and more control as your child learns how to navigate safely. You can only do that by respecting her questions and encouraging her to ask them without fear.

One of the hardest things about being a parent or teacher is believing (to the point of acting on your belief) that truth will stand up to scrutiny. Too often, we associate critical thinking with criticism or even cynicism, something that always tears down,

One of the hardest things about being a parent or teacher is believing (to the point of acting on your belief) that truth will stand up to scrutiny.

never builds up. That's not true logic. The same fear drives modern educators to prescribe textbooks. *The information is all there. Don't question it; receive it blindly. Never move out of the grammar stage.* If we want to make a difference in our children's lives, if we want them to become free adults, we have to be radically different educators. That means we should move further and further away from this textbook approach. We should seek out original documents and let our children do the work of dissecting ideas, questioning them, evaluating them, and then either affirming or negating them. In the example from *The Republic*, note that Socrates never once reaches for an answer key or tells Polemarchus to correct his work using a textbook about justice.

One of the characteristics of the dialectic stage of education that parents find frustrating is that the answer key becomes less and less important. In math, instead of focusing solely on the correct answer, you should be asking your child to show you how he arrived at his answer. In literature, instead of asking only questions such as how many siblings Laura Ingalls Wilder had, you should begin to ask your child to evaluate Pa's decision to move the family west. In science, instead of fixating on whether or not your child achieved the anticipated result in an experiment, you should be asking her why the experiment failed. The focus, then, is not on chalking up another correct answer but on asking the kind of questions that will consistently lead a student to greater understanding.

When you are new to dialectic studies, your primary goal should be to learn how to ask good questions. Down the road, as you become comfortable with the types of questions that lead to orderly thought, you can begin to encourage your student to develop his own questions and to ask them without your prompting. When he can do that successfully, he will be ready to approach the rhetoric stage. (I will talk more about rhetoric at the end of the chapter.) Remember, the art of asking questions takes time, and you should expect to face resistance until your child learns that finding answers to his many questions will take time and patience but is nonetheless possible. If we believe that there is truth to be known and that there are ways to know it, one failed experiment or one as-yet-unanswered question should hold no fear for us. I say "should" because the Socratic method forces both the teacher and the student to grapple with a certain amount of tension. Getting past the first "I dunno" answer requires you to push your child. You have to circle around the first question by asking more questions until your child realizes one of two things: 1) he actually does know the answer, or 2) he doesn't know as much as he thought he did and maybe he should study more.

While both parents and children should learn how to argue effectively, they must also learn how to do so gently and considerately. Here's where it gets a little more difficult. Ms. Sayers refers to the dialectic as the "Pert" stage of learning, which is "characterized by contradicting, answering back, liking to 'catch people out' (especially one's elders); and by the propounding of conundrums. Its nuisance-value is extremely high" ("The Lost Tools of Learning"). If you have ever heard a middle schooler triumphantly correct the teacher who said without thinking, "Thomas went on the field trip with Miss Marshall and I," instead of "with Miss Marshall and me," you might agree with this assessment of the young dialectician! Mutual frustration is common during the teenage years. Children in this age group are prone to become frustrated for one of two reasons: either they think they already know all the answers and there are no more questions worth asking, or they think that the answers to their deepest questions cannot be known. Parents in any age group are prone to become frustrated by the sense that they don't know what kinds of questions to ask, so they cannot possibly model the dialectic for their children.

In order to successfully master the dialectic, parents and children must work to set aside defensive attitudes. As teacher and student, they must first build a relationship based on trust and respect. If they do not, one or both will be tempted to give up and flee the conversation in defeat. My encouragement is that you have already won half the battle by admitting that you do not have all the answers. To paraphrase Socrates in Plato's *Meno*, "You are better and braver and less helpless when you realize you ought to ask questions than you were when you had indulged in the idle fancy that there was no knowing and no use in seeking to know what you did not know." Your task is not to have all the answers; rather, it is to engage your children in dialogue, honestly confronting their questions, and at the same time learn how to model the type of questions you want them to be able to ask on their own.

Before you can ask questions successfully, you will have to get comfortable with tension, which is not something that comes naturally to most of us. Let me give you an example. A conference presenter is speaking in front of an audience of twenty-five people. Three or four of the attendees are doodling in the margins of their notebooks, one is staring out the window, several are checking their iPhones, and another is actively snoring. To regain her listeners' attention, the speaker throws out an easy question: "Can you see any problems with this argument?" No one answers. One minute passes, and then another. Throats are cleared. Armpits begin to sweat. Restless feet tap on the floor. A dozen pairs of eyes are now studiously examining the furniture. Everyone in the room is silently pleading for the speaker to give up and move on. That's how most of us feel about unanswered questions. We don't handle tension very well, but we need to learn how to sit in it together.

For this reason, the Socratic method is inherently relational in nature. Most of the Socratic dialogues feature Socrates sitting down with his pupils at one of their homes. One of Plato's students, Aristotle, founded an influential school of philosophy derived from Socrates' teachings. The school was called the Peripatetic School, not only because Aristotle's followers taught under the covered walkways (Gk. *peripatoi*) of the Lyceum in Athens, but also—according to legend—because they taught while walking (Gk. *peripatetikos*) with their students.

When was the last time you went for a walk with one of your children? In this age of virtual interaction and long days spent in front of a screen, the idea of taking a walk outdoors might seem alien. Treadmills allow us to catch up on television re-runs while

When was the last time you went for a walk with one of your children?

we exercise, after all! Who needs a walking companion? We have headphones! Yet, when someone you know is going through a particularly difficult time—a family member has died, a teenager is slipping out of the house at three a.m., a marriage is floundering—one of the metaphors you might use to indicate support is your desire to *walk with* that person through their struggles. Why is that?

When you walk with someone, you embark on a journey together. The prologue of Geoffrey Chaucer's famous fourteenth-century poem *The Canterbury Tales* is narrated by a man who sets out on a pilgrimage to a shrine at the Canterbury Cathedral in England. Because the road is long and "truly there's no mirth nor comfort, none, riding the roads as dumb as is a stone" (24), he and his fellow travelers agree to tell each other stories to pass the time. In Jane Austen's *Pride and Prejudice*, when Miss Bingley and Elizabeth Bennet want to have a private chat, what do they do? They "take a turn about the room" (38).

Walking is a useful technique in literature for the same reason that we like to imagine Greek philosophers strolling under vine-covered walkways while contemplating the human soul: this is one area in which teaching through technology remains insufficient. To have this kind of meaningful interaction, you need the one sense that technology cannot recreate: touch. A hand on a shoulder or a hug can go a long way to defuse tension between two people. Even if a conversation creates frustration between you as you walk, you are physically together and moving in the same direction. You may be silent or you may talk, but you remain physically close. When you are a mile away from home, you can't give up after the first response of "I don't know." You have to keep asking questions to fill the space. You have to wrestle with the tension and test different ways of reaching resolution. After all, that's what contradiction does: it forces us to reconcile ideas, and that is precisely what the dialectic is all about.

ARISTOTLE'S TOPICS

"I'm sorry. My responses are limited. You must ask the right questions."
—Hologram of Dr. Alfred Lanning, *I, Robot* (2004)

In order to reconcile ideas, we have to be able to think and argue clearly. In order to enable clear thinking and arguing, we need tools to help us ask the right questions. Classical rhetoricians such as Aristotle and Cicero developed a systematic approach to argumentation that was based on the way the human mind functions. They called these rhetorical techniques *topoi* (topics). The five common topics are *definition*, *comparison, relationship, circumstance*, and *testimony*. The topics can help you lead your students to good questions, but don't think about them as defining the limits of your questioning; instead, use them as tools to generate more and more questions as you circle around your subject.

Because every child learns at a different speed, and because dialectical thinking takes time to master, your students may not be able to ask questions related to all five common topics right away. At first, they might just ask questions of definition. Later, as they become more comfortable with definition, they might focus on comparison. Even after they master all five topics, they may not apply all of them to every situation, and they may not ask the questions in the same order.

In part 2 of this book, I will apply the five common topics to individual subjects as a way to organize more detailed conversations about math, science, literature, and more. First, however, I will examine the topics one by one to reach a basic understanding of the type of questions each topic produces. As a model, I will use Plato's discourse

Meno, in which Socrates leads his friend Meno through a series of questions leading to a definition of virtue.

Common Topic #1: Definition
SOCRATES The next question is, whether virtue is knowledge or of another species [division]?
MENO Yes, that appears to be the question which comes next in order.

Earlier, I mentioned that Linnaeus's system of scientific classification was derived from one that Aristotle pioneered. Aristotle did not limit his system to natural science, because he understood, at least in part, that our brains naturally seek to classify objects based on what they are and what they are not. Through definition, we seek to understand the basic essence or nature of a thing. Aristotle breaks definition down further into *genus*—broad classes of things—and *division*, or *species*—narrower subsets of things differentiated from other members of their class. (Today, we more often use those terms in a scientific sense to name living things, as in the classification of man as *Homo sapiens*: *Homo* [genus] + *sapiens* [species].) The following are questions you might ask in order to understand definition:

- What is _____ (history / truth / slavery / literature / writing)?
- What is _____ (science / art / beauty / justice) not?
- Is this _____ (rectangle / fish) a _____ (square / shark)?
- How can _____ (a story plot / a volcano) be broken down into parts?
- What are the essential qualities of _____ (a sedimentary rock / a symphony)?
- What are the characteristics of _____ (a Latin adjective / an epic poem)?
- What are the stages of _____ (a war / a scientific experiment)?

Common Topic #2: Comparison
SOC. Then right opinion is not less useful than knowledge?
MEN. The difference, Socrates, is only that he who has knowledge will always be right; but he who has right opinion will sometimes be right, and sometimes not.

Once we know what something is, we naturally begin to compare it to other things. Why do you think world maps show so many countries and cities and states with the word "new" in their names? Here is an example: In 1664, when England added another colony to its North American holdings, Sir George Carteret was made one of the proprietors. Sir George had formerly been the governor of the Isle of Jersey in the English Channel. So, the only logical name the English royals could find for the new colony was "New Jersey." Do you see how it works? Our brains make sense of new information by comparing it to familiar information. Take another example: When Columbus first reached the Caribbean, he did not recognize that he had reached an entirely new geographic region; he expected to reach the Indies. He incorporated his new experience into his old paradigm, and as a result, he called the region the "West Indies" and the inhabitants "Indians." Later explorers compared Columbus's thesis to newer information about the Americas—again, practicing dialectic—and this time, they realized that Columbus was wrong and modified the familiar information (however, the names stuck).

Rhetoricians divide the topic of comparison into three parts: *similarity, difference,* and *degree*. They ask, "How are things alike?" "How are they different?" "To what degree are they alike or different?" The following are questions you might ask a student in order to help him understand comparison:

- How is _____ (music / a lion / a gerund) similar to/different from _____ (dance / a tiger / an infinitive)?
- To what degree is _____ (Mozart / Shakespeare) similar to/different from _____ (Bach / Dickens)?
- How are _____ (a research paper / the Korean War) and _____ (a persuasive essay / the Vietnam War) both similar to/different from _____ (a poem / the Cold War)?
- Is _____ (honesty / pacifism / capitalism) better/worse than _____ (tactfulness / self-defense / communism)?
- Is a _____ (tornado / question) more or less _____ (damaging / persuasive) than _____ a (hurricane / statistic)?

Common Topic #3: Relationship

Soc. And does any one desire to be miserable and ill-fated?

Men. I should say not, Socrates.

Soc. But if there is no one who desires to be miserable, there is no one, Meno, who desires evil; for what is misery but the desire and possession of evil?

Men. That appears to be the truth, Socrates, and I admit that nobody desires evil.

Soc. And yet, were you not saying just now that virtue is the desire and power of attaining good?

MEN.   Yes, I did say so.

Comparing two things naturally leads us to ask how they relate to each other. Aristotle gives us four categories of relationships to use as a starting point: *cause / effect, antecedent / consequence, contraries,* and *contradictions.* As an example of the first, you might notice that your neighbor has just brought home a new dog, and the new dog barks all the time. A week later, your cat comes home with a torn ear. Before you storm over to the neighbors and demand that they pay for your vet bill, you need to ask a few questions. Even though the new dog arrived before your cat was injured, the dog did not necessarily *cause* the cat's injuries. A second type of relationship asks you to consider the *consequences* of choices or actions. If my son breaks his curfew, he may be grounded. My son's lateness does not cause me to ground him, but being grounded is a consequence of his action. Teenagers need to understand that there are consequences if they wreck a car, get a speeding ticket, or break an expensive electronic device. Ideally, they should have a good understanding of this principle *before* they are placed in situations where their actions can produce irreparable consequences.

The remaining two types of relationships can be confusing. (Chapter 8 on formal logic may help you to understand these concepts.) Two things are *contrary* if they belong to the same basic category and cannot both be true. When we see a photograph of Uncle George, we may say that his shirt is all red, or we may say that his shirt is all blue. These two statements cannot both be valid, but they can both be invalid. Just because we prove that statement A was false does not mean that we have proved statement B to be true. The shirt could very well be green. On the other hand, two statements are *contradictory* if one of them must be valid and the other must be invalid. That cup of coffee is either entirely hot or partially not-hot (logic-speak for the exact opposite of hot). The point of contradictory statements is that there are only two options. If the cup of coffee is not entirely hot, at least part of it must be not-hot.

The following are questions you might ask in order to understand relationship:

- Did _____ (slavery / pollution) cause _____ (the Civil War / global warming)?
- What will happen if _____ (you heat water to a certain temperature / Hamlet kills his uncle / you change the length of one of a triangle's sides)?
- If _____ (evolution / Christianity) is true, what cannot be true?

- Are _____ (the death penalty / American culture) and _____ (Pro-Life movements / Native American culture) mutually exclusive, or can they coexist?

Common Topic #4: Circumstance

Soc.   If virtue was wisdom (or knowledge), then, as we thought, it was taught?

Men.   Yes.

Soc.   And if there were teachers, it might be taught; and if there were no teachers, not?

Men.   True.

As much as we would like to tackle all the questions in the universe, there are some tests that we cannot do—whether for ethical or practical reasons—and there are some laws, like the law of gravity, that we cannot break in everyday life. Part of the dialectic is learning to recognize our limitations. The topic of circumstance deals with basic limitations on what is possible as well as what is and is not probable. The two types of circumstance, according to Aristotle, are *possible / impossible* and *past fact / future fact*. For families, this conversation can blend nicely with a discussion about the consequences of actions and the importance of discipline and family rules. *Past fact / future fact* deals with probability. Do we know that something happened in the past, or are we just guessing? Can we be sure that something will happen in the future, or does the answer depend on our actions now? A child will ask these questions a great deal when he studies history.

The following are questions you might ask in order to understand circumstance:

- Is it possible or impossible to _____ (end world hunger / compare two works of art / solve a math equation)?
- What might prevent us from _____ (winning a soccer game / buying a dog / jumping across the Grand Canyon)?
- Do we know for sure that _____ (the Aztecs killed Montezuma / Latin was pronounced a certain way)?
- If we _____ (raise taxes / read books), can we be certain that _____ (national debt will decrease / our vocabulary will improve)?
- What else was going on when _____ (Dickens wrote *A Christmas Carol* / World War II began / the thirteenth amendment was ratified)?

Common Topic #5: Testimony

Soc.   I think not.

MEN. Why not?

SOC. I will tell you why: I have heard from certain wise men and women
       who spoke of things divine that—

MEN. What did they say?

SOC. They spoke of a glorious truth, as I conceive.

MEN. What was it? and who were they?

Although modern educators often exalt expert testimony above all other forms of
knowledge, it does have an important place in dialectic learning. We need to teach
our children how to recognize valid forms of testimony as well as how to challenge
and expose invalid forms of testimony. Aristotle divides this topic into six categories: *authority*, *testimonial*, *statistics*, *maxims*, *laws*, and *precedents*. An *authority* is
someone who is thought to offer expert opinion on a subject. In a murder trial, a lawyer
for the defense might bring in an "expert witness" to provide evidence about the cause
of death. A *testimonial* is similar, but it is given by someone who, while she may not be
an expert, witnessed or experienced an event firsthand.

Authorities and testimonials provide qualitative evidence, but other types of testimony, such as *statistics*, are quantitative. Although statistics may be useful, numbers
and percentages can be manipulated into pointing to just about anything. When your
child encounters statistics as part of an assignment or while doing research, he should
learn to ask how the statistician gathered and evaluated his data.

Some types of testimony, such as *laws*, are encoded in writing and are thought to
be binding. In human society, laws include contracts, official documents, testaments,
statutes, and constitutions. In science, laws refer to statements that have been proved
multiple times by experiments. In math, a law is a rule that is always true for that
number system.

On the other side of the spectrum are *maxims*, another word for common knowledge. Everyone knows the proverb, "He who laughs last, laughs longest." When you
talk about testimony, you should teach your child to evaluate whether or not a maxim
is based in truth.

The final type of testimony, *precedent*, also changes over time. Precedent could
easily be called the evidence of examples. If you have run through a puddle six times,
each time splashing mud up on your jeans, you can reasonably assume that the same
thing will happen a seventh time. Likewise, history (France under the Germans in
the twentieth century, America under the British in the eighteenth century) tends to

support the argument that people fight back against occupation by foreign rulers. When you base an argument on examples, however, you should always be on the lookout for counter-examples that make the opposite point.

All of these forms of testimony may be useful, but keep in mind that every human is biased in one way or another. Even journalists, who strive to report in an even-handed way, are influenced by their personal beliefs, perspectives, and past experiences. It is up to the dialectician to identify bias and decide if it invalidates a form of testimony.

The following are questions you might ask in order to understand testimony:

- On what type of testimony does this argument rely?
- Should a _____ (work of literature / think tank / historian / politician) be considered an authority?
- What are this authority's biases? Do they invalidate his testimony?
- What does this testimony assume about the world? Is the assumption valid?
- How were these statistics gathered? Who gathered them?
- How recent are these statistics? How many cases were included?
- Should we trust a majority opinion about _____ (history / proper grammar / truth / human rights)?
- Do we know for sure that _____ (chicken soup cures the common cold / cheaters never prosper)?
- Is this example universally true, or are there counter-examples?

TURN TOWARD RHETORIC

So, where are we left at the end of all the questions? In "The Lost Tools of Learning," Dorothy Sayers says, "Towards the close of this stage, the pupils will probably be beginning to discover for themselves that their knowledge and experience are insufficient, and that their trained intelligences need a great deal more material to chew upon." You might be cheering at the idea that your child will be humbled suddenly by how little he knows. No more arguments, no more crowing, no more challenging your authority. Well… maybe not entirely. Another probable consequence of the dialectic is that you will realize how little *you* know. But that's not the end of the story for either you or your children. Sayers goes on to say this:

> The imagination—usually dormant during the Pert age—will reawaken, and prompt them to suspect the limitations of logic and reason. This means that they are passing into the Poetic age and are ready to embark on the study of

Rhetoric. The doors of the storehouse of knowledge should now be thrown open for them to browse about as they will. The things once learned by rote will be seen in new contexts; the things once coldly analyzed can now be brought together to form a new synthesis; here and there a sudden insight will bring about that most exciting of all discoveries: the realization that truism is true. ("The Lost Tools of Learning")

Imagine the doors of a storehouse of knowledge being thrown open and a wealth of knowledge being available at your child's ready disposal because you taught him how to ask the essential questions and that it was productive to ask them. Remember, we ask questions not because we are cynics who believe that nothing is true and nothing can be known but because we believe that truth exists and can be known, at least imperfectly. Our questions are designed to weed out falsehood and cultivate right thinking so that we can share its fruits with those around us. This is the promise that hovers at the beginning of the rhetoric stage. The journey to reach that point is long and by no means easy, but the reward at the end is far better than we can even imagine.

CHAPTER THREE

FREQUENTLY ASKED QUESTIONS

"For such training and toning, either, with translating or composing [Latin], is more than the sum of 'framing sentences.' It's mental horticulture. We plant, and even weed, a small garden patch of the mind when we compose in this taut, conscious way, placing words and clauses with the same care we might expend on planting delicate seeds or transplanting mature stalks. That care becomes not only an exercise in exact thought, but also a loving act. We know we're doing something worthwhile. For one fleeting moment, we push back the chaos and make way for order. *Ad astra per aspera* [to the stars through difficulty]."

—Tracy Lee Simmons, *Climbing Parnassus*

THE PURPOSE OF CLASSICAL EDUCATION

So far, I have given you a vision for what a dialectical education could look like, using the five common topics (definition, comparison, relationship, circumstance, and testimony) to generate questions. When I share these ideas with families new to classical education, I pause at this point, acknowledging that they may have some questions of their own—as they should! In this chapter, I want to walk you through some of the frequently asked questions I receive about the dialectic stage of education.

Do I have to be an expert to answer questions?

I am an amateur educator who answers the question "Why?" for a living. I define myself as an amateur for two reasons. The first is because I have no teaching credentials from any form of higher education, yet I am daily asked to explain why my family or business or home school is engaged in a certain activity. I spend the day teaching from life experience and my passion for Christian education. I can't get away with ambiguous explanations, because usually the person asking wants to model the activity, explain it to an employee, or train a parent interested in using the approach to teach his child. Nothing reveals a dumb idea as well as explaining it aloud. So after I answer "Why?", I often end up hanging my head or kicking myself because I just discovered that I do things without much thought as to why. To explain thyself is to know thyself, and what one discovers is often pitiful. I often do things without thinking about the reasons why, but my answers to "why" inevitably instruct me.

But my self-nomination as an amateur also reminds me that all will be well. Hence, the second reason I consider myself an amateur comes from the true meaning of the word. The Latin root for *amateur* is *amare*, which means "to love." Experts and professionals are paid to do a job. Amateurs are driven to engage in an activity simply because they love it, and they keep trying even when they fail because of their love for the activity. It is easier to be forgiven when you fail as an amateur because no one expects you to be exalted as an expert or paid as a professional. No one pays me to be a parent. I am an amateur at my most time-consuming, influential role: answering "why" questions for our family.

For a serious discussion on the difference between an amateur and a professional, read the cookbook *The Supper of the Lamb* by Robert Farrar Capon. As an amateur cook, Capon can afford to give a chapter to each ingredient in his recipe for a lamb shank. As he exalts and lingers in his love of the tastes, smells, textures, sights, and sounds of food preparation, Capon makes the reader aware of the things he or she loves best, too. All who read it are glad to be amateurs, unhurried by deadlines and unhampered by harsh assessments. Capon confirmed for me what all those around me were saying: I am a lover of questions, whether I can come up with the correct answer or not. Fear of failure hinders most people. I am apparently unafraid of the wrong answer. One of my best friends made a comment in front of me to someone who was nervous about public speaking. My friend said, "Just be like Leigh. She says the wrong thing all the time when she's speaking." The nervous friend laughed uneasily, thinking it was an unkind remark, so my friend added, "Then, when someone asks a question to correct her, she takes the correction and moves on." I am okay with incorrect answers; I have an eternity in which to correct my misconceptions, but my soul will wither if I have no questions.

As adults, we are required to answer questions every day that cause us to assess our reasons for being or force us to make difficult decisions. Just today I had to decide whether to evict a tenant with a bunch of small children (I decided to work with her), answer my son's questions concerning long division, realize I was holding someone else to a higher standard than I hold myself, and brainstorm with a college student who was doing a research project in political science (she repaid me by making dinner). So, I had to choose between financial responsibility and loving my neighbor more than myself, demonstrate why classical educators teach from easiest to hardest concepts, pray my daily repentance for my superiority complex, and discuss the inconsistencies between the Northwest Ordinance and the U. S. Constitution, as a result of the questions I had been asked.

You will never be an expert in all the areas of life that confront you. But if you love your life and the lives of those around you, you can confidently and competently make good judgments.

Can I teach my children to judge well?

The point is that life requires us to use judgment—to answer questions or respond to choices in a manner that reveals the tension of conflict and the harmony of peace. Many seem willing to pay any price for peace in order to avoid conflict. We need more Patrick Henrys to ask us, "Is life so dear, or peace so sweet, as to be purchased at the price of chains and slavery? Forbid it, Almighty God!" Although you will find people who must win at any cost and relish conflict, most folks would rather leave well enough alone. But living does not allow me to leave well enough alone, because my job as a mother is to teach my sons how to use judgment, which does not necessarily mean keeping them safe. Good judgment can cause us to lose friends, employment, and reputation. Good judgment can be as dangerous as bad judgment in a world that just wants us to get along and not make waves.

We live in a world that can be difficult to navigate, even on the best of days. Today was a good day. I ate well, was surrounded by friends and family, stayed dry while it poured rain, and discussed the role of epic poetry with some colleagues. But I also had to confront my desire to break relationship with a person whom I consider a nuisance, and I had to apologize for an offense to a friend. I want to be sure that the time my family spends in academics aids rather than hinders my children's ability to resolve conflict, to seek peace, and to be content with tension. They need to know not only how to answer hard questions but also how to live with circumstances beyond their control without trying to control others. It seems like the purpose of education has become, as C. S. Lewis identifies it in *That Hideous Strength*, the ability for some to control others. Instead, the classical model teaches young people to control themselves. Christian education teaches that self-control is impossible without the aid of the Holy Spirit. The art of the dialectic—the practice of the skill of asking questions—teaches us to be aware of consequences before we make a judgment and then to be able to live with the consequences of our judgments. Living with the consequences can be impossible without the aid of the Trinity.

To modern people, the word *judgment* has negative connotations, which is a shame since we must use judgment every time we make a decision or answer a question. I want to teach my children to judge considerately and wisely. For example, the following question requires a fairly simple judgment: Does $1 + 1 = 2$ or does $1 + 1 = 3$?

For this next question, we must make a more complex judgment that leads to another question: Does $1 + 1 = 2$ or does $1 + 1 = 10$? That depends. Are you counting in decimal? Then $1 + 1$ does equal 2. Are you counting in binary? Then $1 + 1 = 10$.

Here is a still-more complex judgment: Should you go out and play with your friend, or should you play a video game by yourself? Here is a possible dialogue from a child whose friend shows up at the door to play:

> "Wow. I want to go play, but I know my mom will be home in ten minutes to take me to the dentist. I know! Why don't you come in and finish the video game with me?"
>
> "I'm not allowed to play video games except in my own home."
>
> "Well, then, why don't you come in, and we'll write the rules for the next paintball battle until my mom gets home?"

Is this the kind of judgment you want your child to make when offered a choice? Does a citizenry that has to vote based on information about health care or a marriage amendment or a sheriff's election require judging skills? You may choose a politically correct synonym like "discernment," but discernment requires you to make a judgment, so I don't think you can get away from teaching the art of judgment to your children. Think about what happens when we replay the above scene with students who have no judgment.

"Wow. I want to go play, but I know my mom will be home in ten minutes to take me to the dentist. I know! Why don't you come in and finish the video game with me?"

"I'm not allowed to play video games except in my own home."

"Well, no one is here but me. We'll turn off the screen when we hear my mom pull into the driveway."

This is not the judgment we would hope our children would make.

One of my favorite series of books similarly shows how important judgment is for growing boys. In *The Great Brain* series by John D. Fitzgerald, which is set in the 1890s, John's eldest brother, Tom, is The Great Brain. Tom is always scheming ways to make money, have more fun, or solve annoying problems. As a child, he is met with varying degrees of success because he does not always have the experience to judge rightly. Every circumstance prompts a question in his mind, and then the reader has to hang on while Tom tries to figure out the answer. In one important scene, he actually knows the right decision and purposefully chooses to do wrong. He has built a raft and is charging his friends a few cents for a ride when his youngest brother points out that the water is changing color. The author signifies that Tom, The Great Brain, has been taught to use nature as a tool for judgment, yet Tom ignores the danger signs. When Tom attempts to make a little more money and take a few more children for a ride, they almost drown.

What is significant to me as a parent who lives in modernity is the community's response. Tom pays back everyone's monies plus more and is properly punished. His father rebukes him by reminding him, "You knew the water was turning muddy, indicating the possibility of a flood. And yet you jeopardized the lives of six boys for thirty cents." The rest of the community of children properly shuns Tom. In that age, kids were trusted to learn from bad decisions. No one brutalized Tom, as the children knew they shared in the stupidity and took the rides in spite of the danger signs. The community expected nature to school the children.

Okay, fast forward from 1898 to today. Our kids would not have been in the river without a paid guide, life jackets, and helmets. There would have been metal signs telling all of us that there was no lifeguard on duty and no swimming allowed. The county would have insurance on the park, and the river guides would all be certified. And all of us technocrats would have no idea that the color of water means anything, as we are locked up in large, windowless classrooms when we study natural science. Our children's opportunities to exercise their powers of judgment are intentionally limited. The adults have used safety to scare children. So the children compliantly stay indoors

Our children's opportunities to exercise their powers of judgment are intentionally limited. The adults have used safety to scare children. So the children compliantly stay indoors and play video games, where they are safe from their own imaginations, curiosities, and questions.

and play video games, where they are safe from their own imaginations, curiosities, and questions. In fact, there are studies claiming that video games are a safe way to learn how to make decisions so frightened parents can justify buying more.

This world is not safe, but it is glorious. Classically educated students are taught to go outside and study nature. My grandparents' generation worked outside. My generation played outside. My children's generation plays inside. It is time to return children to the great outdoors. We try to choose safety and then realize that there is no such thing. We forget that it is not safe inside the house, either, if we are killing their spirit of inquiry. There is a reason zombies dominate popular culture. We see them and know that they are us.

Whenever adults struggle with thinking new thoughts, we judge the appropriateness of various outcomes. As an educator, it is interesting to watch the development of dialectic skills in a young mind. It is far more difficult to make good judgments when you are young. As adults, we've tackled hard thoughts for many years. We are practiced at it. But a child is experiencing something very new. I enjoyed watching my then twelve-year-old son, the last of our gang, struggle to think, or, really, to learn to think. You know that young children are capable of thinking, but in our home their thought life is often revealed in a conversation like this:

"David, what are you doing?"

"I'm cleaning up my bowl of Jell-O. I spilled it."

"Why aren't you cleaning up the Jell-O on the other side of the kitchen?"

"That's William's Jell-O."

"Well, where's William?"

"Dad took him to the orthodontist."

"Did William spill the Jell-O?"

"No, I did."

"Then why aren't you cleaning up William's Jell-O?"

"Because it's William's!"

Now obviously, as a mother, I am hoping for a different answer, but I cannot expect a child to think like a grown-up. Often, I will look at my boys and say, "Why can't you think like a forty-year-old?" The same judgments that I would like to see them apply in house cleaning, I would like to see them apply to math problems.

For example:

> ME: "If you use a common denominator to add 1/4 and 1/2 and get 3/4, don't you think you should use a common denominator to add 1/4 and 1/7?"
>
> CHILD: "I don't use common denominators, I just add the numbers. And what's a common denominator anyway?"

Unfortunately, too many adults probably can't add 1/4 and 1/7 or identify a common denominator, but then we expect them to understand a mortgage that reads "5 1/4% interest, 5 1/2% APR." How sound has the financial judgment of our populace been lately?

The point of these conversational examples is to demonstrate that all ages in all areas of life need to be dialectic: to think logically, judge appropriately, and choose an outcome. Thinking is a very hard skill to teach a young child. Thinking takes practice and requires lots of stable thoughts in one's head to compare so that the thoughts have pegs to hang on and ways to be sorted. In our family of boys, I have found that they have to work really hard to think between the ages of eight and twelve. They often don't even know where to begin thinking, let alone how to reach logical conclusions or to what ideas they should compare their thoughts. Then sometime around fourteen, it's like a new chemical has been introduced to their brain, and—poof!—thinking becomes possible! They stop and think before answering. They pull out old ideas to use with new ideas. And consideration replaces bickering with each other so that I no longer have to physically separate them during disagreements.

I saw the difference between the grammar student and dialectic student when my younger two were certified for open-water scuba diving. William at fourteen would be given data about atmospheric pressure, could compare it to a previous problem, and come up with a correct answer. David needed to have the calculating process (called an algorithm in math) explained to him for each set of data. Extrapolating data is a dialectic skill. He is not dumb, he is just not experienced at applying information that does not particularly concern him to other ideas that seem irrelevant. "Who cares how many atmospheric pressures there are? Where are the sharks to chase?" On the other hand, William understood that the compressed air is limited and he would like to come back to the surface breathing. So paying attention to details becomes purposeful at the same time his brain is ready to think.

Yes, you can teach your children to judge well. In our culture, we tend to measure their judgment by academic grades. This measure can form your child's view on the outcome of everything if you aren't careful.

Are scores and grades the only way to assess my student?

One of the most frequent questions I hear from parents is, "How will I know if I have done a good job educating my child?" This question reveals a powerful fear felt by every parent, but especially by parents who choose to educate their children at home. The only way to answer this question, according to our present-day culture, is to have your child succeed on a standardized test or receive an offer of admission from a prestigious university. Tests are useful tools for measuring progress and discerning areas for improvement, but they are just that—tools. We must learn to separate our self-worth and sense of accomplishment (as well as that of our children) from the numerical values of a standardized test score. As we begin to think more dialectically about education, we must also consider alternative means of assessing our children's progress.

The dialectic does not give us the answer we want all the time. When people confront the difficulties of life, they often want answers, but life rarely offers anything except more questions. I cherish the conversations, the great classical conversations with my son, my young friend, and my colleagues that I previously mentioned. I think of the infinite variety of questions presented. I'm blessed that I don't need to have answers for every question. I'm content with mysteries—as long as I can ask another question when I think of it. Contentment in questions and mysteries seems to irk the world. We moderns don't seem to be able to do anything without a purpose that leads to billable hours. It reminds me of the story I was told of a businessman who studied Latin every day at lunch. His colleagues asked him what the purpose was of studying Latin. He responded with, "Nothing, praise God!" Can't we ask questions about Latin declensions just because we want to? Must every question have a purpose beyond love of learning?

Dietrich Bonhoeffer, a German theologian, is known for his participation in a plot to assassinate Hitler. When he was teaching in seminary, he was frustrated by the students who asked how they were going to be graded on their prayer life. They couldn't seem to grasp that a mentor could ask you to work at a task just because the task was worthy without measureable results. I experience this same frustration. My publishing company, Classical Conversations MultiMedia, publishes a series of books called *Words Aptly Spoken*, which contains a list of dialectic questions about literature just to kick-start classroom conversations. The only complaint we receive about the series is that it doesn't have an answer key. There are no correct answers to the questions; the books are supposed to encourage you to think of your own questions and maybe discover some answers.

Institutionalized school has taught us to seek answers in order to get the lesson over with rather than to inspire more questions and extend the curiosity of the students. In college, my classmates were often annoyed with me; I kept asking questions, so the professors kept talking, sometimes beyond the bell. One day, there was an audible groan from my classmates. I turned around and said, "Look, I'm paying good money to ask this guy questions. Just leave if you don't want to stay late." The professor gave me a C in the class. (He did not like me, either.) I asked so many questions because the professor insisted on an existential response, in the tradition of Nietzsche, to everything we read. I did not even understand what he was talking about, but I was sure he was wrong. So, I kept asking him to explain how what he said could be true. He did not ask questions to lead an exploration of ideas. I was being told to think a certain way, and he couldn't adequately explain or defend his bias.

Later, a girl came up to me and said that she was proud of me. She said she had had the same questions but was afraid to ask them. I have no idea who she was, as the class held about fifty students. (Who at the state university thought a literature discussion could be held with fifty people? Do we really want our students jumping through hoops and credits so that we can pretend they have received an education?) I wonder what she thinks about three decades later. I thought a goal of education was to give us a voice. Instead, she was afraid to use hers. I wonder if it was because she had been trained to write down the correct answer and for some discussions there are no correct answers, only very interesting questions.

...and for some discussions there are no correct answers, only very interesting questions.

I may be able to see beyond the industrial school paradigm because I never participated in it in a way one could describe as normal. I attended three different elementary schools, skipped from third grade to sixth grade, went back to fifth grade, and then went to three different high schools, including public and private. My mom taught me pretty much everything I know. I can name three influential teachers for whom I am grateful, not because they taught me anything in particular but because they saw who I was and let me do what I wanted in class. Each day they gave me the state-mandated curriculum to complete and then left me alone for the rest of the day to study whatever I wanted. My dad was like Atticus Finch in that we read the newspaper together every day and watched the news and talked politics while I was in elementary school. When my siblings and I got home from school, my mother took us on what she called "adventure walks" and told us the names of all the plants and animals in our suburban yard. I began hanging out with adults after school as soon as I was eleven years old and went to work. These three teachers saw that my parents had schooled me and turned their attentions to other students. Since I was not disruptive and was naturally curious, they were relieved to be able to leave me alone.

All the examples I am giving attempt to make the point that there are more important skills to develop and assess than just academic skills. As Christians, our standard for assessment is, as Jesus said, "Be ye therefore perfect, even as your Father which is in heaven is perfect" (Matthew 5:48). We reduce that standard in most of what we assess because we know it is impossible, so we make other men our standard for assessment. The Scriptures teach that this is appropriate. Paul exhorts us to do things the way he does them. Discipleship teaches the student to do as the master so they can learn even more than the master. Parents are told to teach their children. But in all of these examples two things are paramount: 1) the student is assessing their progress with a human, and 2) the teacher is pointing the student to perfection, to Christ.

As an adult with responsibilities, I know I need to be able to think through difficult situations, but I'm pretty sure my children are not always convinced that thinking hard is worth the effort. That's okay. If everything were easy, they would not need a mother, and they would do only what they like to do. We are all gifted and lean toward using those gifts, so my job is to keep my children on task for the things they ought to do but find difficult to want to do. Through a variety of tools I woo, cajole, threaten, encourage, and persuade my students to focus on difficult tasks, from science to logic and fine arts. One tool never seems to fail: the question.

Through a variety of tools I woo, cajole, threaten, encourage, and persuade my students to focus on difficult tasks, from science to logic and fine arts. One tool never seems to fail: the question.

How do I decide what sources and "experts" to trust?

In order to rightly assess your children's progress, academic or otherwise, you need to question the presuppositions of the people, forms, and content they use to study. All ideas come with presuppositions. In science, we presume something about mankind. In math, we presume something about decimal systems. In education, we presume something about grammatical studies. There are no raw ideas; they all came from someone. Knowing who they came from can help identify the presuppositions.

I want my children to know the delight of asking questions about the creation. Although much of the scientific community rejects the idea of a creator, I want my children to know that the person who presents the facts and theories is as important as the information presented. Thus we also study the history of science, from Hippocrates' medicine to modern-day controversies like stem cell research and reversal theories about the earth's magnetic field. The basic presuppositions of the scientist need to be understood as much as the science.

...I want my children to know that the person who presents the facts and theories is as important as the information presented.

Our family reads from a wide variety of viewpoints when it comes to natural philosophy, and we often discuss the author's intent. We want to know the author's goal in choosing the points presented. We talk about underlying assumptions in the data presented. We want to know who needs the mysteries of life to be answered in a certain way in order to defend their thoughts. We often evaluate information in light of the following quote from Aristotle in *Nichomachean Ethics*: "It is the mark of an educated man to look for precision in each class of things just so far as the nature of the subject admits." And so, through Classical Conversations, I try to introduce students to a broad realm of ideas while giving them the opportunity to practice the ability to store ideas (grammar), the ability to process ideas (dialectic), and the ability to explain and use those ideas (rhetoric). We teach that today's science needs to be held lightly, as new discoveries will replace old ideas, and that parents should engage their family in educational conversations about natural philosophies and scientific interpretation.

I present my students with the idea that science theories are undergirded by the study of natural philosophy, and therefore, the interpretation of facts can change. For example, today we still speak of animals acting on instinct in the same way Aristotle talked about rocks falling to the earth by instinct. Aristotle was wrong about rocks, and I bet we are wrong about animals. Nonscientists assume scientists really understand Newtonian physics and refer to gravity almost as if it is real enough to be photographed, while the real experts aren't sure how to model gravity as they try to unify it with Newtonian and quantum physics.

Our presuppositions also affect our view of what makes something a scientific fact or theory. It's been said that something shouldn't be called a scientific fact until it has been proven for over five hundred years. Our foundational assumptions skew our ability "to see." For instance, the great Scottish essayist Thomas Carlyle commented while addressing a group of scholars, "Gentlemen, you place man a little higher than a tadpole. I hold with the ancient singer, 'thou has made him a little lower than the angels'" (Psalm 8:5). How we view man informs the way we study man.

When trying to illustrate that there is a basis to all our beliefs, even so-called facts, a good question to ask is "What is 2 + 2?" People usually respond with "4," to which I respond, "Don't you want to know what base I am using before you answer?" Everyone presupposes there is one answer to a math problem because we've never been told the presuppositions supporting our decimal system. Our math sight has been limited, I would argue, intentionally. But even if I don't teach my children how nondecimal systems work, I want them to be aware that they exist. You'd think math knowledge would be expanding with our increased use of technology since computers operate with binary and hexadecimal number systems instead of decimal.

As I teach my children science or math or anything else, I want them to know the various ways to "see" facts. I don't want them to step on sharks' teeth without seeing them on the beach, and I don't want them to believe everything they are told because it is on the Discovery Channel or presented by an expert. I teach my children that scientists can extrapolate and hypothesize all they like, but that in order to do so, scientists must make assumptions. I also want to know the assumptions supporting the answer.

I begin my personal framework of scientific ideas with this statement: "In the beginning, God created the heavens and the earth." Upon which axiom do you base your beliefs? Let me know from whence you begin your arguments and then we may have the joy of feasting upon an intelligent conversation about any idea. Otherwise, we may just be speaking past one another by using words with definitions the other one does not understand.

The universe was designed to be studied by observing, defining, and experimenting. These are the basic skills to teach a young scientist. As students mature, they also need to learn how to collect, compare, and contrast data. They also need to know the history of the ideas they are taught. They need to know the origin of facts so they can evaluate the validity of the information. And eventually, they need to have enough confidence in the scientific ideas and their applications that they can pass on their knowledge to others. They acquire this confidence through exploration and questions.

A question is essential to any kind of real learning, whether in science or in history. Unfortunately, students learn that teachers ask the questions, and there is only one right answer, and if I don't know the answer I get a bad grade, and that makes me even less excited about the teacher and his goals, and when do I get to do what I want to do? I have had the privilege of studying with the same dozen students and their parents for seven years. Last year I grudgingly handed them off to another tutor, who was going to lead them through questions for the last two years of high school. It was with great joy that I watched them spend every lunch hour in a circle around their new tutor. They were just full of questions, and he had many more!

Meanwhile, I began working with a new group of a dozen middle-school students. At the beginning of the school year, they went out to play at lunch. And they should. Childhood is very precious. At the beginning of the second semester, a few began coming in early to talk with me. I'll see if they begin sticking around for extended discussions. In the summer, I saw one of the students at a ballgame. His grandparents and cousins from out of town, his classmates, and his friends were all at the game, but for two hours this fourteen-year-old boy sat by me and talked. One question I avoided asking him—and which I try to avoid in all such situations—was, "What are you going to do when you grow up?" (As though a career is the measure of a person's worth or interests!)

After the usual courtesies, I asked him what he wanted to do that day to make a million dollars. By the time the game was over, we had gone over recipes, restaurants, business locations, accounting practices, opportunities for free cooking lessons by top chefs, favorite restaurants, menus, and the crowds they draw. All we did was ask each other questions and laugh as we dreamed. I'm pretty sure he'd like to go to culinary school, but I'm even surer he doesn't have to go. He's passionate enough to teach himself to cook well. Hanging out with cooking colleagues might earn him a degree, but I bet he would do it even if no one gave him a report card or certificate. He is truly an amateur chef.

The next time you meet someone new (any adult), don't ask what he does for a living; instead, ask what he likes to do with his free time. You'll either make him speechless or he won't stop talking. When you are with a student or young person, ask her what gets her out of bed each day. Ask her what makes her angry. Ask her if she enjoys volunteer work. Ask her if she has heard any good sermons or read any good books lately. Just don't ask her how she plans to let society suck the best of her soul out of her body. (Well, actually, go ahead and ask that. It's a pretty

The next time you meet someone new... don't ask what he does for a living; instead, ask what he likes to do with his free time.

good beginning question.) But don't presuppose they define themselves solely by their job skills.

Humans are designed to think. Difficult ideas become much more interesting and approachable when we are curious about them, and curiosity is aroused by questions. So, I teach with the presupposition that I will reach my students better if I can get them to ask questions. Questions change the disliked into the liked, the boring into the interesting, the difficult into a challenge. Such a small thing effects such a big change in attitude, allowing the spirit and mind to explore.

For example, I taught my sons the seventy-two phonograms while they were in grammar school. They learned them while reading, they memorized them for spelling quizzes, they copied them for handwriting, and we drilled them with flashcards throughout their grammar school years. I did my job, and they became readers but lousy spellers. They did well enough on standardized tests, and they did not embarrass me too much when someone else read a paper they wrote. (How is that for a grading system? Not embarrassing? You get an A!) But they really needed to work harder on spelling.

As an avid reader who didn't even know phonograms existed until I was twenty-three, I was determined that my children's education would be more thorough than mine. My elementary teachers gave me whole-word *Dick and Jane* books, which I promptly ignored because I had taught myself to break the phonics code at home with my parents before kindergarten. So, you may say, "See? Whole-word didn't hurt Leigh, and she figured out the phonics without being taught the phonograms, so who needs phonics teachers?" Well, I did. My reading vocabulary as an adult was limited until I learned about phonograms. I would just skip over the words I couldn't pronounce in my head. All the fuzziness became clear when I learned about phonograms as a homeschooling parent, so I taught them to my children. However, I kept having a nagging feeling because although I knew the state assessments verified my boys' reading abilities, I knew my boys really didn't know *why* they could read. They could tell you the sound a phonogram made, but they really couldn't think through its importance or how to use phonics in new contexts. They could read but were limited; their abilities to discover new words on their own and improve their spelling skills were hindered.

Then something glorious happened. In middle school, we learned how to play a spelling game that required the players to think ahead in terms of phonograms and prefixes and suffixes in order to make the other players lose points. My boys are as competitive as the next. All these phonograms were lying dormant in my boys' heads.

Suddenly the questions about phonics were flying so they could win the game. "Mom, is 'au' at the end or the middle of a syllable?" "Mom, when does 'y' change to 'i' and add '-es'?" "Mom, are there any words that begin with 'Mn'?" The phonogram drills mattered to them when relevant questions were being asked. The rote memorization once again paid off. How do you know what questions to ask if there are not copious amounts of ideas in your head? Who thinks to ask about "au" as a rule unless someone has told you it operated under a rule? As a game strategy to eliminate players, I saw my boys teach phonograms to teammates who had never learned them before. It was then that I was certain my boys knew the phonogram rules themselves. Until a teacher sees a student teach another, you can never be sure whether something was learned for a test or whether the student owns it.

Until a teacher sees a student teach another, you can never be sure whether something was learned for a test or whether the student owns it.

Does this mean we have to come up with a creative game every time we want to get our students to ask good questions? The short answer is "Yes!" The long answer is in part 2 of this book. In general, teachers think that creative games are needed to entertain students and that whiteboards and technology hold students' attention. Rather, it is the question that holds their attention. If they have no question, it is harder to pay attention. Thinking is entertaining. Humans long for relationship, and thinking together in an interesting way about hard things is very rewarding. The spelling game required no tools but our brains. We played it in the car where all were trapped, and even those who didn't want to play (because they thought it was a "dumb spelling game") eventually joined in as they felt the joy of the rest of the family. It is hard to resist happiness when it is surrounding you!

How should we use technology?

One of my main presuppositions is that God loves the whole world, so if I am espousing academic principles, they need to apply to mankind and not just wealthy Americans. This is why one of my favorite phrases is "stick in the sand." Our eldest son, Robert, proclaims that I say "stick in the sand" because it was the only toy he was allowed! I actually use it as an answer for those who want to make education unnatural, difficult, or expensive. If I was raising boys on a deserted island, I know I would be adequately equipped to teach with just a stick and some sand.

When addressing the question of technology, it is important to think about the nature of the student, the computer, and the greater cultural ramifications. Some of my favorite books addressing these issues include Neil Postman's *Amusing Ourselves to Death* and Mark Bauerlein's *The Dumbest Generation*.

My neighbor asked me what I thought of one of the popular online academies. I returned his question with another question. I asked, "Do you want the short answer or the long answer?" Since he responded with "Short," I said, "I love the free market and innovations of mankind. So if someone wants to try something new they should go for it." My longer answer, which was actually short because I knew he was a man who had dedicated his retirement to loving folks and would understand with few words, was, "Teaching is an art that requires hard work and dedication. Students are people who are good, bad, and indifferent. There is no such thing as a single solution to educating civilization. Computers are just one more thing."

Having questions is a mark of humanity. As a parent educator who has an engineering background, I enjoy thinking about the tension between reaching the heart of a child and the constraints of time and finances. Everything about thinking involves tension between two ideas. We love it when the two ideas harmonize and come to a resolution, but I think we should also love it when the tension continues and we have lots to resolve. Having questions is a mark of humanity. For the moment, we use technology to communicate, entertain, and research and record academic endeavors. My family uses technology just like everyone else, but we never rest in some kind of numb acceptance of machines taking over our lives. We are aware that habits form us, and relating through a machine mainly forms us into beings who relate to a machine.

We must remember that we are made of flesh, and that is a glorious thing, too. Sometimes we choose to do things the old-fashioned way because the computer robs us of either hard work or social interaction. Sometimes we choose to remove the machine because the human relationship takes precedence in the formation of our lives. At this point our computers don't recognize that my son's eyes are glazed over or that the problem is so hard that he wants to cry or or that to give him a hint will rob him of the sense of accomplishment that comes from doing something with no one else's help. Sometimes my child goes—in less than a second—from being unable to answer a question to having full revelation simply because I saw his tension and touched his arm as a gesture of comfort. Computers are a tool, not an answer.

Technology also tends to remove social cues from the very age that needs as many cues as possible. As a classical educator, I'm always looking for the question. Questions come from frowns, shrugs, hesitations, laughter, and silly faces. Questions come from moving and smell. Good students wrestle with hard ideas. Sometimes answers come from pacing. A wandering child makes me ask if there is anything I can help with. A pacing child makes me stay away until asked a question. At a time when diagnoses of autism and ADHD are rising—as well as the number of medicated students—do we really want to remove even more social cues?

One day, I was in a room with four other women, and I was on the computer interacting with other adults on a conference call. I am in this circumstance often. As usual, my husband came home for lunch, saw we were in the other room, and barged in with his joyful, loud greeting. Normally, all would pause and respond to the greeting. We like folks to feel welcome in our home. Only, this time it was different. The normal social cues masked an entirely different event, and I hadn't warned my husband that I'd be tricking him. I was actually on a call with about a hundred people presenting an elocution lesson that was being recorded for professional purposes. As soon as he stepped into the room with his big heart and loud voice, he was met with a scowl from his wife and shushing from the people in the room. He was quickly waved out of the room, wondering what in the world he had done wrong and was very embarrassed. A lack of visual clues made the man I love feel bad.

Try to see what we are doing to our children. Imagine you are reading a paperback novel. Your hand would be raised and your head bowed. Imagine you are holding an old-fashioned dial phone mounted to the wall. You would be stuck near a wall with a receiver by your head. Imagine you are looking at your wristwatch to check the time. Your arm would be bent sideways and your head would be bowed. All of these images look different but clearly define the person's activity as you see them in your mind's eye.

Now imagine that you are holding a cell phone and you are reading a text, or making a phone call, or checking the time. To a person who just walks by, the body positions all look the same. We need to be aware of the losses as we progress into the future. Are we even aware of the loss in social skills that have potentially increased the numbers of medicated students? We treat all loss of social skills as a physical condition with a physical cause. Maybe we have missed some important skill in social development because we only ask medical questions around disabilities. Maybe we ask the wrong questions about education and child-rearing because we assume children were meant to sit in buildings all day—and now in front of a computer screen instead of a real person.

When I am teaching a young child some information and she asks "Why?", I can say, "Because I said so" for only so long. If she really wants to know, she can wear me down until I have to answer her question. A computer drilling a child never wears down and never hears the question. What does that do to the curiosity of a child? I

I like computers. But I like children more, and it is really important for them to ask questions.

could write a whole book on the wonders of computers and education. I like computers. But I like children more, and it is really important for them to ask questions. It is also important to recognize that cookies and milk, back rubs, and knitting go along very well with questions. Computers are a tool, not an answer.

I have a list of questions for you that relate to technology and education. See if they make you think of more questions.

- Do you want to teach your children to pay attention? If so, how will you do it?
- When we eat and watch TV as a family, which gets the most attention, the meal or the TV?
- Does background music teach us to be inattentive to sound?
- Are you surprised that we can no longer listen to a long sermon or lecture?
- Is suburban life more disruptive than it is contemplative compared to an agrarian lifestyle or an urban lifestyle?
- If a family member is not happy with another, does conflict really get resolved by turning to a screen?
- Has your child ever rushed into the room with good news or an important question only to hear, "Be quiet! I'm watching TV!"?
- Do you watch an entire movie as a family and then discuss it scene by scene, or do you just watch another movie?
- When background noise fills your life, is there room for the questions in your head?
- Do you find your family using the computer to watch operas or research academic topics as much as you watch YouTube clips of dancing cats?

How can I escape the industrial paradigm of education?

There are as many ways to structure education as there are people willing to ask questions. Our ability to define a new paradigm is hindered by our immersion in the current system. We need to rely on history, common sense, a parent's love, and God's Word to jolt us into new visions.

This morning I met with my staff and we discussed models of education and their differences. We talked about ancient Babylonian and Hebrew models, Greek and Roman academies, the Middle Ages, and modern efforts in education. As classical educators, we do not ask how to get our students into modern colleges. That's easy. We don't even ask how to prepare more of our students to get into modern colleges. If you haven't noticed, anyone can go to college these days. It is no longer the herculean academic question it was for previous generations.

Instead, we ask questions about finding scholastic colleagues rather than colleges. We ask how learning institutions were organized in previous centuries. My staff assumes that family, church, neighborhoods, sports teams, artist enclaves, work, internships, apprenticeships, missions, and the military are all sources of academic instruction with different goals, cost structures, logistics, and outcomes. It seems silly to compare our endeavors only to the modern industrial model when there are so many other models. Modern politicians and school administrators talk as though a good education makes one free, but then they constrain themselves to a single model (state industrial) and a single era (global technological). They limit the questions, so they limit the answers. Thanks to the current shifts in the economy and the college bubble (overpriced, too many students there for dorm life, deadening standards, low outcomes), innovators are arising. The restoration of classical education can be counted as one of many different solutions. Online curricula, growth in private schools, tutorial services, cram schools, homeschooling co-ops, university models in high school, and Classical Conversations are all part of a growing trend of intentional parents finding solutions outside of the public school paradigm. The Society for Classical Learning, the Association of Classical and Christian Schools, Classical Conversations, the Association for Christian Schools International, and the parochial school system all offer classical alternatives to K–12 public school.

One of the aspects of education that classical educators reject is the "form" of education. It seems to be a requirement that schools run for nine or ten months a year (even if year-round schools take long breaks) for about eight hours a day, that they hire state-certified teachers over twenty-one, and that the children be grouped by age. Schools structure their schedule around the industrial work week rather than optimum learning structures.

One of the complaints against private education is that it excludes certain demographics. I would argue that the modern idea of certified educators excludes certain demographics from receiving an affordable education. For example, we have made it against the law for a thirteen-year-old girl to be paid to teach at grammar schools. Child labor laws require children to work limited hours a week to make time for studies. Besides, how does one professionally certify a thirteen-year-old? But what better way to make sure our teens are grounded in phonics, sentence structure, basic arithmetic, history narratives, and science facts than for them to teach these concepts to an eight-year-old? If you work with young teens, you must have met many who can run a class as well as an adult. I had the privilege of working with one this past year who was also qualified to teach Latin and piano.

Can you imagine what would happen if the parents of a financially struggling neighborhood paid young girls to teach? They could give that girl a chance to rise above her circumstances by earning a part-time income, pay her much less than they would an adult professional, show the young children that teens can be responsible, give the students a much smaller teacher-student ratio, and save on transportation expenses.

Ah, but what about the adults who need to earn a living teaching? Well, no one is preventing them from running a grammar school either. Are they afraid a kid will do a better job? Aren't there plenty of students to teach? Are we concerned about job protection or affordable quality education? Maybe you think it is an awful idea. Great! How would you improve it? I like dialectic tension. Meanwhile, I also like freedom. As a homeschooling parent, I can hire anyone I want to help me teach my sons, including thirteen-year-olds part time.

Consider what has happened now that education is so expensive. We are using computers to drill students in order to save money and because kids like computers. So we give the machine precedence over a young gifted student. Remember, the machines are also taking jobs away from adult professionals. Some may argue that the young girl in my example should be in school herself. I agree. But why does it have to be all day,

We ask our youth what they are going to do with their lives, but we don't give them real things to do.

every day? Can't she attend to her own academics part of the day and teach part of the day? I know she may miss time at the mall and watching movies and texting, but the student I'm thinking of doesn't do those things anyway. She actually lives a life of service and academics because she thinks life is interesting. We ask our youth what they are going to do with their lives, but we don't give them real things to do. So why are we surprised when they can't answer the question?

What if we had schools that operated during second shift so that parents who work second shift could have their children at home with them during the day? Wouldn't it be great if both children and parents were in bed at the same time, doing chores and reading books in the morning, tossing a ball around after lunch, and then heading away from home at the same time? Learning would be taught by the parent, be caught by the student, and become part of a lifestyle. Evening schools may not be the best for the student, but not having an involved parent is much worse. Perhaps the evening schools could have a lighter academic load and send home morning homework to be done when the family is fresh and the parents can help. No matter how bad this idea sounds, you should know that this disrupted family lifestyle is already happening. Go to Walmart at midnight—it is full of kids because the parents just got off work and picked the kids up from daycare. Children are in school care all day, daycare all evening, and then home for a short night's sleep. Should we be surprised that this lifestyle disrupts family life? Should we expect parents to know what's going on in their child's life if we insist upon separating them all day?

Should we expect parents to know what's going on in their child's life if we insist upon separating them all day?

I guess we could be like Marie Antoinette and say, "Let them get day jobs." At the same time, I like going shopping and out to eat in the evenings. My desire to have access to restaurants and shops until late in the day creates jobs for adults who will work (or even prefer to work) second shift. But then, can I be critical when they aren't involved in their children's homework? Don't many families work two different shifts? Yes. So maybe we should start asking questions about schools at workplaces and schools on Saturday and Sunday. Are there any entrepreneurs out there?

Here is the problem with teaching a populace to ask questions: they ask questions. Think about the current social structure. We think men and women and children should all rise and go to an institution where they are taught to do what they are told. No troublemakers allowed. Then we send our children to college to be taught how adults do what they are told so they can get a career being told what to do. I was born in 1962. This is how my generation thinks. If your child is not in a college, you feel like you have failed as a parent.

Currently, our college graduates are under-employed or unemployed. If they are employed, they listen to music that tells them "It's Five O'Clock Somewhere." In other words, they can't wait to escape this job for which they studied so hard and paid so much. Then we repeat the cycle. Do your schoolwork, get a good job, and you too can be like me and wish you had a different life. Are we sure this is the measure we want for success?

For the next generation, this trend is shifting. A professor from Stanford quit his position in order to start a totally unaccredited online school. He has over fifty thousand adults registered who want to learn from the best in the field of Internet innovation. Khan Academy is changing the face of math for students everywhere—literally. Instead of a teacher's face, you see squiggles on a board. Rivendell Sanctuary in Minnesota, Mandala Fellowship in North Carolina, and the Center for Western Studies in Tennessee are all examples of programs for college-aged students who actually want to study outside the industrial or technological paradigm.

At our Classical Conversations staff meetings, we generate a lot of unusual ideas because we ask a lot of questions, some of which are illegal to ask at a public school. Thankfully, the First Amendment is still alive and well in classical, private education. We ask questions like:

- How was virtue inculcated in other eras and models?
- What are the benefits of teaching boys separately from girls at school?
- Do we want to organize our classes by something other than age?
- What damage is done by the classroom setting?
- How do we assess progress without giving a report card?
- How do we use report cards well?
- Why do schools want to model the family paradigm (small class, loving teacher) instead of encouraging families to do the schooling?
- Why are sports driving the school paradigm?
- Should taxpayers be funding the NFL farm leagues in high school?
- How do math, science, literature, and history teach our students to love goodness, truth, and beauty?
- How do we keep funding low enough that anyone can attend?
- Could we pay sixteen-year-olds to run grammar schools like in the colonial era?
- Why not have college students live with their teacher like in the Middle Ages?
- What about having students make their own bricks and build a school, as Booker T. Washington's students did?
- How do we hire virtuous teachers?
- What is the point of education?

What is the point of education?

Neil Postman wrote a book called *The End of Education*, in which he used the word *end* to question the demise of education, and he also used the word *end* to mean the purpose of education. If we don't know the end (purpose) of education it could mean the end (demise) of education. David Hicks wrote a book called *Norms & Nobility*, in which he argues that the point of education is to make nobility a normative practice. In other words, for the classical Christian educator, it is normal for students to end their formal schooling as noble creatures. This is the point of education.

When I talk to parents about students graduating from middle school to high school, and even more often commencing the college experience, I rarely hear a question posed in light of the previous paragraph. The conversation is always about transcripts and scholarships and employment and athletics. Or it is about a fear that their child will get caught up in the more decadent forms of dorm life. I rarely hear that their son attended this college because he was so excited about his email communications with the science professor that he couldn't wait to sit at her feet. Or, their daughter chose this school because the students embody the idea of a virtuous citizenry. Or, their son told them he is attending their alma mater because he wants to become the same kind of noble man they are. Will any of these kinds of goals prevent your child from getting a professional degree or a skill in a trade? I don't think so.

When Shakespeare has Portia ask Brutus if she dwells "but in the suburbs of your good pleasure" (Shakespeare, *Julius Caesar*, act 2, scene 1), classically trained students know that she is asking the only question most of us care about—"Do you really love me or am I just a convenient pleasure?" Do we really love our children, or are they trophies to display in competitions? The truth is that we love our children more than we seem to be allowed to admit, let alone act upon. Most readers of this book want their children to be noble creatures: to do things well, to love abundantly, to live in humility, and to elevate beauty. But then we try to achieve it through a system that inculcates utility, pragmatism, and conformity. Often, we are content with the status quo out of fear or ignorance of alternatives; after all, we know about the compulsory educa-

tion laws. Our ancestors determined that collectively our children are more members of the state than citizens of heaven. I love my children. Therefore, I declare that they are heirs to a kingdom, servants to the people, and brothers of the King's Son. Of course they will receive an education formed by these presuppositions. I declare that for eternity they will pursue beauty, goodness, and truth.

...the trouble about learning to ask questions is that you'll ask questions. No more accepting the status quo.

Of course they will receive an education developed toward this end.

Remember, the trouble about learning to ask questions is that you'll ask questions. No more accepting the status quo. No more doing what you are told. Know thyself, and be prepared for a life of conflict. C. S. Lewis called man "a glorious ruin." The more

questions we ask, the more ruins we will find in need of repair. But the entire adventure
is glorious.

PART TWO

———————

THE DIALECTICAL ARTS

CHAPTER FOUR

———

READING

"Some books are to be tasted, others to be swallowed, and some few to be chewed and digested: that is, some books are to be read only in parts, others to be read, but not curiously, and some few to be read wholly, and with diligence and attention."

—Sir Francis Bacon, "Of Studies"

Reading dialectically is essential to all other academic disciplines. You cannot be a scientist or mathematician or artist or philosopher or statesman without being a reader. Because children have fewer responsibilities and more active imaginations than adults, childhood provides a unique time to form the habit of engrossing yourself in a book. It used to be a rite of passage to get lost in books. Today, our children may miss this rite of passage because they have an infinite number of distractions at their disposal in the form of TV, music, movies, and social networking. These distractions prevent them from thinking about themselves and their place in the world. Adolescence should be a period of development that gives youth time, space, experiences, and books to contemplate big ideas. They need to experience different kinds of literature, to discuss and to compare. They can begin to compare the themes and styles of different novels and to compare what they read to their own life experiences. This is dialectic. We must protect their ability to do this.

We must help students preserve the experience of good books and good conversations so that they can wrestle with big ideas, but in order to do so, we should consider three questions:

- Why do we want our students to read, and particularly, to read fiction?
- What do we want them to read?
- How do we want them to read?

WHY DO WE WANT OUR STUDENTS TO READ?

The fact that you are reading this book about education means that you appreciate reading and acknowledge that it is an essential activity for children and adults. In an increasingly image-based culture, though, the art and practice of reading are threatened. There is a difference between *illiteracy*—the inability to read—and *aliteracy*—the unwillingness to read. Aliteracy presents a far more real and present danger to our democracy than illiteracy. So, it is perhaps worthwhile to begin a chapter on reading with a defense of reading. Why is it so important for our students to read? Can they get the same information by listening to an audiobook, watching the news, or watching a movie?

The first answer to the question might be that reading is mental exercise. A careful reader must learn to pay attention to the details. An ability to pay attention to details prepares one to be a mathematician or a scientist or an artist. The mental exercise of reading will prepare your student for further pursuits in any field.

The mental exercise of reading will prepare your student for further pursuits in any field.

A second answer in defense of reading is that reading trains children to give their sustained attention to an argument; this is critical thinking. They must give the author space in which to develop his argument, and they must be willing to agree with him as long as his argument is plausible. When the author's argument is complete, and not before, the child must judge the arguments in light of all his previous knowledge and experience as well as the author's contribution. Too often, our political discourse today involves emotional reactions to sound bites. Instead, we need to cultivate patient readers who are willing to listen to an argument in its entirety and then sift through the evidence, judging what is true and rejecting what is not. This is the skill at the heart of the dialectic.

Another defense of reading, especially fiction, is that it cultivates the imagination. While our current educational climate is still receptive to critical thinking, it has rejected the importance of imagination in forming the character. We need to regain an understanding of the importance of a child's imagination. As a child reads, she must participate in creating the world about which she is reading. This is obvious to us in a fantasy novel such as *The Lion, the Witch and the Wardrobe*. She must engage her imagination in producing a mental picture of the strange and wondrous country of Narnia and in peopling it with bizarre and fantastic creatures. It is less obvious to us when our children read a work of historical fiction such as *The Door in the Wall*, which recreates the story of a ten-year-old boy who lives through the time of the Black Death; however, the faculty of imagination is equally important here. Our readers must conjure up mental images of a particular time and place and of a particular ten-year-old boy whose life is fraught with difficulties.

Ignoring the imagination is a profound shame because it is through literature that students form character. Gene Veith writes in *Reading Between the Lines*, "[S]tories instill moral values by giving models for concrete ethical behavior" (61). Students should be encouraged to read a wide variety of subjects—current events, science, history, mathematics, and fine arts. At the same time, teachers and parents should recognize that it is through literature that students can explore the really big ideas that will shape their character. Through reading, they can travel to other times and places, giving them the opportunity to ask questions that go beyond what they can personally experience.

Some of you may still be skeptical about the educational merits of reading fictional literature, particularly when children are in the impressionable early teen years. Would it not be better to read factual books about history and science? Would it not be better for them to accumulate facts so that they can put them to good practical use? You may even be willing to concede the benefits of reading realistic fiction, reasoning that it is close to the facts. Perhaps historical fiction is acceptable because it points to the truth, but surely there is no place in a practical education for fantasy and fairy tales.

Children would beg to differ. They crave fantasies and fairy tales, even as teenagers, precisely because these stories convey truth about the world and help young people to order their experiences. Child psychologist Bruno Bettelheim writes this:

> For a story truly to hold the child's attention, it must entertain him and arouse his curiosity. But to enrich his life, it must stimulate his imagination;

help him to develop his intellect and to clarify his emotions; be attuned to his anxieties and aspirations; give full recognition to his difficulties, while at the same time suggesting solutions to the problems which perturb him. In short, it must at one and the same time relate to all aspects of his personality— and this without ever belittling but, on the contrary, giving full credence to the seriousness of the child's predicaments, while simultaneously promoting confidence in himself and in his future. (qtd. in Veith, 142)

Take as an example the story of Little Red Riding Hood. Children take pleasure in the archetypes of the damsel in distress (Little Red Riding Hood), the treacherous and crafty villain (the big bad wolf), and the dashing and heroic rescuer (the woodchopper). Students recognize that the world is a dangerous place even for the young. They also inherently understand and desire justice. The triumph of good over evil at the end is thus deeply satisfying. By the same token, they would be profoundly unsettled if this story were turned on its head: if the wolf triumphed over the innocent girl. Their analysis of and satisfaction with this simple story demonstrates that they recognize the truth of what should be in the world. They recognize that the world should be full of salvation and protection of the young and innocent, as well as justice. The bad guys should be punished.

Your student's early forays into literary analysis will deepen as he encounters more complex characters and stories. The wolf and the girl are flat characters—immediately recognizable as a type or representative and not as an actual person. Later, he will encounter much more complex villains, like the Nazis in *Number the Stars* or the slave traders in *Amos Fortune, Free Man*. Learning to identify the types in simple stories prepares him for the more complex analysis of characters who make good and bad choices—flawed, human heroes like Achilles in *The Iliad*. Literature provides a means for him to question these ideas and to see possible answers played out. A good cancer researcher tests treatments in a controlled laboratory environment before prescribing them to actual patients. He asks, "What will happen to these cells if I . . . ?" Likewise, literature allows students to test the validity and wisdom of an idea or choice by observing it enacted in a fictional environment before mimicking it in their own lives.

WHAT DO WE WANT OUR STUDENTS TO READ?

We know that asking good questions prepares our children to make wise judgments. We also know that asking good questions requires the exercise of both orderly thinking and imaginative faculties. So, do certain books inspire better questions than others? The answer is a resounding "yes." A book for students at this level must be pleasurable, but it must also be of high moral and aesthetic quality. Too often, parents and teachers encourage reading for reading's sake without considering the content. Perhaps we are nervous about our ability to recognize a good book. On the other hand, sometimes it is necessary for students to reread very easy books in order to quickly and efficiently see past words that otherwise slow a reader down. For example, short common words like "the," "stop," and "not" are barely seen by accomplished readers, but this ability requires practice.

One guiding principle may be a close understanding of a child's readiness. We might all be willing to acknowledge that *The Iliad* is a classic work of literature, but that does not mean that a twelve-year-old is prepared to comprehend it. This might be a work best saved for a more mature reader who can bring a larger vocabulary and broader life experiences to bear upon the reading. (Of course, it is also true that certain books are worth reading and re-reading throughout one's life, so initial, incomplete readings are not necessarily futile.) Instead, coming-of-age stories in which children think creatively and act independently—in short, stories in which children grow up—are excellent stories to inspire and instruct our eleven- to fourteen-year-olds.

If we choose the books wisely, these texts will help us guide our youngsters to wisdom and maturity. Although it may be a lost idea in our culture, this is the purpose of adolescence: to practice becoming an adult. Our loss of this mission can be reflected in simple statements such as, "I need to find some books to help me raise obedient children." Instead, we should say, "I need to find some books to help me raise wise adults." Fortunately for parents and teachers, there are a multitude of coming-of-age books to choose from. See appendix 2 for a list of suggestions.

The Secret Garden is one example of such a "coming-of-age" novel. In the book, two children are deeply wounded for different reasons. One, Mary, is orphaned and must learn to shape her own life and to find joy in it. The other, Colin, has lived as an invalid neglected by his father. So, he must achieve physical as well as spiritual healing. The children transform themselves by taking responsibility for nurturing a secret garden. Reading the story allows our students to see that an important aspect of maturing is to take responsibility for oneself and for a corner of one's world. The novel presents this transformation in such a compelling and appealing way that children who read it yearn for an opportunity to express themselves. They want to create their own secret garden in which they can grow up by nurturing life.

As a parent and teacher, I do not want my children or my students to be limited by reflecting only on their own life experiences. I want them to travel to India during the British colonial rule by reading *A Passage to India*. I want them to meet natives in South America by reading *Through Gates of Splendor*. I want them to experience being stranded on a deserted island through *Robinson Crusoe*. I want them to travel back to India to experience the compassion of Mother Teresa by reading *Something Beautiful for God*. They can only vicariously experience events from the past such as British colonialism. At the same time, there are experiences I want them to have only vicariously. I have them read *To Kill a Mockingbird* because I don't want them to have to live the experience of having a friend who is accused of rape or being the victim of racism.

Parents and teachers often desire to instill a "lifelong love of learning." There are two components to cultivating a love of books. The first is guiding children toward quality literature, the kind of books that accurately depict humanity in all of its glories and failings so that the reader is forever changed by the experience of sharing in the book. The books should be aesthetically pleasing, in other words, well written; they should be morally pleasing in that they depict right solutions to problems. I don't mean here that every book must depict noble and right actions. Sometimes the right solution to

The best books for children and teens are those that you would want to read again and again as an adult.

the problem or the moral behavior is taught by negative example. In addition to these, though, the books must be enjoyable. It may take some time for young readers to find pleasure in books (they might need some remedial training as readers), but don't discount the pleasurable when helping your students to select books. The best books for children and teens are those that you would want to read again and again as an adult.

HOW DO WE WANT OUR STUDENTS TO READ?

The second means of cultivating lifelong readers is to help them become careful, thoughtful readers. Perhaps nothing ignites more controversy in educational circles than the debate between phonics instruction and the whole-language method. As a nation, we have invested much time and money into determining the best way to teach children to read, to teach them to make sense of the letters and to decode words and then sentences. Sadly, that is often the end of reading instruction. Often, we do not know what to do with students once they are reading with ease. We do not view reading as an art with its own set of techniques that lead one from competence to mastery.

Unless we think deliberately about reading, we can forget the hard work of students who labor to understand an author's meaning. First, students must learn to decipher the concrete symbols that make up words. This is the first level of meaning—sounding out symbols and recognizing words. Educators and parents work hard to make sure that students are equipped with this skill. However, we often settle for mastery of this initial skill. Our students are left to flounder with the complexities of language and meaning. As children mature past age ten, they are seldom satisfied with the basic skill of understanding a story. Instead, they want to read a story as a means of understanding the world around them. They read to learn about themselves and about their place in the world. As parents and teachers, we can guide them through this phase of wrestling with big ideas by reading and teaching them how to ask good questions.

> *As children mature past age ten, ...they read to learn about themselves and about their place in the world.*

After students leave formal schooling, books will often be their instructors. Our students should learn to become active readers by reading with a pencil in their hand and engaging in a dialogue with the book itself. Whenever possible, students should own their copy of the books. They should underline character descriptions that remind them of people they know. They should put question marks in the margins when they don't understand the author's point or even when they understand it but don't agree. They should circle words that they don't know the meanings of so that they can look them up later or attempt to define them in context. They should dog-ear a page that was particularly beautiful or moving or disturbing. Their first conversation should be with the book itself. In this age of digital books, we must still teach children to mark up their books by digitally highlighting, making notes, and bookmarking pages.

Then, they can build on their initial understanding by having a conversation about the book with their peers, their parents, and their instructors. As teachers, we can help them in this endeavor by modeling the art of asking good questions. Begin by asking questions and having discussions centered on the grammar of reading, which includes the basic types and elements of all stories. Then you can progress to more complicated questions.

"The 'Who-What-How-What'" by Courtney Sanford

Reading is a big part of family life in our home. We have had many adventures together through children's books we read, read aloud, or listen to on CD. Sometimes I'll ask a few questions to help my children think and talk about what they are reading or listening to. I call it a Who-What-How-What. It sounds like a Dr. Seuss character. If it were one of his characters, I'm sure it would have lots of hair, a long tail with stripes, and live under the couch, but it is really just a way for me to remember four important questions to ask my children about a story.

"Who" reminds me to help my children define the characters. "Who was the story about?" I ask first. This can be a short answer, just a list, or it might launch a discussion about the characters. If we've read the book of Esther, they would list Esther, of course, but also King Ahasuerus, Queen Vashti, Mordecai, and Haman. They will probably want to tell me who they liked and who they didn't like and why. This also gives me the opportunity to teach literary vocabulary such as *protagonist*, *antagonist*, and *static/dynamic* or *flat/round* characters. For students in the dialectic stage, you can gradually decrease the amount of information you hand out. Instead, teach them where to find definitions and examples (a dictionary, a glossary, or a parent-supervised Internet search for literary terms) on their own.

"What" reminds me to ask, "What was the problem or conflict of the story?" For example, in the story of Esther, my children would tell me the problem was that someone wanted to kill the Jews. Terms I introduce during these discussions might be *foreshadowing* and *rising action*, all elements of plot, which this one question will reveal.

"How" reminds me to ask, "How was the problem resolved?" In this case, they would explain how Esther risked her own life and saved her people. We can identify the *climax* and *denouement* (resolution).

The final "What" is the question, "What can we learn from this?" (or "What does the Bible have to say about this?") This helps us pull out the *theme* or *moral* of the story and often launches a great discussion. There are many answers to this question in the example of Esther. My children might answer that we learn that we should be brave and stand up for what is right. I might also ask them if they can remember other Bible verses that relate to these ideas.

As you may have guessed, I use the Who-What-How-What when we read the Bible together to facilitate good discussions. My children keep a journal in which they record the answers to these four questions for every story in *The Children's Illustrated Bible*. They also draw a simple illustration. The journal has become a keepsake and a Bible timeline we treasure. It has also taught my children to ask and answer good questions about the things they read.

HOW CAN YOU HELP YOUR STUDENTS APPRECIATE LITERATURE YOU HAVEN'T READ?

At this point, many parents of young dialecticians will be throwing up their hands and crying, "Wait! But I'm still learning the grammar of classic literature! How can I possibly teach my children? I need tools. I need a workbook!" This will not be a popular answer, but the truth is that you do not really need any special tools. What you need are some good books and some blocks of time to discuss them with your students. (You also need a healthy dose of curiosity.) Be eager to explore guidebooks that give you lots of questions, such as those we asked above, but be very cautious about the guidebooks that give you too many answers. The *Words Aptly Spoken* series is an inexpensive source with many books explored in each guide and many questions to ask about those books. Remember: you don't need an answer key. In the dialectic stage, the questions are far more important.

You can begin by reading some of the great children's literature listed in appendix 2. Follow the same educational path that you expect of your students. Begin with literature written for young adults, proceed to classic short stories, and then move to the great classics of Western civilization. In the meantime, though, can you discuss a book with your children that you haven't read? If so, how do you do it? Sometimes your own ignorance is your greatest ally. You can ask questions about the book and draw your child into thinking about the book as they fill you in on the action and the characters. As we have explored in other chapters, thinking that we have a correct answer can prevent us from asking questions.

Here are some basic questions to get the conversation started:
- Who are the characters in this book? Tell me about them.
- What choices do they have to make?
- What motivates their choices?
- What are the consequences of their choices? Are these consequences limited to them or do the consequences extend to their family? Community? Country?

My friend Jennifer recently had a literature discussion with her son about *The Bronze Bow*. She had not read the book since childhood and remembered hardly anything about it; however, she still needed to help her twelve-year-old understand the book. What you need to remember in these situations is that your child may have more knowledge about a given subject, but that you, as an adult, have more experience and wisdom. Here are the basic questions Jennifer asked her son to get him thinking about the book:

PARENT: Who were the main characters in this book?

STUDENT: Rosh and Daniel.

PARENT: Was there anyone else?

STUDENT: I guess Jesus.

PARENT: Okay. What did each character do?

STUDENT: Rosh was trying to get people to fight against the Romans.

PARENT: What people?

STUDENT: The Jews.

PARENT: How did he want the people to fight against the Romans? Protests? Military action?

STUDENT: He wanted the Jews to kill the Roman soldiers.

PARENT: Was Daniel one of his followers?

STUDENT: Well, kind of. I guess he was trying to decide between Jesus and Rosh.

PARENT: So, does that mean Jesus had followers, too? What did He want his followers to do?

STUDENT: Well, He wasn't going around telling them to kill the Romans. I guess He just wanted them to love their enemies.

Since the discussion went on for a half hour, I won't record it in its entirety. The important things to notice are that the parent/teacher used her own curiosity to ask questions. After the student answered, she asked follow-up questions. In the course of this conversation, she did not ask the student, "What's the plot of *The Bronze Bow*?" Instead she asked, "What happened in the book?" The discussion went on to consider the following questions: "How did the leaders find their followers?" "How did they persuade them to follow?" "What did they ask their followers to do?" "What were the consequences of those actions?" "What did Daniel think about the two leaders?" "How was he changed by meeting them?" After the conversation, the student was able to write an essay comparing and contrasting the two leaders and drawing a conclusion about the qualities of good leadership.

See how doable it is? Even if you missed out on a literary education when you were a teenager, you can still guide your child through a dialectic discussion of a literary work. Simple questions are all you need to engage your teenager in a meaningful way. Using the five common topics (definition, comparison, relationship, circumstance, testimony) will help you lead even more vibrant discussions and will help your students dig deeper into the meaning of a book.

DEFINITION

Definition is not only about defining terms from a dictionary or finding the one true definition of bravery. Definition can also help your students gain a deeper understanding of specific characters and character traits. Let me give you an example from the book *Number the Stars* by Lois Lowry. Imagine that you are trying to define "bravery." Here is a sample conversation that you might begin with your dialectician.

- *Genus*: What is the broad category to which bravery belongs? For our example, let's say that bravery belongs to the genus of virtues. Other virtues would include honesty, patience, humility, etc.

- *Division*: What makes bravery different from other things in its genus? Bravery is a virtue that is exercised on behalf of someone else in response to danger. This definition helps students to understand that the fact that you exercise bravery on behalf of someone else is what separates it from self-preservation and thus makes it a virtue. In *Number the Stars*, Uncle Henrik exercises bravery on behalf of the Jews in response to the dangerous threat posed by the Nazis. Specifically, he risks arrest by hiding the Jews below the deck of his fishing boat and helping them escape Denmark.

To further enrich the discussion, have students contemplate a time in their own lives when they exercised the virtue of bravery.

"Elements of Good Stories" by Jennifer Courtney

Character: Begin a book discussion with questions that help students identify characters. Ask your student, "Who are the characters?" "Can you describe them?"

Setting: To discuss setting, ask, "When and where did this story take place?"

Point of view: To find the point of view, ask, "From whose perspective is the story told?"

Plot: To reveal the plot, ask, "What happens in this book?" "Can you summarize the action?"

Conflict: To uncover the conflict, ask, "What problems do the characters confront?"

Climax/Resolution: To identify the climax of a story, ask, "When does the problem reach its critical or most intense moment?" To identify the resolution, ask, "How did the characters solve their problem?"

Denouement (the unknotting): Help your student identify the denouement by asking, "What happens to the characters after they solve the problem?" "How are they transformed as a result?"

Theme: To help your student uncover the theme, ask, "What does it all mean?"

It is usually best for students to begin literary analysis using the elements of fiction to practice on something familiar such as a fairy tale. This exercise works well in a classroom or at home. Let's try it with the story of the "Three Little Pigs."

- *Who are the characters?* The Three Little Pigs (a group of brothers) and the Big Bad Wolf
- *What is the setting?* A small village in a time long ago
- *What is the plot?* The three little pigs each build their home out of different materials and take shelter there to protect themselves from the big bad wolf. The big bad wolf then goes after each of the pigs in turn. He easily defeats the first two houses (made of straw and sticks).
- *What happens at the climax?* The cunning wolf realizes that he can't blow down the house and begins to come down the chimney.
- *What is the resolution?* The clever little pig sets a cauldron of boiling water in the path of the wolf's landing. It is fitting that he "cooks" the wolf since the wolf has eaten his two brothers.
- *What happens in the denouement?* The third little pig lives happily ever after. (This is, in fact, the denouement of most fairy tales.)

> • *What is the theme?* There is evil in the world, and the wise will take precautions to protect themselves against it.

COMPARISON

Students can use comparison to find the similarities and differences between two characters or between two books or even between a book and their own life experience. For example, you might want to compare Uncle Henrik to the main character Annemarie, who both acted bravely but in different ways. Brainstorm together ways in which the two are similar and ways in which they are different. To compare *Number the Stars* to *The Hiding Place*, you might follow this sequence of questions:

- *Similarity*: What are the similarities between *Number the Stars* and Corrie ten Boom's *The Hiding Place*? Both are novels set in European countries during World War II. Both tell the story of courageous families who helped to hide Jews from the Nazi authorities.
- *Difference*: What are the differences between these two similar plots? In Lowry's book, those assisting the Jews avoid capture. In ten Boom's book, Corrie, her father, and her sister are sent to concentration camps where her father and sister die. How does this one difference change your understanding of the two books? Is the bravery of one family less meaningful (inferior) because they escaped unharmed? How does it change the story that one account is fictional while the other is autobiographical? Is one account more meaningful (superior) because it is autobiographical, not historical fiction?

RELATIONSHIP

By relationship I mean that students will ask questions about the manner in which characters, setting, plot, and conflict affect one another. For the sake of simplicity, we'll only consider cause and effect questions for our literature discussion example. You may also choose to use other relationship-based questions.

- *Cause and effect*: In *The Magician's Nephew*, Digory Kirke travels to an imaginary world. Inside a crumbling and ruined hall, he finds a bell with an intriguing warning. Just like a real boy, he takes the warning as an invitation. He rings the bell and awakens a giant witch. Later, he inadvertently brings her into the world of Narnia. What are the effects of Digory's actions on the country of Narnia? Can an individual single-handedly unleash evil in the world? What responsibility does he bear for bringing her to this fresh, new country?

CIRCUMSTANCE

Circumstance makes students consider what is going on in the rest of the world at the time the book was written or in the time in which it was set. Let's consider the book *Amos Fortune, Free Man*, in which an African prince is brought to America as a slave.

- What else is going on in the world when Amos is captured? What is going on in Africa that makes the slave trade possible? Who is conducting the capture and sale of slaves? What is going on in the American colonies that causes the slave trade to flourish? What ideas did the Quakers have about colonial slavery? How does their ideology impact his interactions with them?

Your child may not have these answers yet, but model asking the questions and searching for answers. As he matures and learns more about the world, he will begin to ask himself this type of question and learn to find answers.

TESTIMONY

Testimony encourages students to think about other ways to advance their arguments. A great discussion to have with your students would be whether or not literature can be a form of testimony.

- Should a work of fiction be considered as valid testimony? Is there truth in fiction? What is the difference between truth about human experiences and "cold, hard facts"? Which one is more authoritative?

The novels of Charles Dickens, particularly *Oliver Twist*, did more to inspire nineteenth-century Londoners to help the poor than a multitude of sermons and pamphlets. Upton Sinclair's dramatic novel *The Jungle* inspired the Pure Food and Drug Act of 1906 and sweeping reforms of factories. The novel *Uncle Tom's Cabin* magnified the evils of slavery and fueled the Abolitionist movement. According to some, Abraham Lincoln called the author, Harriet Beecher Stowe, "the little woman who wrote the book that made this great war." Great literature inspires noble deeds.

WHAT IS THE END GOAL OF READING
LITERATURE DIALECTICALLY?

I started this chapter with the question, "Why do we want our students to read, and particularly, to read fiction?", so it seems appropriate to end the chapter by cycling back to the same governing question. A final answer is that literature inspires good men to good actions like no other medium. Through reading, they are exposed to the really big ideas that have engaged mankind for centuries. They eventually can contemplate truth, goodness, beauty, and freedom. Good literature investigates the experiences that are common to mankind and allows readers to consider the answers to our deepest questions. In his book *Norms & Nobility*, David Hicks lists some of the basic questions that people have asked throughout history:

- What is the purpose and meaning of human existence?
- What are man's absolute rights and duties?
- What is good? What is evil?
- What is the meaning of life? Of death?
- What is morality if every quality of life is reduced to what is convenient or to what brings the greatest pleasure?
- What is truth if all knowledge derives from the scientific analysis of physical data?
  (103)

One lifetime of experience is not enough to equip our children to answer these questions and to become good leaders. Instead, they must experience vicariously the struggles and joys of other lifetimes so that they can approach the world with empathy. Perhaps reading about the Middle Ages and the origins of hospitals will inspire them with a solution to contemporary healthcare problems. So, although we do not talk as loudly about the imagination as we do about critical thinking skills, it is just as essential a faculty to exercise as critical thinking. A good leader must have both: the ability to reason through sound arguments and the ability to imagine a different way of being and feeling.

One lifetime of experience is not enough to equip our children to answer these questions and to become good leaders. Instead, they must experience vicariously the struggles and joys of other lifetimes...

We acknowledge that we want our children to be readers so that they can be self-educated, so that they can develop a fine sense of aesthetics and morals, and so that they can develop the wisdom essential to becoming great leaders. As mentors—parents and teachers—we help them achieve this by exposing them to the right sort of books, by teaching them the techniques of reading actively, and by training them in the art of dialectic conversations.

Through this process, they will be changed. A reader of *Carry On, Mr. Bowditch* should recognize the vast differences between a modern education and a Colonial education. In the process, we hope that he will be inspired to own his education, to actively seek after knowledge, understanding, and wisdom. Through dialectic discussion, we can train our children to stop asking, "What is the right answer?" and train them to ask instead, "What virtues must I cultivate?" Might we inspire them to learn something on their own with just a book and a lot of hard work, the way young Nate Bowditch learned Latin from a New Testament with Latin on one page and the English translation on the facing page? If they are denied a higher education because of life circumstances, will they be inspired to follow Nate's lead and learn science and mathematics from an original source like Newton's *Principia Mathematica*?

Reading literature also builds community. As parents and teachers, we can form intimate bonds with children by loving the books they love and by listening carefully to their ideas. They, in turn, build community with others who have read the same books. They will have a shared set of ideas, almost a secret language, to shorten the distance between themselves and new acquaintances. In early American homes, the access to newspapers, Shakespeare, and the Bible created unity and community. In an increasingly image-based culture, books may very well become a threatened medium. Dialectic discussion of literature will produce not just students who understand literature but also but students who love literature. Perhaps they will become keepers of the books in the same way that monasteries preserved and treasured manuscripts after the fall of Rome.

CHAPTER FIVE

———

WRITING

"I believe that the rounding of the phrase is nothing. But that writing well is everything, because 'writing well is at the same time perceiving well, thinking well and saying well' . . . The last term is then dependent on the other two, since one has to feel strongly, so as to think, and to think, so as to express. "
—Gustave Flaubert, "Letter CCCV. To George Sand" (1876)

I began the section on the dialectical arts with reading because we need the skill of attentive reading in order to study any subject. In the same way, the skill of writing applies to all fields of study. Good writing is all about dialectic processes. If the dialectic is the "thinking" stage, in which analytical tasks and skills are dominant, writing is the dialectical process made concrete: it is thinking mapped out and put into compositions made up of words. We analyze words and organize them into orderly patterns to form sentences. We analyze sentences and string them together to form paragraphs or poetry stanzas. Then, we arrange our paragraphs into essays, and treatises, and plays, and novels—and everything in between. In my community of homeschoolers, our young teens write about many subjects, not just literature. We also write about science, history, and current events. (This is especially good for boys—if they are writing about some weird or disgusting animal, they actually enjoy writing. And if they are writing about Attila the Hun and his favorite weapons, you have a very engaged young man!)

There are many ways you can foster the dialectic skills of writing in your students and help them to become masters of the art of writing. Part of the responsibility lies with your own attitude toward writing. Just as we need to model the love of learning, we need to model the love of writing. Homeschooling pioneer Laurie Bluedorn asks, "Do you like to write? Do your children ever see you writing anything besides what is absolutely necessary?" (*Teaching the Trivium*, 403). If the answer to this question is "no," then you need to begin to find ways to model an interest in writing for your children. It doesn't have to be complicated. You can model by journaling, by showing an interest in writing forms and techniques, and by expressing an admiration for good writing. When you exhibit a positive attitude about an activity, and then confirm that you have acquired that attitude by engaging in the activity yourself, it will be a powerful encouragement to your children to follow in your footsteps. Introduce writing to your children early, and teach them that it is a responsibility for them to learn to write well, just as it is a responsibility for them to make sure they can do math, study geography and history, and learn about language as they go about the task of understanding the world in which they live.

More than anything, when young writers are learning to be dialectic, they need practice in "thought experiments," which are really just explorations of topics through *You as the teacher need to understand the critical importance of asking questions in the process of dialectical writing.* asking questions and examining their answers. This is what Socrates called the "life of inquiry." You as the teacher need to understand the critical importance of asking questions in the process of dialectical writing. Help students to practice asking all kinds of questions about their own writing, and although at first you will have to model asking questions for them, encourage them, as soon as it is possible, to ask their own questions.

Assist students to recognize that even asking questions that do not seem fruitful is productive, for it not only helps them simply practice the dialectical activity, but it will also help them to develop the skill of recognizing which kinds of questions are more fruitful than others. In addition, allow students to make mistakes and ask questions that end up "going nowhere" (i.e., resulting in answers that are not actually useful to their endeavor). Realize that the process of asking questions in and of itself is worth drilling and practicing, and that whether or not the questions are the "right" ones or lead to the "right" answers is secondary to mastering the skill. Students will learn soon enough to stop asking questions that do not lead to substantive results. They will learn best from the experience of working through it.

THINKING DIALECTICALLY ABOUT WRITING

The art of writing well focuses on the three following questions: 1) What am I going to say? 2) How am I going to arrange what I say? and 3) How am I going to present what I am going to say? Although all writing presents one's ideas to another person, writing as a dialectic skill is mostly related to the first two questions: how to decide what to write and then how to arrange it. Students add to the factual knowledge they learned in the grammar stage about the building blocks of writing (vocabulary, the parts of speech, usage rules, syntax, paragraph composition, etc.) and style (parallelism, alliteration, metaphor and simile, etc.) as they play with different forms of writing.

Some of the most important parts of studying writing dialectically will take place before your student ever composes his first original sentence. When adolescents approach writing, they are often eager—even anxious—to set pen to paper (or cursor to screen) and begin the physical act of writing. Likewise, once they have written a sentence, they treat it as though it were carved into stone or tattooed on their foreheads. This, from a generation that has never used correction fluid or retyped an entire page on a manual typewriter because of one error! I know a tutor who made one of her students write a sentence and then immediately scratch it out with red pen, just to conquer a fear of rewriting. By the end of the exercise, the student was laughing, but she grudgingly admitted that it was possible that she might be able to write another sentence as good or maybe even better than the first.

When you think about writing, tell your children what author Mark Twain wrote in one of his *Notebooks* (1902–1903): "The time to begin writing an article is when you have finished it to your satisfaction. By that time you begin to clearly and logically perceive what it is that you really want to say." Remind your student that even great writers often revise their books for years before they are satisfied. Remind yourself that marking up a composition is not about passing judgment on your child's capabilities or worth. It is not about assigning a one-time, high-stakes grade. Rather, when you or your child edits his writing, you are indicating how much confidence you have in his potential. You have so much confidence that you are willing to spend time and effort to make his writing better. In this way, you are showing your child that you value what he has to say so much that you want it to be well said, and you want him to value his own writing in the same way. That's why the dialectic student should spend copious amounts of time brainstorming and outlining before ever writing a sentence, and then he should write, rewrite, edit, and write the same ideas again in order to master different forms of writing.

"Brainstorming" by Courtney Sanford

Writing doesn't have to start with a blank sheet of paper and writer's block. That is what most people say they dread most about writing, isn't it? In my home, papers never begin that way. They begin at the whiteboard. I have a large whiteboard on my dining room wall. (You won't see that in the home decorating magazines, but they are really wonderful, and if you know me well enough to be in my dining room, then, you would know I homeschool and you wouldn't think it strange at all. It is beautifully trimmed, and if I have guests for dinner, I write or draw something relevant and thought provoking on it. I highly recommend that you hang one somewhere in your house, if not in the dining room.)

Before beginning a writing assignment, we brainstorm together and fill the whiteboard with our thoughts, opinions, and ideas until it is entirely covered. Once all our ideas are on the board, we can sit back and look over them all, choose the best three ideas to form a thesis, and then the writing will come easily. Is helping a student come up with ideas for a paper "cheating"? Absolutely not, in my opinion. I am modeling and guiding my student in the asking of good questions, organizing his thoughts, and having a great conversation of ideas. Later, I will expect my student to be capable of doing this on his own, but he'll never do it on his own if he doesn't have a form to guide him and a lot of practice under his belt. Plus, these are some of my favorite times spent with my children. We really enjoy the conversations. They cause us to think deeply and often laugh aloud or cry together. (Okay, I'm the only one who cries openly over the characters in books during a discussion. I could cry now remembering Corrie ten Boom's father or the tragedy of *Little Britches*.)

There are several ways to get your brainstorming session started. If we already have a prompt to start our paper, we begin with the prompt and try to put every possible answer to the prompt on the whiteboard. Then we can sit back and discuss which answers are the strongest points for a paper.

If the assignment is open ended, we pick a favorite character and form a "should" statement about one of that character's actions or decisions. For example, we could ask ourselves, "Should Corrie ten Boom have hidden the Jews in her house when she knew it was illegal?" I write the question at the top of the board. Then I draw a vertical line down the center of the board. One side of the line will be all the reasons that "Yes, she should have." And the other side is for all the reasons that "No, she shouldn't have." We then try to fill both sides. Sometimes we have to get the book out and look for more "evidence." Sometimes we really have to play devil's advocate to come up with evidence that opposes our own opinion. Once all the ideas, pro and con, are on the board, we can sit back and compare the two sides. Which one has the stronger case? Which points are strongest? Which points show biblical truths and which do not? After this discussion, my children have no trouble choosing their favorite three points. When I have had more than one student in the brainstorming session, they choose different points and often choose different sides of the argument. This results in very different, but thoughtful, well-developed papers.

Another form for brainstorming is to compare two things: two different characters, or one character at two different points in his life, two different situations, two different choices, or whatever is compelling from the literature or prompt. Write the two items on the board, one at the far left and the other at the far right. Under each item, you will brainstorm and list how they are different. In the middle, make a column for how they are similar. For example, if you are comparing Hester Prynne to Arthur Dimmesdale from *The Scarlet Letter*, you would write "woman" under Hester and "man" under Dimmesdale. One of the things they have in common is that they are both Puritans, so I would write "Puritan" in the center column. The first few items on your list will come easily, but to fill the board will take some effort and thinking.

Give brainstorming a try with your own children. The results are great—great discussions, great relationships with your teenagers, and no more writer's block! This is just one simple technique that rains down many blessings. I believe the blessings are so great because this falls in line with how God intended for parents to teach their children: through relationship, throughout the day, using questions and answers.

Students in the dialectic stage of writing need to acquire and practice using models of form and structure—templates, if you will, like the ones that come already set up on our word processing or spreadsheet software. Templates act like outlines, which specify certain "fill in the blanks" by asking different questions, depending on what the template is designed to achieve. The significance of forms cannot be stressed enough. Stanley Fish writes this in *How to Write a Sentence*:

[W]ithout form, content cannot emerge. When it comes to formulating a proposition, form comes first; forms are generative not of specific meanings, but of the very possibility of meaning. Despite the familiar proverb, it is not the thought that counts. Form, form, form, and only form is the road to what the classical theorists called "invention," the art of coming up with something to say. (27)

In the classical tradition of education, students used the five common topics to generate content to write about, but the topics can also help your student learn good writing techniques. Although at first it may seem that requiring students to follow a series of questions limits freedom, in reality it liberates them. By asking and then answering questions derived from the five common topics, students will discover a wealth of information with endless possibilities for their writing. Stanley Fish puts it this way: "Tie yourself to forms and the forms shall set you free" (33).

"Tie yourself to forms and the forms shall set you free."
—Stanley Fish, *How to Write a Sentence* (p. 33)

DEFINITION

Whether your child is writing a literature essay, a scientific research paper, or a creative story, he will need to begin by asking basic questions to define his goals in writing this paper and the parameters of the specific assignment. Start with the generic components of an essay. What are the common features of an introduction? A conclusion? Should they state opinions, provide background information, or make a specific claim? What is a *thesis*? Do all writing assignments require one? What is a body paragraph? Does every paper need to contain three of them?

Next, define the form of this particular assignment. Is the project creative or factual? One type of writing allows the writer to use his imagination to tell a story or convey an idea, while the other relates an argument, a set of facts, or a true story. If the project is factual, is it a book report or a persuasive essay? A book report asks the student to provide a summary of someone else's writing, while a persuasive essay asks the student to develop an original argument. If the project is creative, is it a poem or a short story? A poem could be written with meter and rhyme or in free verse. A short story could be narrated from the perspective of one character or from the perspective of an omniscient narrator. How long does it need to be? If it is a five-page paper or story, the topic or plot can be more complex than it can be if the project is only one page long. As you ask more and more specific questions about the definition of the assignment, your student's understanding will become gradually clearer.

The next step is to define the topic about which your student will write. Sometimes a curriculum may provide a topic for the student, but sometimes the student may be asked to come up with his own. In that case, begin by asking your student more questions of definition. If he is writing about a work of literature, ask him to define the plot of the book. Ask him to identify the main characters and ask basic questions about the setting, conflict, and themes of the novel. (For more ideas, see chapter 4 on reading.) Any of these categories may help your student define his topic.

When your child is just beginning to write compositions, do not expect him to tackle complex, controversial topics right away. Begin with simple either/or topics so that he can focus on the forms of writing. Andrew Kern, author of *The Lost Tools of Writing*, suggests that "should" questions provide particularly fruitful topics because 1) they deal with philosophical, not factual differences of opinion, so there is room to argue; 2) students can make an argument on either side of the issue; and 3) these questions require no outside research beyond the book and the student's personal opinion. For this reason, we often teach beginning writers to start with the persuasive essay as a basic form of writing. From a "should" question, your student can easily choose his thesis, or main claim. Either the character or historical figure *should have* done an action, or the individual *should not have* done the action. That statement is what your child's persuasive essay will attempt to prove.

Once a student has defined the writing assignment, encourage your child to think about how this will differ from earlier writing experiences.

COMPARISON

One of the best ways a dialectician can prepare to write well is by analyzing and comparing the work of other excellent writers, so do everything in your power to provide your students with a rich literary environment. Laurie Bluedorn writes, "If nothing literary is going in, then don't expect something literary to come out" (*Teaching the Trivium*, 403). Keep books in your home, and in addition to modeling writing for your children, make sure to provide other models of writing through good literature. The classics that have withstood the test of time are excellent examples—think of great biographies like Plutarch's *Lives*, philosophies such as Aristotle's *Ethics*, sermons like Jonathan Edwards' "Sinners in the Hand of an Angry God," plays like those by

Shakespeare, novels by Jane Austen, short stories by Hemingway, mathematical treatises like Euclid's *Geometry*, scientific works like Newton's *Principia*, and famous speeches like Lincoln's "Gettysburg Address" or Martin Luther King's "I Have a Dream."

Encourage your students to pay attention not just to the plot and the characters of their favorite novel but also to the writing. Sometimes this is a difficult assignment for speedy readers, so you may have to train them to slow down their reading habits. Copying individual sentences from a book onto a separate page may help. So may underlining or highlighting parts of speech or transition words. Bring life to this hard work by inviting your students to wonder why Charles Dickens might have written such long sentences while Ernest Hemingway wrote such short ones. Ask them why Martin Luther King used so much repetition and why Lincoln did not just say "eighty-seven years ago." Hold a race to see who can diagram the opening sentence of the Declaration of Independence the fastest, and then compare your answers. Ask each family member to find a favorite sentence, and then talk about what makes that sentence so much fun to read. Spend time comparing the crafts of other writers, and your own craft will improve proportionally.

In addition to comparing writers and sentences, spend time comparing genres and forms of writing. Talk about the different demands of newspaper writing and novel writing. Ask your student to rewrite a children's novel as a news story. Rewrite a scene from a novel as a play and read it aloud as a family. This exercise does not have to be tedious. For a humorous example, tell your students about a comic writer named Sarah Schmelling, who gained Internet fame a few years ago when she rewrote Shakespeare's *Hamlet* as if it were a Facebook news feed. Find a genre that interests your child, and encourage him to tell a classic story using the conventions of his chosen form.

When your student is confronted with a writing assignment, he can also use comparison to gain greater understanding about his task. For example, if he is writing a book report, you might ask him to find three examples of book reports (covering different books, not the one about which he is writing). Have him study each of the examples and compare the structure and style of each one, looking at the length of sentences, the length of paragraphs, and the length of the report as a whole. Ask him to compare the structure of each argument. Does each book report begin by giving a synopsis of the book, or do some of them begin with an engaging "hook" instead? How does each book report conclude? Does the writer pass judgment on the book? What kind of title does each author use? Does the author use specialized language such as jargon or slang? Then, when your student begins writing his own book report, he will have a basic form to imitate.

As you move toward the rhetoric stage, when young writers will focus on style and developing original arguments, comparison becomes even more important. Imagine that you are writing a poem about a dog. You want your reader to understand more about the dog than you can convey by defining what it is: a basset hound, brown-haired, eighteen inches tall, seven years old, female, called Rosabelle. So, you begin to tell your reader what Rosabelle is *like*. You make a comparison. Maybe her tail wags like a windshield wiper on high speed. This is a literary device called a *simile*, an explicit comparison. Or, you might say she whirls across the room when you walk in the door. You are not explicitly saying that Rosabelle is *like* a helicopter with her long ears, but your words make that implicit comparison. This is a literary device called a *metaphor*. Both of these rhetorical tools use comparison to create vivid word pictures for your reader. As your student moves toward the rhetorical stage, these and other literary devices will contribute to his personal style and voice as a writer.

RELATIONSHIP

Once your student has a basic form and structure in mind for his essay, he will need to arrange his thoughts in a logical order. The young writer deals with questions of relationship from the level of sentences to that of paragraphs and finally to the essay as a whole. He must learn how to tie thoughts together, how to contrast ideas, and how to connect one paragraph with another. Here, drilling the grammar of writing (parts of speech, verb conjugations, grammar and usage rules, diagramming sentences) is essential if your student is to progress in the dialectic stage. A 2012 article in *The Atlantic* featured a New York public school that decided to tackle its academic problems by putting writing back at the heart of its curriculum. The administrators and teachers wanted to know why students struggled so much with basic writing tasks. Here's what one history teacher found:

> He pointed out that the students' sentences were short and disjointed. What words, Scharff asked, did kids who wrote solid paragraphs use that the poor writers didn't? Good essay writers, the history teacher noted, used coordinating conjunctions to link and expand on simple ideas—words like *for, and, nor, but, or, yet*, and *so*. Another teacher devised a quick quiz that required students to use those conjunctions. To the astonishment of the

staff, she reported that a sizable group of students could not use those simple words effectively. (qtd. in Tyre, "The Writing Revolution," 2)

What the history teacher noticed was the students' inability to relate one idea to the next in an organized fashion. They were missing the relationships—the glue—in writing. Coordinating and subordinating conjunctions tie clauses together to form sentences. Transition words such as "next" and "however" and "first" connect sentences and paragraphs together in meaningful ways. If students do not understand these concepts, how can we expect them to write well?

Thankfully, you don't have to be an expert writer to guide your student; you can help him improve his writing by asking questions of relationship.

Thankfully, you don't have to be an expert writer to guide your student; you can help him improve his writing by asking questions of relationship. For visual learners, I use the image of a bridge across a river. Place yourself in the position of the reader and ask, "So, in this paragraph, you've told me about X. Now you want to talk about Y. How can you help me get from X to Y? Use transition words to build me a bridge." Or, use a different example. "Your friends are talking about X, but the conversation is lagging, so you want to change the subject to Y. At the same time, you don't want to be rude by changing the topic abruptly. How could you ease the conversation from X to Y?" These simple questions will encourage your child to think about the relationship between ideas and remind him that writing is not a one-sided task. His writing is meant to be read, and what is more, his ideas are worth reading.

Another way to practice the concept of relationship is for dialectical students to write a lot of outlines in complete sentences. Distilling every step in an argument to a single sentence, first, requires your student to understand the skeleton of his argument. If he cannot explain it to you, ask more questions to help him clarify his ideas: "What do you mean when you say X?" "What I hear you saying is Y, but could you put it another way?" "I'm not sure how this fits into your argument. Can you give me an example?" "I feel like we're missing a step here. How did you get from Y to Z?" Let him play the teacher and you will find out how well he understands his argument.

Furthermore, writing outlines will bring the key ideas closer together in space, placing them next to each other so that your student can see whether or not they make sense in that order. Ask him why he arranges his points in that way. Assume he should have a reason and he may be more willing to admit that he does not know. Then encourage him to think about cause and effect and antecedent and consequence. If he is writing an essay arguing that slavery is wrong, giving historical examples, ask him whether he wants to arrange his examples chronologically or by using a different organizing principle. Then ask him what difference it makes one way or the other. Always frame your questions around the assumption that his ideas will be read by someone. Will one version of the outline help his reader follow his argument more easily? Will one outline make a stronger emotional claim on the reader?

At this point, you can turn to the question of purpose and audience, encouraging him to think about what this particular essay should accomplish and what outline will best enable him to reach that end. Then, when he sits down to write the body of his essay, expanding his outline, he will be primed to consider the relationship of the sentences within each paragraph and the relationship between paragraphs. If the student understands why he has placed his paragraphs in a particular order, he will find it easier to write transitions that reflect that organizing principle.

CIRCUMSTANCE

Once your student has a form, a topic, and an outline, he will need to identify his audience and the circumstances surrounding this assignment. Who will be reading this paper? A teacher? A parent? His peers? An expert or celebrity? Each of these audiences has different expectations and background knowledge. If he is writing for a teacher or his classmates, he may not need to provide background information about the plot of the book because everyone who sees the paper will have read the book already. By contrast, if he is writing for a celebrity or public official, he may not know if the individual has read the book, so he should include a brief synopsis to provide his reader with necessary information. Likewise, while his peers may be most comfortable reading an essay written in casual language that uses contractions, slang, and sly remarks, his grandfather may not appreciate a paper that includes the acronyms FWIW or IMHO. The tone of the paper will depend heavily on the audience for whom it is written, so it is important that he identify the audience before he begins to write.

Finally, our budding writer will need to determine his purpose. Ask him if this piece of writing is designed to inform, entertain, or persuade. (These are not clear-cut categories; some pieces of writing will serve more than one purpose.) The purpose of the composition will inform style and content. If he were writing a eulogy for a respected civil servant, he would not want to include a joke about the presidential election. His purpose was to inform mourners who did not know the official well about the man's character and life's work or to persuade mourners who did know the man that his accomplishments should not be forgotten. A political joke probably does not advance this purpose and may, in fact, sabotage it. Consider also that a journalist may lose credibility if she interrupts her story on land disputes in Arizona to urge readers to vote for a certain political candidate. Her role is understood to be that of an informer, not a persuader. Likewise, a humorous after-dinner speech would take on an entirely different tone if the speaker ended by requesting a toast to the memory of his recently deceased uncle. Ask your student what elements of style will help him advance his particular purpose in writing.

TESTIMONY

Depending on the type of essay your student is writing, he may need to rely on evidence of one kind or another. The amount of research will depend on the form of the writing assignment. Creative writing may require little or no secondary support, while fact-based writing may require testimony ranging from quotes from a work of literature to statistics from an official government report. Your student should ask, "What type of testimony does my assignment require?" "How can I find that information?" and "How should I incorporate this information into my paper?" Practice using computer-based research, libraries, and reference books as well as logic. Your student's arguments will become more nuanced and well balanced as he learns to test his ideas (comparison) against those of other writers and thinkers. Likewise, your student should be learning to ask, "Who says?" when he encounters an argument written by someone else. As he gathers research, teach him to ask questions about his sources: "Who is this source?" "What is her background?" "Is she an expert or an eyewitness?" In the slavery example above, for instance, the student may read testimony from a plantation owner about benign aspects of slavery. What can the student say about this source? If the author is using statistics to prove a point, where do the data come from? What method was used to calculate them? This is an opportunity for your argumentative child to put to good use all of his natural skepticism.

As your child writes his own papers, however, be aware that he may also begin to ask questions about other kinds of authority, particularly if he enjoys creative writing and wants to abandon the hard work of good grammar and spelling in favor of creative interpretations. What then? Refer back to the section on circumstance and ask him questions about the difference between creative writing and formal writing. How can your student modify his writing to fit the needs and expectations of his audience? When you correct your student's work, remember, as Littlejohn and Evans write in *Wisdom and Eloquence: A Christian Paradigm for Classical Learning*, "it is not sufficient to just grade papers. As conscientious teachers in the liberal arts tradition, we must correct papers. We serve students as editors, respecting their style and voice, but holding them accountable for good grammar, sound logic, and meaningful expression in their writing" (113). Personal style and voice are built on knowledge of good form. Remember the notion of memory work discussed earlier in this book. We memorize English grammar for the same reasons that we work to master logic symbols and phonograms. We overlearn rules of English so that if, later, we make a conscious decision to break them, we can defend our choices.

Invite your creative child to participate in a conversation about when it is appropriate to stray from accepted rules of grammar and punctuation, and when it only confuses and alienates your reader. This is an opportunity to talk to your child as an adult about courtesy and consideration for others. Andrew Kern of the CiRCE Institute enjoys talking about the idea that even the details of grammar are reflective of Christian character. Did you ever think about the fact that grammar *Did you ever think* is a form of kindness? We love our neighbors by following *about the fact that* conventions of English grammar that have been agreed *grammar is a form* upon by the community. Who would think that grammar *of kindness?* could introduce such an important conversation? That is the joy of the dialectic stage, in which your child's natural argumentativeness opens the door for the kind of adult conversations that truly matter.

PUTTING THESE SKILLS ONTO PAPER

I mentioned earlier that the five common topics can also help your child generate content to write about. Let's take these techniques and apply them to an imaginary essay that you have assigned your child to write after he reads *The Magician's Nephew* by C. S. Lewis. For the sake of an example, pretend that he is writing a persuasive essay on the topic of temptation. He has decided to argue whether Digory should have rung the bell when he was in Charn with Polly.

He has an issue, whether Digory should have rung the bell, and so we want him to define his terms. Who is Digory? He is a boy, a human; his father is overseas in India; his mother is sick; he lives with his aunt and uncle; he is friends with Polly, the neighbor girl. What is the bell? It is a bell, located in a great hall, in a rundown place called Charn; a nearby inscription reveals that to ring it could bring danger but that not ringing it will make you go mad.

Your son might feel that this is enough information to settle the issue and get to writing. There is plenty more to consider, however. He should compare Digory with another character, like Polly. How are they the same/different? What do they have that is the same/different? What do they do that is the same/different? They are both humans, but Digory is a boy while Polly is a girl. They both have families, but Digory's mother is sick while Polly's parents are healthy. They both read the inscription about the bell, but Digory wants to ring the bell while Polly does not. (More could be said, but this can get him started.)

Your son should then consider the circumstances at the time Digory is tempted to ring the bell: Digory's mother is sick, the city looks rundown and scary, Polly is scared, they are in an unknown land, and Digory has hurt Polly's arm.

As your son turns to the relationships in his issue, he discovers that Digory's uncle's deceit has brought them there, where this odd bell and the pillar's inscription now tempt Digory. Your son will also know that ringing the bell brings about a specific danger: the release of the Empress Jadis. Digory, however, does not have this key information.

Finally, your son should consider the testimony or authority of others. What happened to Macbeth (if he's familiar with the story) when he listened to the witches who tempted him? What happened to Adam and Eve when they gave in to their temptations? What was Aslan's reaction to Digory's ringing the bell?

Your son will need to consider the evidence he has amassed from these questions and answers to decide whether or not Digory should have rung the bell. Now he has the information he needs to be able to formulate a thesis and its supporting arguments, which he can then arrange and write as an essay.

Finally, encourage your son to read his composition aloud, and also read it silently side by side with him. Interact with your son, have conversations about his topic with him, discuss questions with him, and ultimately, edit what he has written for grammatical accuracy, clarity, good organization, and style.

You do not need to be an expert to discuss your son's paper with him. The feedback you give him as you interact with him will be worth volumes. Rather than simply marking the errors in the paper, ask, "Why did you use a semicolon instead of a comma?" or "What is the relationship between these two clauses? If it is cause and effect, what conjunction should you use to indicate that fact?" Remember the example

I gave early in this book about Socrates' teaching style? Be like Socrates and allow your son to identify his own errors, and then ask him how he can fix them. In this way, you teach him that it is okay to ask more questions as he gets excited about the different ways to write an individual sentence or a conclusion. In addition, you express your confidence in his ability to improve as a writer. Over time, you will teach your son to internalize what Stanley Fish calls "a grammatical 'sixth sense' that enables you first to sense that something has gone wrong and then to zero in on it, and finally to correct it" (*How to Write a Sentence*, 22).

Leading your child through the questions generated by the five common topics is teaching him how to think. This is is a form that he should learn to imitate and use for himself as he writes more essays. The five common topics provide a form that will give you confidence in teaching him dialectically and will give him confidence as he learns something new or attempts to communicate what he has learned. Do not excuse your math genius or technically minded student from learning to write well. He will need to be able to communicate his ideas to others, whether he pursues a vocation as an inventor, a CEO, a chemist, a doctor, or a professional athlete.

Leading your child through the questions generated by the five common topics is teaching him how to think.

Writing according to this pattern has one more distinct advantage: your child is not just learning how to write, he is learning to make judgments. As one writer of the French Renaissance, Michel de Montaigne, noted, it is the teacher's principal end "that he imprint not so much in his schollers mind the date of the ruine of Carthage . . . nor when Marcellus died . . . that he teach him not so much to know Histories, as to judge them" (qtd. in Hicks, *Norms & Nobility*, 4). I want my children and students to know facts and dates from history or literature so that they can pass judgment on them. As they learn to judge them, they learn to judge rightly, and as they learn to judge rightly, they learn to live well with self, with neighbor, and before God. In the book *Climbing Parnassus*, Tracy Lee Simmons says,

> The educated mind must first know how to do, how to form and build, something. Education is the result; training is the method. Grammar, Usage, and Composition lend the starter sets for constructing that educated mind; they are the bricks and mortar, hammer and nails. But master architects draw the plans, not amateurs. Quintilian defined proper usage in language as "the agreed practice of educated men." Time and experience have validated his judgment. For centuries men and women of discernment have seen the

claim's truth played out daily. To speak, write, and think well, one must learn from those who have expressed themselves better than had others throughout history. One learns how to think well by constant exposure to the greatest thoughts expressed with the finest, most apt words. Literature was the treasure chest; Grammar and Usage were the keys unlocking its lid (162).

It is often the case that the greatest of achievements are built upon the seemingly smallest of skills. The greatest ultimate artifact of the dialectic promises to be a human life lived wisely, creatively, and with virtue—no matter the context of career, financial achievement, or fame. We can teach the dialectic well by teaching good writing skills.

Students who learn to write in an organized, structured way will be able to make significant contributions to their culture, civilization, and country. They will be able to write persuasively in many areas of interest to them (politics, economics, art, science, history, technology, vocational manuals, even sports), and they will be able to write beautifully for the pleasure of others. Students who can write and read well will also reap the rewards of living richly knowledgeable, imaginative, and creative lives. That is, they will understand their own history and culture well. They will have access to the wealth of knowledge that our civilization has produced, and they will be able to share it with others and pass it on to future generations.

CHAPTER SIX

———

MATH

"And he made a molten sea, ten cubits from the one brim to the other: it was round all about, and its height was five cubits: and a line of thirty cubits did compass it round about."

—1 Kings 7:23

Math is the perfect tool for teaching dialectic skills because math teaches children how to ask specific questions and articulate precise answers that they can prove. As Dorothy Sayers says, solving an algebra problem is like reading a mystery novel. Both require us to become intimate with the suspects and discover the unknown. Math is advantageous over a novel in teaching children to be sleuths because most math mysteries can be uncovered in just a few minutes. Solving equations fits well with our children's attention spans.

Algorithms and memorized facts are preparatory for the forensic skills required to solve an algebra problem or build a geometry proof. Just as you have to know the nature of the crime before you can see past the obvious to identify the culprit, you need math drills to steep yourself in the environment of math thought. When the basic facts are obvious, we have mental space to investigate the obscure, the unknown, and the unfamiliar.

...solving an algebra problem is like reading a mystery novel. Both require us to become intimate with the suspects and discover the unknown.

To persuade you that your mind already knows this method of thinking dialectically and mathematically, let me give you a few examples that are less sterile and academic. The word *algorithm* simply means a step-by-step procedure or set of rules used for a particular type of calculation. What other activities have this kind of point-by-point instruction? How about a family baking lesson? When you look at a recipe for baking powder biscuits, you see a series of numbers and symbols. To produce edible biscuits, you have to interpret the symbols and follow the directions in the correct order. This requires reading over the recipe and making sure you have all of the ingredients before you start baking.

Begin by asking, "What do I know?" If you are an experienced cook, you probably know that "Tbsp." is the symbol for a tablespoon, which is a larger unit of measurement than a teaspoon (tsp.). You know how to read the lines on a measuring cup. You might even know that four tablespoons of butter is the same thing as half of a stick of butter. Then ask, "What do I not know?" Perhaps the recipe tells you to "cut" the butter into the flour, and you have never heard that verb used in this particular context. So, ask, "How can I find out?" You could find the word "cut" in a dictionary, but that might not help you define it as a baking term. The recipe might give you enough information, but you might also need to consult another cookbook or a glossary in the back of the book you are using. If your child is baking for the first time, he might need to ask you or another more experienced adult how to proceed. But once you have answered these three questions to your satisfaction, you can easily follow the directions to reach your desired outcome: delicious food! After baking biscuits many times using many different recipes, you will be familiar enough with the basic ingredients (flour, milk, butter, baking powder) and methods (cut, sift, knead) that you can tackle more complex recipes or even create your own.

How about a family carpentry lesson? When you look at an instruction booklet for assembling a bookshelf, you see a series of numbers, symbols, and shapes. To produce a sturdy bookcase, you have to interpret the symbols and follow the directions in the correct order, so you need to read over the instructions and make sure you have all of the required tools and parts before you start assembling. Once you have asked and answered, "What do I know?" "What do I not know?" and "How can I find out?" to your satisfaction, you will be able to build a useful product for the family library. Eventually, after building bookshelves many times using many different kits and blueprints, you will be able to design and build your own unique creation that will become a family heirloom. The same thought processes that allow you to build or bake successfully will allow you to guide your child through increasingly complex math equations.

One reason parents may shy away from higher mathematics is that it lacks the tangible outcome of a biscuit recipe or a blueprint. Yet math is a gateway to the thoughts that are deeper than all other thoughts. Math is not just foundational; it can take a student back to the foundations of the world. In Lewis's *The Chronicles of Narnia*, the White Witch knows the deep magic. She knows that a traitor's blood can be redeemed by a willing substitute and triumphantly agrees to let Aslan substitute his life to pay for Edmund's crime. But she does not know the deeper magic. She doesn't know that if the substitute is innocent, the sacrificial altar will be broken, time will run backwards, and all will be healed—all creation, not just the traitor or his substitute. This love of the deeper magic,

> *Math is not just foundational; it can take a student back to the foundations of the world.*

the mystery behind thought, the metaphysics that informs functionality, is what drives me to study math. The mathematician regularly dwells in the abstract and therefore has the privilege of seeing more of the unseen.

This privilege takes hard work and dedication over an extended period of time. As Christian discovered in *The Pilgrim's Progress*, there are no alternatives to the narrow road that leads to the Celestial Palace. We moderns want that special pill, that new video program, or that popular textbook to take us to depths of knowledge that can only be accessed by hard work. We want the path to be easy and understandable. Yet as Christians, we should know that the path will be long and difficult. I do the same thing that so many others do, buying videos titled *Flat Abs in 20 Minutes* or *Italian in 8 Easy Lessons*, knowing all is a delusion. Yet I waste my money, emotionally feeling as if I have done something. Remember this the next time you switch curriculums when you have a perfectly good one on the shelf. The author of the book or video could produce the material because they did the hard work that makes it look easy. The privilege of hearing God say, "Well done" comes from the doing well.

HOW IS MATH LIKE READING?

Let's begin by asking a simple question: "What is five minus two?" Notice that I asked you to answer a question, not to solve a problem. A father who homeschools his children said to me, "Of course we hate math. Who wants to solve problems? I don't want my life to be any more problematic than it has to be. Just the word 'problem' makes me anxious." This father works in a software company and is very familiar with math, so think of how much more anxious nontechnical people feel. So, instead of asking you to solve problems, I will ask you to answer many questions about math sentences. Equations are really sentences written with symbols full of abstract meaning.

Equations have both nouns and verbs and are very similar to sentences that follow the subject-verb-predicate noun pattern. For example, "Three is five minus two" can be written as $3 = 5 - 2$. "Three is two less than five" can be written $3 = -2 + 5$. You can see from these examples that math is a structured language. The first sentence was pretty easy to translate, but the second had unusual nuances. Math requires a student to have excellent reading skills. He has to know that "two less" means "minus two." In addition to the nuances, he has to know that the symbol "-" is packed with meaning: less, minus, and difference.

Those who read well understand abstract meanings. "Her world was colored by the war's devastations" does not mean that the war used a crayon to change the color of her living room. This sentence uses "coloring" as a metaphor for "influencing" or "having an effect on someone." Furthermore, learning math is similar to learning Chinese in that we have to learn not only a new vocabulary but also a new alphabet that, at first glance, looks like unfamiliar squiggles. Math has its own symbolic form.

Learning math is similar to learning Chinese in that we have to learn not only a new vocabulary but also a new alphabet.

One reason children may find word problems frustrating is that we have to translate our familiar English language into the language of mathematics before we can begin to answer the question at hand. Think for a moment how children raised in a bilingual home naturally switch from one of their native languages to the other, while children raised hearing only one language struggle to grasp another language when they study it in school. Unfortunately, very few of us are fluent in mathematics ourselves, so we do not raise our children to be naturally bilingual in mathematics. Instead, they have to learn the hard way, as we did. Does that mean that no one can become fluent in a foreign language unless they are born hearing it? Of course not! Instead, we use deliberate study and, when possible, immerse ourselves in the language and culture we are trying to learn.

The same principle applies to math studies. Thankfully, we do not have to travel to CERN in Switzerland or MIT in Boston in order to immerse our families in mathematics. Math surrounds our daily lives; we just have to learn to see it and point it out to our children. When you go to the grocery store, ask your child to help you find the best bargain for bread. Two different brands each cost $3.99 a loaf. How do you know which is the better value? Point out that the net weight of one loaf is 1 lb. 8 oz., while the other is 1.5 pounds. To find the best value by weight, your child will need to know the definition of a pound and an ounce. He will need to be able to use fractions (what part of a pound is eight ounces?). He will need to compare fractions to decimals, understanding that 1.5 is the same as 1½. And even after he solves the word problem you have just identified, you can talk about how math affects marketing in this situation. Why would one bread manufacturer use one number form instead of the other? And just like that, a simple exercise in frugal living turns into a multifaceted math lesson that opens your child's eyes to the world of numbers that he inhabits.

As in this example, beginning mathematics requires us to study symbols that represent abstract concepts and to study how they relate to one another. Understanding math becomes easier when you can read the alphabet (symbols), memorize the proper vocabulary (facts), internalize the few—really, very few—structural rules (laws and operations), and learn to ask questions that lead to clarity. The dialectic stage, the questioning, reveals for the student the unreadable symbols, unmemorized facts, and misunderstood laws and operations. The questions force us to continue mastering the grammar. This is why it is acceptable to have the wrong answer if you are practicing the dialectic. The wrong answer gets us to the next question. Learning is more difficult if we don't ask questions after coming to a wrong conclusion. When teachers merely grade a student's work, they are robbing the student of the opportunity to ask questions and discover for herself her flaw in thinking. For me, the best use of the dialectic in math is when a student solves an equation correctly and still asks questions because she sees alternative plots (formulas) and endings (final numbers), just like in a mystery story, a shopping trip, or a carpentry project.

MATH AND THE COMMON TOPICS

Many parents grow frustrated as their children enter the upper grades, feeling ill-equipped to teach math or help with homework. This is not a reflection on parents but rather a reflection on the way we teach math. Teaching math dialectically leads students beyond an understanding of how to solve particular problems in a particular textbook; it teaches students to think about how math works and how to use numbers in relationship to one another. Students will learn how to untangle an equation into all of its grammatical components and to focus on how to truly understand a problem, instead of just focusing on how to get the correct solution. The solution matters; it will just be derived more accurately as the student understands more. We can learn to rejoice in the tension often caused by math studies if we recognize that it is normal to be frustrated with new ideas. The joy comes after we understand the difficult. Wrestling and subduing a problem can be gratifying, especially as we see more of the beauty of math.

Mastery of the basic operations and number facts is foundational to appreciating math. Good teachers ask questions that help students discover that they have already been taught the answers. Your basic role during the dialectic stage of math education is to help your student take basic grammar (the numbers, operations, and laws) and expand its reach to word problems, unit conversions, and basic algebra and geometry. We need to cultivate our students' ability to think clearly and appropriately about every math equation they encounter. This requires an intentional effort from both parent and student to understand the concept, not simply to reach the correct answer.

Good teachers ask questions that help students discover that they have already been taught the answers.

In writing, we used the questions suggested by the common topics to plan and compose a persuasive essay or speech. In other words, we used them to generate proofs to help convince an audience that our position on a given issue was correct. As we investigate the dialectic in math, we are going to learn how to use these common topics to ask math questions that guide our students' understanding.

In order to help more of us appreciate math questions, I will use both simple arithmetic equations and algebra problems to explain the dialectic. Keep in mind that algebra, in comparison with arithmetic, emphasizes the dialectic. *Algebra* is an Arabic word for "reuniting broken parts." Algebra teaches us to find the first logical question, write down the answer, ask and answer the next logical question, and repeat until we identify the unknown variable. The dialectic then teaches us to verify the answer by working the problem backwards. If we find that the answer is incorrect, we may find ourselves taking a little side trip (scribbling on the side of our paper, away from our neatly written steps) as we seek different answers since our first attempt took us down the wrong path.

Algebra introduces the idea of unknowns and uses relationships to solve for unknowns. This involves logical relationships expressed in a mathematical sentence: the equation. Attending carefully to the math equation is the first step in solving a math question. The common topics help us to observe accurately and to begin to analyze math problems.

When you see $6 + 4y (3 + 5)$, you can learn to ask questions like these:

Definition: I see + symbols and parentheses. What do they mean? What are they?

Comparison: I see numerals that represent different quantities. I also see the letter "*y*." Can I follow the equation from left to right in order to understand the expression correctly, or do I need to restructure the equation?

Relationship: The 4 is outside the parentheses but is added to the 6. Do I associate it first with the 6 or with the parentheses?

Circumstance: Do I have enough information to solve this problem?

Testimony: What laws do I need to know in order to understand this equation?

What does the answer key say? Can I use it to teach myself the solution?

This may seem like overkill for such a small equation. Who has time to teach a child to ask all those questions for every math equation she is asked to manipulate? The student does not have to ask every question every time. Most of the time, she *should* just find the answer as quickly as she can. Speed and accuracy are valuable tools. But every now and then, the student should slow down and examine the obvious. She should spend time getting to know equations, meditating on them and appreciating their structure, noticing their simplicity and beauty. She should pray to discover basic principles that may make a difficult problem easier to solve. She should be guided through a mathematical environment by someone who loves both the child and math. Teachable math moments occur when the child, rather than the author or the parent, has a question. When that happens, drop everything and use that time to fall in love with math with your child.

Teachable math moments occur when the child, rather than the author or the parent, has a question.

The problem with these teachable moments is that, often, parents and teachers do not love math, so they have a hard time cultivating that love within their student's soul. We love what we know. We know what we spend time with. You may not love math, but I bet you love your child. Spend time with your child enjoying math games, struggling over new concepts, and developing the habit of daily problem-solving, and you may surprise yourself. Unfortunately, our own discomfort with math gives us an excuse to abandon our children to the private torture of math studies—abstractions beyond the maturity of, well, the adult doing the abandoning. We expect our child to do something we will not even do; then, we are surprised that all is not going well. I know some of you birthed children with an affinity for math and are not struggling like the other ninety-nine percent of families. Some of my boys are good at math, and some are not. As I have taught each of them, I have discovered that it is equally as delightful to help a struggling student learn a basic concept (sometimes that student is me) as it is to help a competent, confident student wrestle with an unfamiliar law. I like doing both because I love spending time with my children when they have questions.

DEFINITION

Aristotle classified objects based on what they are and what they are not. When we begin learning about a new idea, we naturally think in broad familiar categories (*genus*) and then consider how the thing we are learning may be different than other items in the same category (*division*). Mathematical questions using *genus* and *division* are:

- What is an integer? A number that can be negative or positive and is whole.
- What is a fraction? A number that is broken into a numerator and denominator.
- What is a decimal? A number that represents base ten.

Depending on your familiarity with mathematical terms, each of these questions may generate more questions: What is a whole number? What is a numerator? What is a denominator? What is base ten? Before you panic over the slew of questions, think back to the baking and carpentry examples we used earlier. Here, you are really dealing with the same three questions: "What do I know?" "What do I not know?" "How can I find out?" The glossary in the back of your math book is your best friend when you are thinking about the common topic of definition. Model good research skills for your student by asking him to look up unfamiliar terms and to copy the definitions until the terms are mastered. We are all grammarians when we encounter new information.

Another way to define a term is to ask how it is the same and how it is different from other family members. If you had to explain to someone what *complement* means in the context of geometry angles, you could ask:

- What category does *complement* belong to? A sum of degrees.
- What other things belong to that group or category? *Supplement.*
- How is *complement* different from *supplement*? *Complement* means the number of additional degrees required to reach 90 degrees, and *supplement* means the number of additional degrees required to reach 180 degrees.

Ask defining questions often enough that both you and your students naturally memorize them. Memorizing makes difficult things easier because it allows you to retrieve knowledge from your brain rather than always having to refer to glossaries. (For more tips on memorization, I recommend you read books like *The Core* or *How to Develop a Brilliant Memory Week by Week* by Dominic O'Brien, a world memory master.)

> *Memorizing makes difficult things easier because it allows you to retrieve knowledge from your brain rather than always having to refer to glossaries.*

Now that we have begun to define some terms, try to answer this question from geometry: What is the complement of 50 degrees? The answer is much faster to calculate if you memorized the fact that complement goes with 90 degrees and supplement goes with 180 degrees. (One mnemonic device to remember this is "C is before S in the alphabet, just as 90 comes before 180 on the number line.") Memorizing the definition of a complement allows understanding to occur much more quickly because your brain was not distracted by the need to flip pages or look up terms. So, we ask, what do we know? We know that 50 plus its complement must equal 90. In symbolic form, we would write $50 + C = 90$. Next, what do we not know? We do not know what "C" equals. How do we find out? We isolate the unknown in the equation by subtracting 50 from both sides, which gives us the equation $50 - 50 + C = 90 - 50$. We can simplify this equation as $C = 90 - 50$. So, the answer must be that the complement of 50 equals 40 degrees. We can verify our answer by working backwards. If $C = 40$, then according to our original equation, 50 plus 40 should equal 90. It does! Because we knew the definition of a complement, we were able to answer the question.

But definition does not only help us to answer math questions correctly; it can also enable us to understand more fully the nature of arithmetic and the language of mathematics. A sequence of defining questions will help you understand what I mean. You can hold a conversation with your students by asking defining questions.

"What is arithmetic composed of?" "Numbers" is a good answer. "What is a number?" A number is an abstract notation of a quantity. Did you know that numbers can be expressed by different forms? Most of us are comfortable with whole numbers: 1, 2, 3, 4, and so on, but many things in life cannot be expressed in neatly displayed whole numbers with a few digits. Can you think of other number forms that we use in everyday life?

"What are fractions?" Think of them as fractured numbers, a part broken out of the whole. You can talk about fractions when you are serving an apple pie for dessert. If you cut the pie into eight pieces and then Freddy ate one piece of the pie, what fraction of the pie remains? Your child can count that seven out of the eight original pieces, or 7/8 of the pie, are left. The *denominator* (eight) is the number that tells you how many parts the original whole was divided into. The *numerator* (seven) tells you how many parts of the original are present.

"What are decimals?" *Deci* means "tenth." Decimals deal with numbers, wholes and parts, using ten digits and never more than ten digits. Last week, I went into a store to buy groceries. My bill was $20.53, a decimal number. To read this number, I need to understand that the number "2" is in the tens column (I need two ten-dollar bills), the number "0" is in the ones column (I don't need any one-dollar bills), the number "5" is in the tenths column (I need five dimes), and the number "3" is in the hundredths column (I need three pennies to settle my bill).

Are there counting systems that use more than ten digits? Are there systems that use less than ten digits? Of course. When do we use other counting systems? What number system do computers use? Clocks? Neither use decimal.

We could keep going, or we could go back and ask, "What else is part of arithmetic?" Operations? We are using the word *operations* in a special sense again, so we need to define our terms. It is difficult to understand math if you believe an "operation" only refers to something a surgeon does in a hospital, just as it is difficult to understand baking if you believe "cutting" only refers to slicing bread with a sharp knife. Part of defining arithmetic operations might mean naming a few operations that are familiar to you. Addition and subtraction? Addition and subtraction are foundational verbs of math. They tell the numbers what to do. Other operations can be seen as derivatives of these two operations. Adding, which is an act of joining quantities, and subtraction, an act of removing or comparing quantities, become multiplication and division as we advance in our studies. Joining, removing, and comparing are all acts of relationship, so we might define *operations* as "the different relationships between numbers." Adding is counting quickly. Multiplication is counting even more quickly. For example, it is slow to say 1, 2, 3, 4, 5, 6, 7, 8, 9. It is a little faster to say 3 + 3 + 3 = 9. And it is even faster to say 3 × 3 = 9. All three methods take you to the same place on the number line.

What else is a major part of arithmetic? How about math laws? What are laws? Laws are rooted in the nature of the mathematical operation being performed. Laws reflect the way numbers and operations relate to reality. Therefore, laws further define how to appropriately honor relationships that are true to the nature of numbers and operations. We'll think more about rules and laws in the section dealing with authorities.

So, we know that mathematics is composed of numbers, operations, and laws. When approaching any equation, here are the common questions to ask:

- What number forms are being used?
- What operations are being performed?
- What laws need to be honored or applied to solve this problem?

Now that we have defined the main categories of math words, let's continue by considering the next common topic: comparison.

COMPARISON

We learn by comparing, by asking, "How are these alike, and how are these different?"

Perhaps the most natural form of thinking is comparison. We can learn more about the nature of numbers, operations, rules, and laws by comparing them to one another.

Let's begin by comparing numbers. The difference between the idea of numbers and numerals is critical in math but rarely understood. Numbers are an abstract idea. Numerals are the form they are written in. Since this comparison is always explained in math texts, yet rarely grasped by students, I am going to use the phrase "number form" to mean numeral when I want to emphasize the difference.

For example, the idea of the number four can be expressed with the numerals IV if you are a Roman, 4 if you use Arabic, 4.0 in decimal, 4^1 in exponent, and so on. There are infinite ways to use *numerals* to express the idea of the *number* four. Students think they understand the number four but then feel confused when it is introduced in a new form using more numerals than just "4." I have had students see an equation like $3 + 4^1$ and ask what to do with the 4^1. I ask, "Well, what do you do any time you add 4?" We have to get comfortable with the details of the numerals we use to represent the ideas of numbers if we want to understand abstract math.

Remind your students that you will use simple equations to teach the questions so that they will know how to use the questions when they are solving difficult equations. A good teacher explains one hard thing at a time. When there are two or more new or difficult concepts, it is better to break them down into familiar examples, teach the new concept in the easier form, and then apply the idea to the original, more difficult form. I will often ask a struggling student, "May I treat you like a first grader for a minute? I want to explain something that you understand

A good teacher explains one hard thing at a time.

well so that you can apply it to something that is difficult." I need to set my students up to attend, or they may ignore me because the example is too easy, and they think they already know what to do.

For example, if I write the decimal equation $1 + 1 = 2$ on the board, it is almost too easy for an older student to see the whole idea at once. I have to ask them to attend to the components of addition and equality and numbers, or they just gloss over it. What

Comparing easy grammar to a difficult new concept is a very effective teaching tool.

if I want to explain that in binary $1 + 1 = 10$? This kind of equation is best understood if I can compare the familiar decimal counting system with the strange binary system. The concept of binary reveals to the student that they really only understand addition and equality in decimal. I would use $1 + 1 = 2$ in decimal to compare to the binary. Comparing easy grammar to a difficult new concept is a very effective teaching tool.

Here are a few simple examples of comparison questions to ask:

- Express the same number using three different numerals (whole, decimal, and fraction) and write them out. Ask the students to compare the numerals. Ask them, "How are these numerals alike?" "How are they different?" For example: 3, 3.0, and 9/3 use different numerals to represent the number three.

- Now express different numbers using the same form of numeral (whole, decimal, or fraction). Ask the students to compare the numerals. Ask them, "How are these numbers alike?" "How are they different?" "How are the numerals alike or different?" For example: 4.0, 6.0, and 19.0 use decimals to express different numbers.

Teach your students to observe the number forms being used. Different number forms are embedded with different rules. Can your student identify and attend to the number forms being expressed? Paying attention to number forms is an essential ability as students move forward in their math studies. The nature of whole numbers allows the operations to be executed with the greatest ease; the nature of fractions adds a layer of complexity; the nature of decimals adds a different layer of complexity. But all these forms of numbers use common digits and symbols.

We can use comparison to not only learn more about the nature of numbers but also about the nature of operations. Let's learn a little more about addition, subtraction, multiplication, and division by comparing them.

- Compare addition and subtraction: $3 + 5 = 8$ with $3 - 5 = -2$

How are the equations similar? They have the same numbers on the left side of the equal sign. How are they different? They have different numbers on the right side of the equal sign. How are addition and subtraction similar? Both equations change quantities. How are they different? One equation increases quantity and one decreases quantity.

- Compare multiplication and division: $3 \times 5 = 15$ with $3 \div 5 = 3/5$

  How are these equations similar? They have the same numbers on the left of the equal signs. How are they different? They have different numbers on the right side of the equal sign. How are multiplication and division similar? They change quantities. How are they different? One equation increases quantity and one decreases quantity.

- Compare adding and multiplication: $3 + 3 = 6$ with $3 \times 3 = 9$ and $2 + 3 = 5$ with $2 \times 3 = 6$

  How are these equations similar? How are they different? How are adding and multiplication similar? How are they different? How is multiplication like adding? How are they different?

- Compare subtraction and division: $5 - 3 = 2$ with $5 \div 3 = 5/3$ and $3 - 3 = 0$ with $3 \div 3 = 1$

  How are these equations similar? How are they different? How is division like subtraction? How are they different?

Notice that none of these examples asks you to solve a math problem. Rather, you and your student are using questions to build essential knowledge about the language of math. Answering questions and solving problems will follow, but how can you answer questions if you do not even speak the language? Math, like Latin, French, Chinese, Russian, or English, requires study in sequence.

RELATIONSHIP

Another way we learn is by finding the relationships between one thing and another by asking, "What causes _____?" "What is the effect of _____?" and "What comes first?" In math, the nature of the operations and the order of the operations defines the relationship between the numbers, so proper ordering of an equation is essential in expressing the problem, and proper ordering of the operations is an essential part of answering the question correctly, whether you are studying arithmetic or algebra. Try out these exercises to grasp the kind of questions you might ask to help your student understand mathematical relationships:

- Perform this relationship: 3 + 5
- Perform this relationship: 5 + 3

  What effect did changing the order have on the answer? Why?

  (Later, after studying laws, you might also ask, "What law did I just observe?" We will discuss laws in detail when we get to the common topic of testimony.)

- Perform this relationship: 5 − 3
- Perform this relationship: 3 − 5

  What effect did changing the order have on the answer? Why?

  Is there a law to be observed?

  What do I learn about the nature of addition and the relationship of the order of its terms?

  What do I learn about the nature of subtraction and the relationship of the order of its terms?

- Perform this relationship: 3 × 5
- Perform this relationship: 5 × 3

  What effect did changing the order have on the answer? Why?

  What law did I just observe?

- Perform this relationship: 3 ÷ 5
- Perform this relationship: 5 ÷ 3

  What effect did changing the order have on the answer? Why?

  Is there a law to be observed?

What do I learn about the nature of multiplication and the relationship of the order of its terms? What do I learn about the nature of division and the relationship of the order of its terms?

CIRCUMSTANCE

Through the common topic of circumstance, we learn by asking, "What is going on at the same time?" In a simple form, we ask, "What concept was just taught to me? Do I see that concept in the problems I have been assigned?" Some may also think of this topic as context. Thinking in context helps us to think more deeply about a topic or idea. Any time you approach a math problem, you should begin by asking several questions: "What am I being asked to find? What information am I being given? Do I need all of the information given? What operations or relationships help me rightly relate the information given?" Sometimes in math we are not given enough information to solve the problem. Conversely, sometimes we are given information that we do not need. We have to learn that some math problems are not solvable with the information given, and in other problems, we may have to slog through unnecessary information for a solution. Here, mathematical skill overlaps with reading ability. Practice analytical reading, and your child will become a better mathematician. Practice mathematics, and your child will become a more analytical reader.

Example 1: Enough information

Sara had three red balloons that she bought for a dollar each. Sarah also had seven blue balloons that cost fifty cents each. How much money did Sarah spend on balloons?

Is it possible to solve this problem? Only if we have enough information. What are we looking for? How much money Sarah spent on her balloons, right? So we gather information: Sarah spent $3 on red balloons and (7 × $.50) on blue balloons. We want a total of money spent, so what operation allows me to get a total? Addition, right? Addition is the act of joining quantities.

Now I must use the language of symbols and numerals to write a mathematical sentence, an equation that reflects this reality and shows this relationship. Here is the equation that helps me find my solution: $3 + (7 × $0.50).

Would an alternate equation—$3 + 7 × $0.50—correctly show the relationships of the information given? Why or why not? We will run into this question again under the topic of laws.

Example 2: Not enough information

If a circle's radius is half of the diameter, what is the area of the circle?

Begin by asking and answering some basic questions, as we have practiced. Is this problem solvable? Only if we have enough information. What are we looking for? The area of the circle. What information have we been given? That the radius is half of the diameter. What operations or formulas help me rightly relate the radius to the area? I would need to know the connection between the radius and the area of a circle: $A = \pi r^2$.

Can I solve the equation now? Although I know the connection between the radius and the diameter, I cannot find the area of this particular circle because I do not have the actual measurement of the radius. So, with the information given, this question is not answerable.

Example 3: Too much information

Forty apples cost $5. Bill has six apples. How many apples can Sarah buy for $80?

Is this problem solvable? Only if we have enough information. What are we looking for? How many apples Sarah can buy for $80. What information have we been given? Forty apples cost $5; Bill has six apples. Do we need all of the information given? Remember what I am looking for: how many apples can be purchased for $80. Which piece of information will help me solve my problem—the cost of 40 apples, the fact that Bill has six apples, or both? Bill is not relevant to the question.

When too much information is given, the students have to learn to think about and seek connections between the answer being sought and the information being given. Students are practicing distinguishing between information that helps us solve a problem and information that can be used as a distraction. Do you see how this activity of the mind trains the mind to perceive distractions and to weed them out? This is an elementary form of practicing discernment, which is closely related to understanding.

TESTIMONY

Another element of understanding comes from looking to experts and asking, "What do authorities say about this concept? What laws and maxims govern this concept?" In the nature of mathematics, and, in particular, arithmetic, students will find certain laws and rules that have been discovered through the ages, of which students are the beneficiaries. Here are the essential laws of mathematics:

Laws of equality:

- $2 = 2$
- $2 < 3$
- $2 > 1$
- $2 \neq 3$

Commutative laws for addition and multiplication:

- $x + y = y + x$

- $xy = yx$

Associative laws for addition and multiplication:

- $x + (y + z) = (x + y) + z$
- $x(yz) = (xy)z$

Distributive law:

- $x(y + z) = xy + xz$
- $x(y - z) = xy - xz$

Identity laws:

- $a + 0 = a$
- $a - 0 = a$
- $a \times 1 = a$
- $a \div 1 = a$

As your student investigates the algorithms (procedures) of math, the laws need to become second nature. As I discussed in the first few chapters, rote memorization, rather than impeding creative thought, actually forms the basis of understanding. The only way to be certain that your student understands these laws is for him to repeat them back to you aloud. Notice that in doing so, he is translating the symbolic language of mathematics into the English language. During the dialectic stage, repeated practice translating mathematical equations from symbols to words and back again will cement the forms in your student's mind and solidify his understanding of mathematical concepts. To moderate this process, you simply need to ask a lot of questions, using the common topics to guide you.

Math laws are one form of testimony, but today's parents and teachers have access to many forms of authority as guides and resources. Parents who are nervous about teaching math can take encouragement from the knowledge that they do not have to approach math as solitary superheroes. One option is to find another parent (or an older student) who loves math and ask him to be a tutor and

Parents who are nervous about teaching math can take encouragement from the knowledge that they do not have to approach math as solitary superheroes.

mentor for your student. If finances are an issue, see if you can work out an exchange. I know families who pay for math tutoring with firewood, home repairs, foreign language lessons, or technology training. If possible, don't just drop your student off at the door. Ask permission to sit in on the lessons and take this opportunity to educate yourself alongside your student. Doing so will accomplish two things: first, your child will see that you value math enough to learn it for yourself; second, you will be better equipped to teach your student during the rest of the week. Other resources that are available to you at no additional cost are the glossary and the index in the back of a math book. Teach your student to use these resources to find information about a concept he does not understand. Parents can model this habit for their students simply by being willing to say, "I don't know the answer. Where can I go to find out?"

LEARNING TO LOVE MATH

Learning to ask good questions is essential to a classical education, but ultimately, the knowledge of math is its own end. Stratford Caldecott writes in *Beauty for Truth's Sake*, "[Math] is not to be valued for the power it gives us over nature, or even for the moral improvement it may bring about in us. It is to be valued for its *beauty*" (28). I know math because I love it. I love its Author, its symmetry, its reliability, its mystery. Symmetry, for example, is one of the fundamental principles of beauty and is best recognized and understood through mathematics. The Fibonacci sequence, the powerful meaning and beauty of numbers like one (unity), two (diversity), three (harmony), and so on help us to understand the universe in which we live and to see its magnificent beauty. I believe, with Galileo, that

> [T]he universe . . . stands continually open to our gaze, but it cannot be understood unless one first learns to comprehend the language and interpret the characters in which it is written. It is written in the language of mathematics, and its characters are triangles, circles, and other geometric figures, without which it is humanly impossible to understand a single word of it; without these, one is wandering about in a dark labyrinth. (*Il Saggiatore*, 237–238)

Usefulness is just the grace given to all who love anything intimately. I solve math equations because they balance, because they give us a mystery to talk about, and because I am a social creature who reflects our Creator. I cannot stop talking about math, because it is so beautiful. Learning to ask good questions using the five common topics helps students learn to think, which in turn helps them to see beauty. In short, math studies allow us to know Him and to make Him known.

CHAPTER SEVEN

GEOGRAPHY AND CURRENT EVENTS

"People who can use their [moral imaginations] are hard to herd around. They can form societies of their own. They become men and women, not human resources. They can be free."

— Anthony Esolen, *Ten Ways to Destroy the Imagination of Your Child*

The task of exploring our universe should be easier than ever in this era of global interconnectedness. Information is ubiquitous, and access to it is nearly effortless, thanks to Internet search engines and other technologies. Unfortunately, access to information alone is not enough. Having access to information has not translated into knowledge; rather, the means by which we access information have become distractions. These distractions, however, delight us. They delight us too easily because we do not even know what questions to ask in our pursuit of knowledge. They delight us because we do not even have the requisite curiosity for pursuing knowledge. Technology delights us because it distracts us from the gaps in our education and provides us with the opportunity to be entertained instead of challenged.

Our inability to ask questions is a result of our lack of curiosity. New knowledge about a particular field should result not in satiety but in a hunger for more knowledge of that subject. So, how do we develop this curiosity?

Curiosity is a byproduct of knowledge. In other words, it takes a little knowledge to

...it takes a little knowledge to create the desire for more of it.

create the desire for more of it. Geography is the perfect subject with which to practice this cycle of learning. Starting with a wide-angle lens, your child can acquire a few pegs of knowledge about the world such as the seven continents. Then, he can zoom in on any one of those pegs and gather more complete knowledge to hang on it. He can learn the names of the countries in that continent. From there, he can add to his knowledge of the physical world, knowledge of its history, its literature, its cultures, or its art. This, in turn, will lead to even more questions.

In *The Core*, I discussed how to raise a child who can map the world by heart. A mental map of the world is essential because it gives your student the context in which he can understand history, stories, political events, or his immigrant neighbors. Knowledge of geography will breed curiosity because it will show him what he does not know. If your student knows nothing about geography, he will not be inspired—or curious—to rectify his ignorance when he reads about an unfamiliar place, precisely because he is unfamiliar with all places. Why? He will be less likely to recognize his ignorance as ignorance. When your student knows the world map by heart, however, and happens upon a location with which he is unfamiliar, he will recognize his deficiency. He will know, instinctively, that he knows many other places but not this one, and he will be inspired—he will be curious—to fix it.

As your child moves from curiosity to questions, he will begin practicing and learning to ask better and better questions. It is at this point that you should introduce more information. As your child enters the dialectic stage, you should present information that is well suited to and requires knowledge of geography: the current event. The current event brings new information to the student, information about which he can ask questions.

A current event related to a specific area of the world, Afghanistan, for example, would require him to access his knowledge of geography. As he searches his mind, exercising the faculty of memory, he pictures Afghanistan and its location on the map. He may also remember where it is relative to bodies of water, deserts, and mountains. As he continues to think through the event that is taking place there, he might run across a specific area in Afghanistan, such as the city of Kandahar. Unfamiliar with Kandahar, but knowing that he is armed with knowledge about the geography of Afghanistan, he will be more inclined to discover the geographic details of Kandahar. His curiosity will generate questions as he pursues the information. He may take advantage of the technologies that can provide him with an answer, or he may seek out a map or globe if one is available. He may even seek out one of the maps he has drawn as part of his efforts to map the world by heart. He may wonder if he has ever labeled his maps with Kandahar in the past and has just happened to forget doing so. Even if he does need technological aids, he only turns to them because his prior studies first generated the curiosity.

In order to inspire the student to dig deeper, we must help him to develop the dialectic art of asking geography questions. The first step is to identify what type of information we are seeking and then to ask questions appropriate to that end. Once we have done that, we teach him to do the same thing, primarily by modeling it to him.

This aspect of the dialectic can be just as frustrating when you study current events or geography as when you study math or writing. Initially, your student will not know why you have suddenly begun pelting him with questions. His reaction may be to avoid the question, to assume ignorance. He will not realize that the question is designed to draw on the knowledge he already has in order to bring him to a potentially new conclusion or observation. You will have to be patient and encouraging. You cannot ask an abstract geography question and immediately answer it yourself when he proclaims ignorance. He is waiting for you to give him the facts, as you did in the grammar stage when he was a consumer of information only. Nor can you answer your own question if he sits there in silence. You must patiently wait for him to sort through his own body of geographical knowledge to discover the answer. If patience does not bring forth an answer, you may need to reword the question or ask an entirely different question to help him make the connection.

Your child may also fail to understand that the seemingly innumerable questions you are asking him do have an end. Or, he might understand that there is an end to the questioning, but he might assume that the goal is to reveal his ignorance of geography. It will take experience to correct that misunderstanding. Telling your student what you are doing will likely not work. He will need to experience a successful discovery several times before he recognizes that the exercise is intended to help him, not embarrass him. Socrates was a master of this technique in teaching people, but he often had to encourage the people whom he would engage in dialogue by asking them to suffer his "stupid questions" as he pursued their "brilliant answers." In time, the experience of suffering your stupid questions and arriving at his own brilliant answers will help your student to recognize the true goal of the exercise.

Eventually, your student will develop the faculty of asking questions for himself. Through the questioning process, not only will he learn geography, but he will also learn to ask better and better questions. Using the five common topics to ask questions about current events and geography, we can model inquisitiveness to our children and direct their natural curiosity toward productive inquiries about the world around them.

DEFINITION

We begin with the common topic of definition. You can use definition questions to help your child build a bridge from the grammar, the facts about geography that he has memorized, to the dialectic, the connections between those facts. When you first seek to define a geographical term, begin broadly with its location or physical features, for example, and then move toward a narrower understanding of each term. The depth and detail you achieve will vary depending on your child's maturity and experience. An eleven-year-old might still be working to master the names of countries and capitals. For this child, to define "North America" might mean naming the major countries, rivers, mountain ranges, and bordering oceans. A fourteen-year-old, on the other hand, might have narrowed his focus to the United States. His definition might include the fifty states, their capitals, and some of the major physical features, but it might also touch on history and government, weather and climate, or industry and agriculture.

If we were to return to our original example with Kandahar, we might ask, "What is the city of Kandahar?" There are innumerable answers to this question, and you should not be discouraged if you don't get the exact answer you have in mind. A fairly complete answer would be that the city of Kandahar is located in the south of Afghanistan. It is east of one of the rivers running through Afghanistan. It is southwest of the capital, Kabul, and south of the mountain range that runs through most of Afghanistan. It is west of the mountain range that runs along the Pakistan-Afghanistan border. It is the site of an American military installation, as a result of the war in Afghanistan, which followed September 11, 2001. As a teacher, you might like this lengthy and complete answer, but it is unlikely you would hear it early in your dialectic exercise.

More likely, you would hear answers like these: it is a city; it is a city in Afghanistan; it is a city on a plain in the south of Afghanistan; or, it is where my uncle is stationed in the Army right now. These answers are all acceptable. With these answers, however, you can initiate new questions, more specific questions. Is Kandahar the capital of Afghanistan? No, Kabul is the capital. Why is your uncle stationed there? He is there fighting the Taliban. Why is he fighting the Taliban? President George W. Bush sent American troops there after 9/11. These are all acceptable answers that generate new questions, which in turn help to connect dots of knowledge in your child's mind.

As we ask questions related to definition, though, we should ask questions about the term under consideration (the city of Kandahar) that will bring us to greater knowledge of the term. So, once your child has identified a feature of the city, ask to what group it belongs. Answers might include, "It is an urban center," "it is a single location with a large population," or "it is a center of trade." At this point, your student is identifying the features of cities in general. Ask him which of those groups is most helpful in defining the city of Kandahar.

Let's say he chooses to identify Kandahar as an urban center. Now you want him to think about other terms that would also qualify as members of the group "urban center." He might answer with "New York City," "London," "Paris," and—if he is a fan of *Batman*—"Gotham City." Next, ask why all of those terms qualify as urban centers. You might hear any number of observations at this point. The more you practice the skill of definition, the more observations your student will make. Your student might say that these are all cities with tall buildings or that they are all densely populated. Then

The more you practice the skill of definition, the more observations your student will make.

we would want to know what makes Kandahar different than the other terms in the group. If your student did not name any other Afghan cities, he might just reply that Kandahar is located in Afghanistan. But if he did name other Afghan cities, he will have to be more creative in his answers; he might say that a foreign military force occupies the city. Any answer, so long as it is factually accurate, is acceptable.

Now your child has defined Kandahar as an urban center currently occupied by a foreign military force, and he has done so without using a dictionary or encyclopedia. You can engage in a further exercise by breaking the city down into its parts. Kandahar has lots of buildings, a stadium, and lots of markets. It has a population of over half a million people, most of whom are Pashtun. It is okay if you and your student need to access information from outside sources, such as encyclopedias or the Internet, at this point. We want dialectic learners to satisfy their curiosity, not squelch it. In this way, they will develop a habit of seeking answers, so they will continue to learn and want to learn.

This exercise can be done with any term in current events. You might ask your child to define 9/11 or former President George W. Bush. You might ask him to define other terms related to a specific current event, but you will want to be careful not to push him into defining terms that are too abstract—not because it is impossible to define abstract terms but because it can be very difficult. Remember, the philosopher Plato could not define the term "man" to his own or anyone else's satisfaction. Confronting your student with a degree of difficulty that even Plato could not manage can discourage and even stifle the very curiosity we are trying to encourage.

COMPARISON

As we continue asking questions, we will move beyond definition into comparison. Comparison may be the easiest method for generating questions from your student. Children compare from birth. The newborn knows whether his mother is holding him or not, based on comparison with others. He may not articulate the similarities and differences, but he recognizes them. Even in the definition exercise above, the student was required to compare his term to other terms to see which other terms would fit in the group. Then, he had to compare the terms within the group to see what made his term different than the others. We are always comparing. You are comparing as you read this line. You are subconsciously recognizing the similarities and differences in every letter that appears on this page in order to identify them and string them together into words, phrases, sentences, and paragraphs. As you engage with your student in the study of geography and current events, you will stimulate dialectic conversations using questions of comparison.

It is difficult to select a specific current event to write about because I cannot predict when you will read this book; I do not know what events will be current for you as the reader. When you consider the events I am using as examples, understand that I am doing so knowing they are not actually current for you or for me!

Let's say you are studying the geography of the United States with your children. One of your children wonders why Oklahoma has such an odd shape, why it has a panhandle and Kansas does not. Using the tools of definition above, you lead her through a series of questions that results in defining Oklahoma as a Midwestern state and defining a panhandle as a narrow strip of land protruding from the main body of a geographical territory. She may come up with entirely different definitions, which is fine. We just want to encourage factual accuracy. You will also want your student to define Kansas. Now you will need to help her compare the defined terms through a series of questions. Encourage your child to word her questions in a way that simplifies comparison. The original question might have been, "Why does Oklahoma have a panhandle?" In that case, it would be less than helpful to compare Oklahoma to a panhandle. If, however, you bring Kansas into the question, comparison becomes more helpful and useful. To compare thoroughly, I suggest using nine questions that break into three categories of three. This is one helpful way to structure a comparison, but you can also develop your own sequence of questions.

	Oklahoma	Kansas	Both
ARE	How is Oklahoma different? *South of KS*	How is Kansas different? *North of OK*	How are they similar? *States in the Midwest*
HAVE	What does OK have that KS does not? *A panhandle*	What does KS have that OK does not? *A border with Nebraska* *More land area*	What do both have? *A border with CO* *A border with MO* *Native American names*
DO	What does OK do that KS does not? *Primarily cattle ranching*	What does KS do that OK does not? *Primarily grows grains*	What do they both do? *Food production*

Kern, Andrew. *The Lost Tools of Writing*™ *Student Workbook* Level 1. 4th ed. Concord, NC: The CiRCE Institute, 2013. Page 67. Used with permission.

First, ask three questions about what the two terms *are*: "How is Oklahoma different from Kansas?" "How is Kansas different from Oklahoma?" "How are Oklahoma and Kansas similar?" These questions should generate several answers each. You might notice along the way that some questions—although different—will generate the same answers. Again, that is okay; we are really practicing the skills of question-asking and dot-connecting.

The next set of questions you will ask concern what both terms *have*: "What does Oklahoma have that Kansas does not?" "What does Kansas have that Oklahoma does not?" "What do both Oklahoma and Kansas have?" The chart provided an answer for each of these questions, but your child should easily be able to come up with five to ten answers for each; although, it is possible that one set might generate answers more easily than another.

Finally, ask what both terms *do*: "What does Oklahoma do that Kansas does not?" "What does Kansas do that Oklahoma does not?" "What do both Oklahoma and

Kansas do?" I have limited my answers to what the states produce: cattle, grains, and food. You could, however, allow your student to fill in the chart not with what the land of the states produce or do, but what the people of the states do. You could end up with answers such as "They are mostly Presbyterians," "they vote," "they work," or "they wear cowboy boots."

RELATIONSHIP

Having defined your terms and compared them with good questions, you should ask your child to consider the relationships between them, keeping in mind the ultimate question about the Oklahoma panhandle. You are looking for other events that may be related to the shape of Oklahoma in a causal or noncausal way. Start by asking broad questions, and then get more specific.

"What happened immediately before and after these two states were given their shapes in the second half of the nineteenth century?" The Missouri Compromise happened before (as did the American Revolution, the War of 1812, Columbus's discovery of America, and many other events). The War Between the States happened after (as did the assassination of John F. Kennedy, the moon landing, and the sinking of the *Titanic*). Notice that we are not looking for cause and effect yet; we just want to know what else is going on here. Now, we should try to limit the answers to *immediately* before and after so that there is more likelihood for relevance. It is not necessary that the answers be directly related by anything other than proximity of time and space.

Your student should now move into an area of assessment or judgment regarding the relationships established. In the writing chapter, we called this a *thesis*. Your student now gets to decide which prior events caused the main event and which did not. Did the Missouri Compromise affect the shape of Oklahoma? In fact, it did. The Missouri Compromise, and later the Kansas-Nebraska Act, prevented any slave state from extending north of the 36°30′ parallel. On the other hand, did the shape of Oklahoma cause the War Between the States? Probably not. Rather, the Missouri Compromise may have contributed to the start of the war as well as the shape of the state. As you can see, some sequential events are related by cause-and-effect, while others are not.

At the end of these questions, we still do not know why Oklahoma has a panhandle, but we have eliminated several incorrect answers. Eventually, guiding your child to outside research (again, modeling this habit for your student), you might discover that the panhandle shape of Oklahoma was a result of Texas ceding its territory north of the

36°30′ parallel; it was also a result of the Missouri Compromise and the subsequent Kansas-Nebraska Act. The purpose of its panhandle shape was to prevent the further expansion of slavery in the new territories. The panhandle was initially not assigned to a territory, causing it to be known as "No Man's Land" for some time, and it was eventually settled through squatter's rights and the Homestead Act.

CIRCUMSTANCE

You may notice, as we move into circumstance, that you begin to see some of the same questions asked repeatedly but from different angles. That's okay! Repetition imprints the questions in your student's mind, until asking certain questions feels like second nature.

The following questions, concerned with circumstances or context, should also generate several answers each. What was happening in that area of the country when the states were given their shapes? The population of the American states and territories was expanding westward through the Midwestern territories. Ask again, "What was happening at the time these states were given their shapes?" Several states were debating and fighting and compromising over the status of slavery.

You may notice… that you begin to see some of the same questions asked repeatedly but from different angles.

Under circumstance, we also want to consider if other potential answers to our main question are possible, and why or why not. Is it possible Oklahoma could have been formed without a panhandle? Why or why not? Where would it—the territory that makes up the panhandle—have gone if not to Oklahoma: Texas, New Mexico, Colorado, Kansas? Depending upon the nature of your original question or thesis, you may also consider the probability—not just the possibility—of a certain answer. Is it probable the panhandle land would have been given to another territory? In our question, that seems to be an unnecessary line of thought because we know the result. It is improbable because it did not happen.

When you are teaching through this with your child, these questions will be more sensible because you will be using them with current events that are actually current. When I first wrote this chapter, the 2012 presidential election had not yet happened. If I used the election as my current event and considered the likelihood of Gary Johnson (a third-party presidential candidate) getting elected, I would need to understand how each state nominates their candidates during the primary. As you read this, you will know whether it was probable or not that Johnson was elected because you are reading this after I wrote this chapter. You will want to use current events that allow for those kinds of discussions. The question "How…?" often leads to "Should…?".

Lastly, in regard to circumstances, you may ask questions related not just to whether or not the question is possible or probable, but whether a certain action should even be attempted. This question often makes sense when the possibility or probability question has been answered in the negative. "Is it possible Gary Johnson will be elected president in 2012?" If I were to answer no, speaking before the election, then I could ask, "Should Gary Johnson even run?" This can be an especially thought-provoking exercise. If the purpose is only to win an election, then my son's immediate answer would probably be, "No." However, he may see another purpose in running for president: to bring about a national conversation on a particular issue such as ending abortion or legalizing drugs. He might argue that Gary Johnson should run for president even though it is neither possible nor probable that he will win.

As we discussed in the writing chapter, "should" questions give students two clear sides of an issue to argue. Although we teach them to consider both sides of a question,

… "should" questions give students two clear sides of an issue to argue.

it is also necessary for students to take a side, even if it means playing the devil's advocate. Only by accepting a dogmatic position will students be able to ask the questions they need to ask, provide answers to questions that need answers, and evaluate authoritative testimony honestly. They may later change their opinion about the issue, but they must learn to take a side in order to stimulate good conversation.

"Should" questions come with an additional benefit: they introduce our students to issues that really matter. Someday, our children may be the next politicians, lawyers, and thinkers who govern our society. Thinking about current events in the light of "should" questions prepares our children to be the kind of leaders who will answer these questions with confidence in whatever role they serve as adults.

TESTIMONY

The last common topic, testimony, may be the most interesting and fun for your dialectic student. There are basically two questions involved: "What do the witnesses say?" "What do the experts say?" Keep two things in mind at this point. First, some analysis needs to be done on the credibility of the witness or expert. If your authority is based on an eyewitness account but your witness has 20/400 vision and was not wearing corrective lenses at the time, your testimony of authority may be called into question. Likewise, if your expert testimony is about the effects of marijuana use on humans but your expert's education and experience is with dogs, your testimony of authority may be called into question. In considering the probability of President Obama's re-election, we might have considered the testimony of experts (there were no eyewitnesses at the time unless you consider eyewitnesses who watched how he was campaigning); our expert witnesses might have taken into consideration the historical precedence of Democratic presidents winning a second term. They might have taken into consideration the state of the economy—unemployment numbers, taxes, consumer confidence, and deficits—and then done an analysis of his likelihood based on how those numbers have affected past elections. Pollsters on both sides of the election did just that.

In this age of global communications, we have the distinct advantage that news about current events can be disbursed in many different ways, bringing new voices to the conversation. Think about the influence of Twitter, YouTube, and other social media platforms on the revolutions of the Arab Spring in 2011. News moves at unprecedented speeds. When an earthquake occurred in central Virginia in 2011, my fellow residents of North Carolina heard about it on Twitter seconds before they felt the ground shake. What we have to remember is that the speed of information also means that it is easier than ever to spread misinformation. For example, in June 2012, CNN and FOX News reported on a highly visible Supreme Court case deciding whether it was constitutional to require individuals to have healthcare coverage. In their rush to report the decision, both networks announced, erroneously, that the Supreme Court had struck down the individual mandate. In the days that followed, their mistake became as big of a story as the Supreme Court decision itself. We must teach our students to consider carefully the credibility of any eyewitness statements or expert testimony they believe or pass on.

Second, expert testimony does not need to come in the form of human experts. There are many things that serve as an authority in our lives and have an impact on our culture and the way we think. These authorities can be found in the form of literature, statistics, laws, or proverbs. For example, if the current event was a consideration of whether the Federal Reserve should lower interest rates in order to encourage spending and discourage saving, then expert testimony, an authority, might be Benjamin Franklin's maxim, "A penny saved is a penny earned." If we were asking a student to consider whether artists should

...expert testimony does not need to come in the form of human experts.

accept monies from the federal government in the form of grants from the National Endowment for the Arts, an authority might be the proverb, "He who takes the king's coin becomes the king's man." Does the artist fear becoming an artist in service of the governing authorities? Will the artist become so by virtue of having accepted the grant? Conversely, did the initial grant give the artist a boost that led her to achieve success later on? Allowing and encouraging your student to reach into the body of literature with which they are familiar in order to bring authoritative testimony to the table can make the discussion that much more fruitful—and entertaining!

"Capital Punishment and the Common Topics" by Matt Bianco

A couple of years ago, my son's ninth-grade class engaged in a dialectic conversation around the question of whether the United States government should continue executing murderers. The students defined their terms: the U.S. government is a legislative, judicial, and executive body that administers justice to the citizens of its states. They defined *execute murderers* as the act of ending the life of one who has purposely and maliciously ended the life of another.

They then compared the U.S. government to other national governments: it is one of the only first-world countries that still executes murderers. In that statement, they acknowledged similarities with other governments: America is a first-world nation. They acknowledged differences with other governments: America executes murderers.

They considered relationships that affect the government's decision to execute murderers: the Constitution allows it, the Bible teaches it, murderers forfeit their own lives when they choose to forfeit someone else's life. The class also considered the purpose of the government. Based on their definition, the government's purpose is to administer justice. Their definition required examination of a new term: justice. They then had to define and consider the purpose of justice in order to answer the question.

They continued on to circumstance. In what context do we execute murderers? Is it possible to discontinue executing murderers? What would the consequences of such a decision be? Is it probable that America would discontinue executing murderers? In light of those questions, should America discontinue executing murderers?

Then they considered authoritative testimony of the question. What do the political, judicial, and social experts say on the matter? What does literature teach us about execution? In Shakespeare's *Henry V*, King Henry executes three friends for crimes against the state, against him. In Shakespeare's *Julius Caesar*, Brutus executes Caesar because of tyranny he might commit. In America's own history, assassins have executed presidents for their perceived inability to govern well. In the Bible, Noah is taught to execute murderers, and Israel's law includes provisions for the death penalty. What is the purpose of execution in each of these instances? What is the result of execution in each of these instances? What are the similarities and differences between America's government today and the governments in these authoritative testimonies?

Some of my son's classmates made the argument that justice is intended to punish the murderer, to make him pay for his crime, and to deter future murderers. My son argued that justice is intended to be restorative, to return the criminal to a proper role in the community.

The first group made the additional argument that the norms of biblical and historical literature authoritatively encourage the death penalty as punishment, payment, and deterrence. My son argued, in regard to the Bible, that it only proffers the death penalty in the case of near-absolute certainty of guilt and where the victim (or his nearest family) is willing to initiate the death penalty by casting the first stone. The executioner would have to take responsibility for his own motivation and for the possibility that he might be taking an innocent life. My son went on to suggest that this very personal form of execution was actually more of an encouragement toward mercy than it was a promoter of death. With these arguments in hand, he proposed that the American government should not execute murderers because of its inability to establish near-absolute certainty of guilt (based mostly on historical precedent) as well as its unwillingness to encourage mercy from the offended victim.

This dialectic process of asking good questions encouraged a pursuit of knowledge that led to a more spirited, honest, and earnest discussion of the death penalty in America than what most adults will hear from the mainstream media. We do not often hear this kind of conversation coming from our politicians or leaders, nor from community leaders or experts. This class of ninth graders, however, was able to burst into the conversation and add thought-provoking voices to it simply because they learned to ask good questions. My son and his peers defined their dogma, joined the conversation, and in some cases, transcended their initial position. They engaged in education, and they enjoyed a life that was livable in the process. As youth, they were respected and taken seriously because they had been taught how to be respectful and serious via the dialectic.

THE SPIRIT OF INQUIRY

Dialectic conversations that are a result of knowledge, curiosity, and questions are an essential part of the learning process about geography and current events. This should help us to see the necessity of people, of neighbors, in the education process. It is difficult—but not impossible—for students to engage in dialectic alone. I would argue that it is not impossible because the students can engage in dialectic with the authors of and the characters in the literature they are reading. I can argue with Bilbo Baggins as to whether he should keep putting on the ring. It is difficult, however, to engage in that form of dialectic for very long because the potential answers Bilbo can provide are limited by the number of things J. R. R. Tolkien has written. Once I ask a question he has not answered, I have finished the discussion. Engaging in dialectic with other humans—with other students and teachers—provides me with an ongoing discussion of questions and answers.

Dialectic discussion respects and honors the nature of my student. I treat him as a human being rather than as a machine or just a source of production. I allow him to think and reason, to question and answer, and to exercise curiosity and encourage a spirit of inquiry. By studying geography and current events, he recognizes his need for others and learns to love his neighbors. He loves them because he needs them to

Dialectic discussion respects and honors the nature of [the] student.

ask questions, because he needs them to dig out answers to his questions. He loves them because they love him by needing him to ask questions and explore possible answers to their questions. We want, however, to do this with a spirit of inquiry aimed at finding knowledge. We do not want to encourage a dialectic conversation that is aimed at winning for the sake of winning. Winning does not always equate to knowledge. It can feel like intellectual bullying. If you have ever listened to competing news stories or read opinion columns about a contentious current event, you have experienced this bullying. Again, keep in mind that more knowledge can sometimes be gained through the asking of the question than through the receiving of a right answer.

As the student continues to learn by asking and answering questions about geography and current events, he learns that there is sometimes more truth and value in the question itself than in the answer. Sometimes, the journey of discovery is more important and valuable than the discovery itself. Let me give you an example. The Internet may be able to tell our students about the geography of Israel and Palestine. Thanks to technology, they may be able to locate facts almost instantaneously. Students can find the answer to almost any question, but will the information have meaning? Will it belong to a larger body of knowledge about the world that allows them to live and judge wisely? Not necessarily. On the other hand, consider the experi-

> *Sometimes, the journey of discovery is more important and valuable than the discovery itself.*

ence of a group of students who travel to Israel and Palestine. They walk over the varying elevations of the land, see the arid places and those with access to water, and talk to people who have been displaced by the ongoing conflict in that region. They are drawn by their own curiosity to ask questions about the way nations are defined, about the way two countries compare to each other, abut the relationship between one country and the rest of the world, about the circumstances surrounding a nation's birth, and about the testimony of people with conflicting opinions. Even in situations when on-the-ground experience is not possible, your goal in teaching geography and current events dialectically should be to bring each topic to life for your student by asking good questions and guiding him on a journey of discovery about the world in which he lives.

When you do that, you show your student that knowledge is possible, that education is meaningful, and that life is livable. Knowledge is possible because there are questions with answers and means by which to reach them. We can know something through reason, through dialectic and contemplation. Long before the invention of satellite, the ancient Greeks speculated that the earth was round. We can also know something through perception, through fact or actual instances. Later, Greeks in the time of Aristotle noticed that different stars were seen in the north than were seen in the south. From this, they concluded that the earth was round. Finally, in addition to reason and perception, we can know something through re-presentation, through artistic and rhetorical expression. More than a thousand years later, by circumnavigating the earth, Ferdinand Magellan was able to demonstrate what those before him had only postulated. Although Magellan did not survive the journey, the surviving sailors returned to present Magellan's story and their own to the curious world.

Precisely because there is knowledge to be had, education is meaningful. Our children can see the example of those who worked hard to reconcile competing ideas about the world. They can imagine themselves in a similar role. When students can see the purpose behind rote memorization, they have a new incentive to work hard: so that they can participate in the important conversations that geographical facts inform.

It follows, then, that life is livable because we have neighbors to relate to, neighbors with whom we can engage in the dialectic. Our students have the tools to work through the tensions and conflicts they see in everyday life. They have the right questions to ask, even if they might not find answers to all of their tensions and conflicts right away. They may have to meditate on them—contemplate them—for long periods of time. Students may need to seek out authoritative input from witnesses and experts, from literature and science, and from precedents and proverbs. Along with your student, you may have to abandon preconceived ideas in order to attain resolution. As you consider current events and geography through this lens, you may be surprised to find that it is hard work. There is a lot to consider, and the communities with whom you engage will bring different questions and different answers to the same topic. They will stretch you and push your student. In doing so, they will help everyone to develop the ability to ask poignant and precise questions. This is what we want for our children.

When our students have matured and become the adults we hope they will, they will be difficult to herd around. As men and women, not resources, they will be free—free and able to start new societies as well as to magnify the virtues of established societies. They will ask reflective questions and participate in a conversation that will encourage both freedom and community. There is a democratic nature to this kind of education: it empowers everyone. In current events, even more than other areas of study, we should practice the dialectic, promote a spirit of inquiry, and teach our children to delve into the common topics. They need to define, compare, and relate so many ideas when it comes to ideals that affect a whole body politic. If, however, we encourage a spirit of inquiry and teach lessons in question-asking, we will empower our students to join the classical conversations of mankind, to seek and discover knowledge, and to promote freedom and justice. All this, because we taught our children how to ask good questions about geography and current events.

CHAPTER EIGHT

LOGIC

"Many, however, in their passionate desire to win a reputation for eloquence are content to produce showy passages which contribute nothing to the proof of their case."

—Quintilian, *Institutio Oratoria*

At the end of the geography chapter, I used logical proofs to convince you that knowledge is possible and that it makes education meaningful. But, you probably did not recognize what I was doing as a logical proof because I used everyday language to do it. Logic has its own language and symbols because it is a theoretical science, much like math, but at its core, it is concerned with the pursuit of truth. Many view the theoretical sciences as among the least important because a practical benefit of studying logic is not immediately seen. Aristotle argued that this belief was flawed; in fact, he maintained that theoretical sciences were the most important. Peter Kreeft explains in *Socratic Logic* that "their payoff is more intimate, their reward closer to home" because they improve our very selves (8).

Although many parents and teachers claim that they want their students to learn logic—what moderns call "critical thinking skills"—the art can be difficult to teach due to its precise mathematical nature. Formal logic has been called "math with words." Few

Formal logic has been called "math with words."

are aware that the purpose of formal logic is to teach the *forms* of thinking. Just as people today believe you are either naturally good at writing or you are not (as if it were somehow an inborn ability), many believe you are either born a logical thinker or not; I would argue that both logic and writing are crafts that can be taught and mastered through practice. You can learn to be a better thinker. Thinking is intentionally taught through formal logic. Students learn how to reason well through the use of definitions, laws, syllogisms, and truth tables.

Logic is synonymous with the word *dialectic*. The study of logic includes clear thinking, sound arguments, and consideration of abstract ideas in an orderly, systematic way. The art of argument is well suited to the dialectic brain of a youth. Dialectic students possess certain characteristics and natural abilities that allow them to exercise the skills of reasoning. In other words, your dialectic student is primed to learn logic. Students ages eleven to fourteen are hungry for independence. They are no longer content to be spoon-fed information. Instead, they want to begin understanding the world around them. One of the ways they do this is to take one side of an issue and argue with those who hold the opposite opinion. Logic teaches them to look at all sides as they prepare to argue.

The dialectic student's naturally developing abilities include analyzing and evaluating information, making connections between pieces of information, comparing and contrasting ideas, and integrating ideas. Because dialectic students have reached this stage of development, we as parents and teachers need to be prepared to meet the challenge. We must work diligently to sharpen the skills of sound reasoning, of good discernment, of thorough analysis of ideas and thoughts, and of correct argument. Study of formal logic will not only sharpen these essential skills in us, it will also prepare our students to consider ideas thoughtfully and to use those ideas to build greater understanding of the world and their place in it.

Why study formal logic? Because logic helps us to do the following:
- see what is true and what is false
- distinguish good reasons from bad ones
- develop a habit of thinking in an orderly way
- make wise judgments
- recognize truth in advertising
- decipher campaign speeches, recognizing fallacies and poor rhetoric
- recognize fallacies in arguments with others

- avoid accepting the false reasoning of others
- become persuasive communicators who captivate others with our words

Logic studies enable us to experience the world in richer, more meaningful ways; in short, logic studies make us free.

PERSISTENCE IN LOGIC STUDIES

The keys to studying logic include persistence, diligence in completing exercises, and respect for the sequential nature of the study. As with mathematics, you will not be able to master the next concept until you grasp the current one. You cannot "forget" your last lessons in the pursuit of the new lessons. You will not easily be able to take a week off and pick back up where you left off. I encourage parents to think of logic studies as being rated PG: Parental Guidance expected.

Learning logic is a process; there are patterns to be discovered and rules to employ with impartiality. Following the correct procedure and asking the right questions will lead the student to the proper analysis of the argument every time. There is beauty in the objectivity of logic and irony that in this "rote study" we can find truth. Yet, the mastery of any subject, logic included, begins with the grammar stage. Students who wish to master logic cannot skim over the grammar stage of logic; rather, they must study and memorize the vocabulary, fundamental laws of thought, and rules of procedure. As parents, we must commit to mastering the grammar of logic, for ourselves and for our students. Consider teaching your student the basics of formal logic over the summer or as part of her regular class schedule. The resource list in appendix 2 includes several excellent courses of study, starting from the grammar stage and progressing upward.

Following the correct procedure and asking the right questions will lead the student to the proper analysis of the argument every time.

Our goal in using the five common topics with any subject is to formulate sound and beautiful arguments. The study of logic hones in on the first half of that equation—soundness.

DEFINITION

The teaching of any subject most easily begins with definitions; in fact, it is often the starting point. Philosopher and psychologist Raymond McCall has defined the study of logic as "the science of right thinking" (qtd. in Cothran, *Traditional Logic I,* 7); it is also called "the distinction between correct and incorrect reasoning" (7). The common topic of definition is critical to sound argumentation because it requires precision of thought.

To help students develop precise thinking, logic teaches them to distill their ideas into a form called a *syllogism.** In the math chapter, we talked about math equations as a type of sentence that uses symbols rather than words to express ideas. In logic, a syllogism is similar to an equation: it is a way of distilling ideas so that their presuppositions become clear. When your student begins to study logic, he will learn to write a categorical syllogism, a fancy name for a series of statements about categories of things. The most famous example goes like this:

All men are mortal.

Socrates is a man.

Therefore, Socrates is mortal.

The first statement is called the *major premise.* It asserts something about the category "men." The second statement is called the *minor premise.* It asserts that an individual (Socrates) belongs to the category "men." The third statement is called the *conclusion.* If Socrates belongs to the category "men," he must necessarily share the characteristic of being mortal. Not all syllogisms are as simple as this one, but you should always start with simple examples when teaching a new idea.

A logician uses tools, such as truth tables and truth trees, to test the validity of complex statements. These mathematical tools are comparable to very simple calculators. A *truth table* is a diagram that shows how the truth or falsity of a complex statement varies depending on the truth or falsity of its component parts. Like a calculator, a truth table tells you that if you input a certain value for each part of the statement, you can expect to receive a certain value as the output for the statement as a whole. Truth tables deal with two basic values, true and false, so they are comparable to a binary system in mathematics.

A *truth tree* is used to test the validity of a statement by assuming that the argument is invalid and following that assumption to its logical conclusions. This assumption will lead to contradiction when applied to valid arguments, but it will produce no conflict if the argument is actually invalid. (If you study formal logic, you will work with these concepts extensively.)

---

* Syllogism: a form of deductive reasoning consisting of a major premise, a minor premise, and a conclusion.

Because logic is such a precise subject, logicians dwell in an environment where the correct use of words is paramount. In formal logic, students *formally* practice definition through the use of genus and species. All of what I am describing in this chapter has been taught using examples or definitions in the other subject chapters, but formal logic courses emphasize the entire grammar of dialectical studies. *Genus* and *species* are words used regularly in a logic course. While discussing the history of manufacturing, you may discuss different kinds of furniture from different regions, but in a logic class, the same ideas would be discussed using almost mathematical precision. Let me give you an example:

- *Genus*: Furniture

  Species: table, chair, sofa
- *Genus*: Logic

  Species: informal, formal
- *Genus*: Statements

  Species: supporting, nonsupporting

Precise definitions like these become crucial when you start to learn about common fallacies in logical thought. Our children may use the cliché "but everyone will be there" when they want to attend a social event. In doing so, they are extending the term "everyone" to mean, "I want to go where you don't want me to go and I can't think of a logical reason so I will use a popular fallacy that makes you look like the unyielding parent of a much-maligned child." (If our children had mastered English grammar when they were younger, they might have been able to express this meaning without a run-on sentence!) You can integrate logical definition into your daily life by pausing the irritable child's tirade and asking, "Everyone? What do you mean by 'everyone'? Everyone on the planet? How will they fit into the room?" Your daughter may respond with indignation—"Mom, you know what I mean!"—but the question may also help to dissolve tension and produce laughter. Eventually, your efforts to model questions of definition for your child will help her to define, identify, and correct the fallacies in her arguments. She wants to win the argument, after all! But remember, logic students will also delight in calling out your fallacies, so you will need to stay on your toes as well. In this way, learning logic has the potential to challenge and benefit the whole family.

COMPARISON

In formal logic, we use specific forms of comparison. Two of the most important techniques are called *extension* and *intension*. Extension is used to broaden definitions, and intension is used to narrow our definitions. Often in disagreements, each party is *Often in disagreements, each party is using a different definition of the same word.* using a different definition of the same word. For example, academics argue over literacy rates without first defining the extent of literacy to which they are referring. Do they mean the intensive definition of proficiently literate, or the extensive definition of functionally literate? What do they mean by proficiently or functionally literate? Or, in another example, imagine that you are disappointed because you wanted a wristwatch from your grandmother for Christmas, and she gave you your grandfather's old watch and fob. You did ask broadly for a watch, but you should have been more intense in naming your request! In conversations about politically charged terms, we may use examples as another method of comparison. "Nation" may mean "Cherokee," "Lumbee," and "Arapaho," or it may mean "Mexico," "Canada," and "Iceland."

Comparing words is easy to teach as a game while driving in the car. You can refer to one game as Extension/Intension. Ask a child to give you a noun, any noun, but it must be a noun. Maybe they say "cat." Ask a different child to challenge with the word *Extension* or *Intension*. Say the other child chooses, "Extension." Then, the child who gave the noun has to see how many logical extensions he can make from that noun. Reverse the roles on the next word, and whoever made the most extensions or intensions is the winner. Or, make it noncompetitive and include everyone in the car with a goal of finding as many words as possible. To extend "cat," you may think of the words *feline*, *mammal*, and *animal*. If the noun was "calico," then *cat*, *feline*, *mammal*, and *animal* would be extensions. But the extension for "calico" could be entirely different if you lived in a family of cloth-makers. *Muslin*, *fabric*, and *textile* could have been the extended words if you had a weaver in the car!

Games like this are a light-hearted way to teach your child how to define his terms, how to compare the subtle differences of synonymous words, and how to improve his vocabulary with ever more precise words. Not only his logic but also his writing, reading, and mathematics will improve proportionally.

RELATIONSHIP

Perhaps the most visual way of understanding the possible relationships between logical statements is to use the *square of opposition*. Use of this tool is very helpful to students because it visually demonstrates the relationship of statements. Do not be frightened by the new words and symbols in the square. Tell your brain that this is just like looking at the math equation $1 + 1 = 2$ for the first time. You have to become a detective to learn the language and then the difficult becomes understandable.

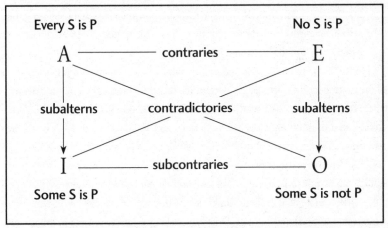

Figure 1—Square of Opposition. *The Stanford Encyclopedia of Philosophy (Fall 2012 edition).*

There are four types of logical statements: *A, E, I,* and *O* statements. Placing these four standard categorical statements on the corners of the "square" is the first step. Each statement is made up of a subject (S) and a predicate (P), just like a sentence in English grammar. The letters used to represent these four types of statements come from the first two vowels in each of the Latin words *affirmo*, which means "I affirm" or "I assert," and *nego*, which means "I negate."

- "A" statements are the *universal affirmative statements* in the form of "Every S is P." These statements assert something positive or affirmative about all the members of the subject group. We use the letter "A" for these statements because it is the first vowel in *A-ffirmo*. The A statements are easy to remember because of the words "all" and "affirmative." Here is an example of an A statement: "All dogs are horses."

- "E" statements are the *universal negative statements* in the form of "No S is P." These statements assert something negative about all members of the subject group. We use the letter "E" for these statements because it is the first vowel in *n-E-go*. Here is an example of an E statement: "No dogs are horses."

- "I" statements are the *particular affirmative statements* in the form of "Some S is P." They assert something positive about some members of the subject group. The name comes from the second vowel of *aff-I-rmo*. An example of an I statement is, "Some dogs are horses."

- "O" statements are the *particular negative statements* in the form of "Some S is not P." They assert something negative about some members of the subject group. The name comes from the second vowel in *neg-O*. An example of an O statement would be, "Some dogs are not horses."

Notice that I am not looking at the truth-value of these statements, just at the form of the statements. The form helps to determine that the sentence is actually a statement. There are only four ways to say this statement about the dog and the horse. Statements are a special form of sentences because a statement is either true or false. It is worth repeating: all statements have truth-values. All sentences do not have truth-values. Can you tell that the previous two sentences are statements? "All statements have truth-values" can be true or false, as can "All sentences do not have truth-values."

It is not enough to analyze single statements; we must examine statements in relationship to one another. Statements can relate to other statements in many ways, which allow statements to be used as propositions in arguments. Statements may be related as contrary, contradictory, subcontrary, and subaltern. Look back at the square of opposition to see these relationships demonstrated visually.

Contrary statements deal with absolutes. As such, they cannot both be true, but they leave open the possibility of a third, non-absolute option. In the square of opposition, A and E statements are contrary. Logic students would memorize these relationships, but you can also understand them using common sense. I'll give you a scenario to demonstrate what I mean. You have five coins. An A statement would be, "All the coins are pennies." An E statement would be, "None of the coins are pennies." If A is a valid statement, then you can see that E is not valid, and vice versa. However, it is possible for A and E to both be false: some, but not all, of the coins might be pennies.

Two statements are *contradictory* if one of them must be valid and the other must be invalid. A and O statements are contradictory, as are E and I statements. In the scenario I used above, the A statement was, "All the coins are pennies." An O statement would be, "Some of the coins are not pennies." These two statements directly contradict each other. If the O statement is valid—one of the coins is a nickel—all of the coins cannot be pennies, as the A statement asserted. If the A statement is valid, then all five coins are pennies, and the O statement cannot be valid. Likewise, the E statement was, "None of the coins are pennies." An I statement would be, "Some of the coins are pennies." These two propositions cannot both be valid, and they leave no third option.

Subcontrary statements deal with particulars. As such, both may be true, but both cannot be false. In the square of opposition, I and O statements are subcontrary. Let's keep using the same example. Our I statement said, "Some of the coins are pennies," while our O statement affirmed, "Some of the coins are not pennies." Both of these statements can be valid—we might have three nickels and two pennies—but they cannot both be invalid.

The final type of relationship, *subaltern*, is represented by A and I statements and E and O statements. If A is true, then I must be true as well, but not vice versa. In other words, if "All of the coins are pennies," then it necessarily follows that "Some of the coins are pennies" is also valid. However, just because we know "Some of the coins are pennies" does not mean that we can assume that "All of the coins are pennies." Likewise, if E is true, O must be true, but not vice versa.

Understanding the relationship between statements allows the student to understand what is being said—and not being said—in a given conversation; it also allows students to determine what can be logically asserted and what cannot be logically asserted in a given situation. At this point, we are still not talking about truth-value; we are talking about logical validity. Look at my dog sentences. "All dogs are horses" is obviously false, but the fact that it contradicts the statement "Some dogs are not horses" is not so obvious. *All, none, some,* and *not* are very precise words that we need to use accurately. True and false are big parts of the logic story, and we will talk more about them later, but they are not the only part in determining a sound argument.

Remember, we begin with simple, even silly statements like these because they allow our students to focus on the form of the argument rather than getting caught up in the argument itself. Your student is not likely to become emotionally involved in an argument about whether or not dogs are horses or coins are pennies. If, however, we started with an argument about the death penalty, or evolution, or world hunger, your student might be unable to analyze the logical validity of the argument calmly because the topic would evoke an emotional response. That does not mean logic is good for only "cold" topics; rather, the cold topics serve as practice for the conversations that truly matter, when your student will need to be able to combine orderly thought with emotional appeal.

Mastering logical relationships requires regular practice, but incorporating the basic forms of logic—the definition of a statement, the types of statements, and the relationships between statements—into regular life is not as difficult as you might think. Practice the basic forms in your daily conversation by pulling a sentence out of a news report, an editorial, or an essay you are studying. Look for the key words "all," "no," "none," and "some" to help you find clear statements to analyze. Write the sentence on a whiteboard or piece of paper, and ask your student to eliminate modifiers and extra information until she is left with a simple sentence. Then, ask her to identify whether it is a statement or just a sentence, and if it is a statement, what kind of statement it is. Ask her to identify the subject (S) and predicate (P) of the sentence. Finally, ask her to create the other three types of statements that would complete the Square of Opposition.

Here's an example from the Declaration of Independence: "We hold these truths to be self-evident, that all men are created equal, that they are endowed by their Creator with certain unalienable Rights, that among these are Life, Liberty and the pursuit of Happiness." For the sake of this exercise, we might eliminate from the sentence everything except, "all men are created equal." Is this a statement or just a sentence? Can it be true or false? Yes, so it is a statement. What kind of statement is it? It takes the form, "All ____ is ____," so it is an A statement. What are the subject and the predicate? The subject is "men," and the predicate is "are created equal." How would you create E, I, and O statements from this one? "No men are created equal," "Some men are created equal," and "Some men are not created equal."

You might use this exercise in a conversation about the way the founders justified slavery, or you might go on to talk about the women's movement and the Seneca Falls Declaration, or the "separate but equal" doctrine of segregated schools in the twentieth century. The possibilities go on and on.

CIRCUMSTANCE

Circumstance relates to possibilities of thought. As stated before, there are some sentence structures that are not statements. Their truth-value is impossible to determine. Logic teaches students to write and to recognize logically valid statements. Statements are sentences that are either true or false; they have a "truth-value" that can be evaluated. Some sentences that might appear to be statements are not statements at all because they have no truth-value. Questions, commands, self-reporting sentences, and nonsense sentences are not statements because their truth-values cannot be determined. The following are examples of the four types of sentences that are not statements with a truth-value.

Logic teaches students to write and to recognize logically valid statements.

- "Do you like chocolate?" A statement is not even given.
- "You must like chocolate." Force allows for no evaluation.
- "I like chocolate." Opinions or preferences are not logical statements.
- "Chocolate likes me." Nonsense—a thing cannot have preferences.

Nonstatements prohibit logical analysis. When you say, "I like chocolate," I would be a fool to argue. After all, they are your taste buds. In an argument, questions, commands, preferences, and nonsense sentences interrupt and divert the argument away from its purpose. It is difficult to have a meaningful debate about the nation's immigration policy if one individual keeps saying, "I just don't like immigrants!" Likewise, you cannot seriously consider the question, "Is justice the most important quality in a free society?" if one person responds with a hypothetical question every time he is asked to give his opinion. Of course, I do not mean that nonstatements serve no purpose; this book would be meaningless without questions, and parenting would not be parenting without the occasional command. What I mean is that these types of sentences do not play a role in formal logical arguments. The important thing is for your dialectical student to learn how to distinguish between statements with a truth-value and sentences that serve other purposes.

TESTIMONY

It is difficult to play a sport if you do not know the boundaries of the playing area or the rules of play (even Calvinball, from the comic strip *Calvin & Hobbes*, had one rule: you cannot play the game with the same rules twice). In the same way, it is difficult to analyze a logical argument without certain foundational parameters. In logic, the parameters are set by the three laws that govern all of logic. These laws act as a presuppositional authority to truth and non-truth in logic. Of course, we know that God is our ultimate authority, but as all things reflect His character, it is to be expected that every subject would have laws that govern its particulars.

- The *law of the excluded middle* tells us that any statement is either true or false.
- The *law of identity* tells us that if a statement is true, then it is true.

- The *law of non-contradiction* tells us that a statement cannot be both true and false.

These simple laws seem to state the obvious, until you want things to go your way. Then the situation no longer seems so black and white. These laws are applicable in all areas of analysis, and we often refer to them when explaining the fallacy behind a logical argument. Let's examine them one at a time.

The law of the excluded middle tells us that any statement is true or false: there is no middle ground. This first law teaches students to take a stand, accepting responsibility for their own ideas, as well as for the consequences of those ideas or actions. When you ask your son if he broke the neighbor's window with a baseball, he should learn to say a firm "Yes" or "No," rather than saying, "Well, sort of . . ." The first law teaches logicians to deal with absolute truth, rather than relativity.

The law of identity tells us that if a statement is true, then it is true. This second law teaches that nouns (people, places, things, and ideas) have one nature, one essence. Things cannot possess characteristics that are inconsistent with their nature. When Abraham Lincoln reminded the Republican convention in 1858 that a house divided against itself cannot stand, he was using this principle by quoting a biblical passage (Matthew 12:22–28), in which Jesus corrects the faulty logic of one of the Pharisees' accusations, saying, "Every kingdom divided against itself will be ruined, and every city or household divided against itself will not stand." The second law of logic teaches that there is an essential unity in Creation, reflecting the unity of the Creator, so when you teach your children this law, you are affirming that they have a nature to be honored.

Finally, the *law of non-contradiction* tells us that a statement cannot be both true and false. Put another way, a statement and its opposite cannot both be true. When your daughter breaks curfew, she cannot give each parent a different, contradictory explanation and expect to get away with the lie. The third law teaches your children the value of consistent actions and a consistent worldview.

LOGIC THROUGHOUT THE CURRICULUM

Logic trains the brain to think clearly about all subjects by ordering information into usable form.

One mom recently shared with me that her thirteen-year-old daughter always complains about studying logic. This young dialectician whines, "But I'll never use this!" to which her mother replies, laughing through the tears, "I know honey, but you could be the first!"

This mother and daughter are not alone in their sense that logic is an academic exercise with little pragmatic value. So, what is the practical use for logic? Why should parents and students attempt to master this intimidating subject? Will it really prove to be useful? I say an unequivocal, "Yes." Logic trains the brain to think clearly about all subjects by ordering information into usable form. This is a skill we all need to acquire. We use principles of logic to master mathematics, to study literature critically, to understand history, to hone the skills of observation and evaluation used in the sciences, and to appreciate and produce art.

As already stated, logic is math with words. The same principles that guide clear thinking in logic inform our thinking in mathematics. The same laws of thought that govern logic guide the practice of algebra. Proofs in logic are parallel to proofs in geometry. Students who study logic in the dialectic stage reinforce the foundational principles that may make math not just doable but artful; logic students are able to find not only the answers to the problem sets but also the important forms that give structure to math.

True study of literature requires critical analysis of characters, plots, themes, settings, literary devices, and symbolism. The tools of logic—defining terms, determining relationships, analyzing cause and effect—make literary criticism and study rich and effective. Clear thinking skills make it possible to divine connections between themes and a character's actions in novels, and between actions and consequences in a story. Patterns of orderly thinking help students as they read critically and as they write with structure, order, and persuasiveness.

Logic skills also make the study of history more compelling. An understanding of cause and effect propels students from the grammar of knowing what happened to whom, into the dialectic understanding of why events transpired, and toward the rhetorical extrapolating of what is likely to occur in the future as a result of current actions. The study of logic allows students to evaluate the past and to use those conclusions to make wise judgments in order to affect the future. The skills of logic shape students into persuasive speakers and debaters, and these abilities make them able influencers.

The fundamental skills used in the practice of the sciences are sharpened through the study of logic. The skills of defining terms, of careful observation, of clear thinking to discern relationships between ideas, and evaluation techniques used to determine causation carry over from logic training into the disciplines of physical science, biology, chemistry, and physics. Logic students embrace order and form; these skills make obser-vation of experiments and producing lab reports easier and more natural.

Logic even has its influence on the study of the arts. The skills of clear thinking help students develop plans for executing art projects, be they graphic arts, music, dance, or sports. They help the artists attain their ideals by making their visions realities. Logic and the arts also share a similar need for practice; just as the practice of logic skills and procedures leads to mastery over that discipline, so practice in the arts leads technicians to become artists.

Exploring relationships is another key focus of logic. Dialectic students must under-stand how statements are related to one another in an argument, how valid arguments are constructed, and how to recognize truth as opposed to validity in an argument. What forms can statements take? How can they be combined into arguments? What combi-nations produce "good arguments"? What is the difference between a valid argument, a coherent argument, and a true argument? Thinking about thinking benefits everyone.

"Logic in Literature" by Matt Bianco

The following are excerpts from Atticus Finch's closing arguments in the Tom Robinson case in Harper Lee's *To Kill a Mockingbird*. Atticus is the defense attorney for Tom Robinson, a black man, who has been accused of beating and raping Mayella Ewell, a white woman. Atticus, fighting for a justice he knows he will not win, against a prejudice he cannot singly overcome, closes with these remarks:

> Her father saw it, and the defendant has testified as to his remarks. What did her father do? We don't know, but there is circumstantial evidence to indicate that Mayella Ewell was beaten savagely by someone who led almost exclusively with his left. We do know in part what Mr. Ewell did: he did what any God-fearing, persevering, respectable white man would do under the circumstances—he swore out a warrant, no doubt signing it with his left hand, and Tom Robinson now sits before you, having taken the oath with the only good hand he possesses—his right hand. (204)

Atticus is using sarcasm to draw some logical conclusions for the jurors. Mayella Ewell was beaten by someone's left hand. From that, we can draw two conclusions that we could put into good logic language.

Some (of Mayella's) bruises were made by a left hand.

Tom Robinson cannot use his left hand.

Therefore, Tom did not make Mayella's bruises.

Or,

Some (of Mayella's) bruises are bruises made by the left hand.

Mr. Ewell is left-handed.

Therefore, Mr. Ewell bruised Mayella.

What questions could we ask about these two syllogisms? What types of statements are being made? Is each proposition a statement with a truth-value? Have the laws of excluded middle, identity, or non-contradiction been violated? Are the syllogisms valid? Certainly, it can be seen as valid that Tom did not create the bruises, being without a viable left hand. It cannot, however, be proved that Mr. Ewell is the cause of Mayella's bruises, unless he is the only left-handed person in the world!

Atticus continues,

> The witnesses for the state . . . have presented themselves to you gentlemen, to this Court, in the cynical confidence that their testimony would not be doubted, confident that you gentlemen would go along with them on the assumption—the evil assumption—that *all* Negroes lie, that *all* Negroes are basically immoral beings, that *all* Negro men are not to be trusted around our women, an assumption that one associates with minds of their caliber. (204)

Here, he presents the state's lies in a series of A (Every S is P) statements. To be clear, Atticus is not saying that these are true but that the state's witnesses are confident the jurors will hold these prejudices to be true. Why does he call the jurors "gentlemen" then mock them by referring to "minds of their caliber"? Are these statements true or not? Does society really want to hear the truth when it is inconvenient? Atticus uses logic to succinctly reveal the evil in the jurors' hearts. He is using A statements—universal affirmative statements—to sway a jury, to clearly show them the despicable way in which they think.

As you discuss *To Kill a Mockingbird* and others like it, ask your children to define terms, to compare, to consider relationships and circumstance, and to consider testimony. Ask them, "Where else do you see logic at work in literature and the world around you?" It is certainly present; we just lack the habit of looking for it.

Logic is useful in all sorts of practical ways; it shapes our thinking in both academic and everyday life circles. But, logic is not just useful because of what it helps us to produce in our endeavors. Logic improves our very selves, making us more of who God made us to be than we ever supposed we could be. Logic empowers us to be truly in the image of God.

In Genesis 1, we are told, "In the beginning God created the heaven and earth. And the earth was without form…" Then the rest of the chapter is about God creating the forms and filling the earth with things we can name. Likewise, we reflect His image when we find the forms and fill them with things we can name. We have math FORMulas, Latin forms, concrete forms, plastic molds, as well as logical forms, musical forms, and sentence forms. Logic ties the forms of statements into logical arguments, just as algebra ties forms of equations into logical proofs. Dialectic students discover the forms inherent in creation as they ask questions and discover that there are limited forms of answers, which contain infinite constructions.

Formal logic is one way to introduce the discovery of these ideas to a student of any age. It may be difficult to see the value in studying logic, even though I have highlighted the benefits it offers to clear thinking and wise judgment. Some students will not like logic initially, either. They might decide they like a specific branch of logic, like informal logic or material logic. Formal logic, however, is necessary for many of the reasons already stated—especially, however, because it makes us free and conforms us more to the image of God.

CHAPTER NINE

———

HISTORY

"Modern men and women who lack a sense of place and continuity with the past are driven by ephemeral appetites and the passion for immediate self-gratification.

"The true rhetorician employs memory . . . strives to demonstrate that we live in continuity with those who have gone before us, who also knew suffering, and that therefore there is reason to have courage and hope even when things seem at their worst."

—Vigen Guroian, *Rallying the Really Human Things*

In a chapter on history, you would expect to hear the argument that we must study history to avoid the mistakes of the past. That is a good starting point. We do study the past to be aware of old mistakes, bad ideas, and things gone wrong, in order to avoid unnecessary repetition of those very things. In *The Core*, I quoted George Santayana: "Those who cannot remember the past are condemned to repeat it" (165). This authority reminds us that the study of history is essential to avoid mistakes already made. C. S. Lewis argues that we study the old books not because our forebears were more clever or devoid of having made mistakes but because they did not make the same mistakes (qtd. in *Classical Christian Education Made Approachable,* 41). Just examining the different mistakes they made is instructional, whether we repeat them or not.

This cautionary motivation is only one half of the equation, however. We must also study the past to acquire a sense of the great story in which each one of us has the opportunity to participate. Our predecessors did not always make mistakes. Sometimes—maybe more often than we care to admit—they made the right choices. When they did, we should imitate them. At other times, they made the wrong choice for the right reason. By studying the history of such cases, we can avoid a past mistake while learning from the reasoning behind it.

As parents and instructors, we often teach our children through our own personal histories. Whether formally or informally, we include our own history as something from which they can learn how to live, and live well. We speak as authorities, as eyewitnesses, of the mistakes we have made in order to dissuade our children from making those same mistakes themselves. Likewise, we want our students to study history because they are experiencing events in their own lives that are informed by historical people and events. Their relationship to history is that they are *in* history! They need to learn their story and where they fit into it. They ought to learn to respect history because of how it can impact their own lives.

Now, you may be thinking, "That's not the effect of my child studying history. My child memorizes dates so that he can pass a test at the end of the year." Bear with me for a minute while I challenge that way of thinking. Your student may believe he is only studying history in order to pass a test, but history is subversive, and it is instilling in him, subtly and slowly, a way of thinking about life that will affect the decisions he makes and the systems he defends. Unless he learns to ask questions, he won't even know how or why it happened. Let me give you an example. Your student may be preparing for a test, but he may also be wondering whether it was okay for Brutus to assassinate Julius Caesar in light of John Wilkes Booth assassinating Abraham Lincoln. While he memorizes the date "1865" and the Shakespearean phrase *"E tu, Brute?"*, he is forming an opinion about political assassinations and correct responses to power. If your student is trained only to memorize the facts of history and not to ask the questions aloud, he may not see or experience the fullness of history and his place in it. He may not realize how it is shaping his opinions. Our goal as parents and teachers,

> *…history is subversive, and it is instilling in him, subtly and slowly, a way of thinking about life that will affect the decisions he makes and the systems he defends.*

during the dialectic stage, is to give our students a safe outlet for their questions and to encourage them to ask more.

Together, you and your student must move beyond the grammar of history—the bare facts—into the dialectic of history. In this chapter, you will learn to guide your student as he questions the way historical events relate to one another, analyzes their causes, considers their circumstances, and interprets their results in light of future consequences. Knowing the fact that Napoleon attacked Russia does not tell him that it was a mistake unless he also knows the outcome of the war. Your student needs to go beyond the facts of Napoleon's attack and into questions about the attack. This is where he will learn about poor and good judgments. This is where he will learn about the consequences, both intended and unintended, of past actions. As I walk you through the questions that encourage dialectical thinking about history, I hope to persuade you that, while studying history can be as reductionistic as passing a test, it can also be as glorious as motivating your student to discover and emulate modern-day heroes.

HISTORY AND THE COMMON TOPICS

Memorizing basic facts gives us a starting point for studying history dialectically. As in other subjects, your student must first input data before he can begin to process and analyze it. My younger two boys memorized a 161-point timeline of historical events and figures when they were between the ages of five and eleven. When they were young, for the most part, they were happy to parrot the names and dates in order, without pausing to ask questions. As they approached middle school, however, their natural curiosity began to inspire questions—not just "what?" but also "why?". The bare facts were less satisfying. In addition to memorizing the dates and nations involved, they began to wonder about the relationship between World War I and World War II, and about the circumstances surrounding the American Revolution.

Use your child's knowledge of historical facts to jumpstart a dialectical discussion. You might start with a particular period of history, with a specific event, or with a certain historical figure. I find it helpful to begin with a sentence such as "In 1776, the Continental Congress published the Declaration of Independence in Philadelphia, announcing the colonists' intent to form a new nation." Or, you might start with an individual from this period such as Patrick Henry. We could simply leave our students with these facts, as if Patrick Henry and the Continental Congress were part of some sort of American Historical Figures trading cards set. Many textbooks teach history in just this skeletal way. But we want more for our children. We want them to know who Patrick Henry was because we want his life to inspire them to action. (And, contrarily, we want our students to know who Adolf Hitler was, to avoid wrong actions like his.) We want our students to know why the Declaration of Independence was such a revolutionary document in American history. To take your students to the next level, you must guide them through the questions that will put Patrick Henry and other historical facts into a story—a story that is also your students' story because it is part of their American past. (If they are not Americans, you could, of course, use different examples.) The five common topics will help you devise the right questions.

DEFINITION

Begin by asking your student to define his terms. In the sample sentence above, your student might need to define "Continental Congress," "Declaration of Independence," and "colonists." To guide this process, think about 1) the broader category to which the term belongs, and 2) the characteristics that distinguish this term from others in its category. What makes this term unique?

Your student might know some of the answers off the top of his head, but he might also have to practice research skills in order to find out. Research becomes even more important for older students. (We will talk more in the section on testimony about the kinds of resources that should be considered authoritative.) In the math chapter, we talked about using the glossary in the back of the book to find definitions of math terms. History books from the library or from your private collection may not have a glossary, but they should have an index that lists key words, names, and concepts discussed in the book. Teach your child to use this index to locate information about his topic. Encyclopedias, and sometimes dictionaries, can also help your student define his terms. Don't be afraid to get creative. In the process of defining the Declaration of Independence, look for images of the original document or paintings of the signers. Read the document itself. All of these artifacts help your student form a broader defini-tion of historical events.

In the second example, you might ask, "Who was Patrick Henry?" Answers to this question will probably consist of biographical data gathered from biographies and historical records. Your student might reply that Henry was an attorney, planter, politi-cian, and Founding Father from Virginia who lived from 1736 to 1799. If your student can be induced to define Patrick Henry in terms of story, then all the better. What do

I mean by a definition "in terms of story"? Let me give you an example. What role did Patrick Henry play as a Founding Father? With some digging in either your student's memory or some external resource, he may recall that Patrick Henry is known for the famous quotation, "Give me liberty, or give me death!" Now, instead of just a collection of facts, your student has the beginnings of a narrative. As your student practices definition, Patrick Henry becomes a character, more than simply a name on a page.

In the process of defining who Patrick Henry was, your student may also need to define the broader genus of "Founding Father" or "Republican politician" as it was understood prior to the American Revolution. Likewise, in the process of defining "colonists," he might encounter information about British and French colonies in other parts of the world. Then, he would need to determine what separated Patrick Henry from his contemporaries and what made the American colonials different from Brazilian, Indian, Australian, and Guamanian colonials. These lines of questioning will lead your student naturally to the next common topic, comparison.

COMPARISON

Comparison happens naturally when we study history. Your job as the parent or teacher is to make this implicit process explicit. Give your student models to compare. For example, when asking questions about the Declaration of Independence, ask your child to read the Magna Carta and identify what is the same and what is different between the two documents. Or, compare the Declaration of Independence to the Declaration of Sentiments presented at the Seneca Falls Convention in 1848, demanding equal rights for women. If possible, choose examples that belong to the broader genus that your student has identified during the definition process (in this example, the genus might be "statements expressing basic human rights").

Your job as the parent or teacher is to make this implicit process explicit.

Similarly, ask your child to compare Patrick Henry to one of the other Founding Fathers or to a figure from later in the nation's history. How were they similar, and how were they different? What did they both have that was the same and different? What did they both do that was the same and different? You might want to identify some of Henry's contemporaries, both allies and adversaries, in the debate over freedom. Here, encourage your student to read biographies of Jefferson, Madison, and Hamilton. In a comparison of Patrick Henry and James Madison, your student might find that they both fought for American independence (the same), but that James Madison supported replacing the Articles of Confederation with the Constitution (different), while Patrick Henry opposed the ratification of the Constitution (different).

Older students may want to define the ideals of freedom fighters from other time periods or geographical regions. Locke, Voltaire, Gandhi, Martin Luther, Martin Luther King, Jr., and others come to mind. In comparing Henry to freedom fighters from different eras or regions, the same questions can be asked, moving beyond biographical comparisons to geographical, political, and cultural differences that were formative to the character's response to a historical event.

RELATIONSHIP

Sometimes, in the course of comparison, your student may find that one term had a direct influence or relationship to another term. In the example we have been using from the Constitutional Convention, your student may wonder if any of the Founders had read the Magna Carta and used it to craft their Declaration. Now you are moving into the common topic of relationship. Ask your student, "What is the relationship between the Magna Carta and the Declaration of Independence?" Your student may need to conduct further research in order to find out that the American colonists were well informed about British common law through Sir Edward Coke's *Institutes of the Laws of England*, some of which was derived from the Magna Carta. Ask your student to consider whether this is an example of cause and effect, antecedent and consequence, contraries, or contradictions.

In the Patrick Henry example, you might ask, "What was the relationship of Patrick Henry to his place in history?" You aren't necessarily asking your student to consider Henry's relationship to another person (although you could be) but to the time period and events in question. What beliefs caused Henry to oppose the Constitution? Was he rich or poor? Was he school-educated or street-educated? Did his parents inculcate this love of liberty? Did his church preach freedom? What caused the early Americans to feel that a new Constitution was necessary? What were the effects of ratifying the Constitution? What happened to Patrick Henry after the Constitution was passed? How did his speech affect the French Revolution? What impact did his speech have on later figures like Gandhi or Martin Luther King, Jr.? How are modern Americans affected by the Bill of Rights that Henry fought for? All of these questions about relationship help your student to create connecting threads between the events, people, and artifacts that form our knowledge of history. In the process, he should be learning to think about his own role in history as it relates to the people and events around him.

CIRCUMSTANCE

When your student begins to consider the common topic of circumstance, he should ask questions about the context surrounding his topic. As much as we like to think our decisions are made freely and independently, the cultural, social, political, and economic climates surrounding a historical moment assert a powerful influence on events and individual choices.

When your student begins to consider the common topic of circumstance, he should ask questions about the context surrounding his topic.

In the example about the Constitutional Convention and the Declaration of Independence, you might ask your student, "What happened in 1776 to make the colonists likely to rebel?" You might also ask what circumstances made it possible for the American colonists to declare their independence. As you discuss this question, you might point him to the colonies' geographical distance from England, their intellectually engaged citizenry, or their religious heritage and determination to be free. Give your student the opportunity to stake a claim and defend his opinion. Gently challenge him by offering alternative points of view. In doing so, you can model respectful debate for him, and you can also help him to wrestle with the complexity of historical events.

In the Patrick Henry example, you might ask, "What was happening in the time and place that Patrick Henry was living, and in the time and place in which he opposed the ratification of the Constitution?" What factors made it probable that Henry would speak out? What factors probably discouraged him from taking a stand? Consider what Henry risked by speaking out. Did his wife and children pay a price for his aggressiveness? How did the circumstances of the local slaves and slave owners affect his thinking? How did his peers understand the word "liberty" when he made his famous claim?

To analyze circumstance well, older or very interested students will probably need to do additional research in order to appreciate the circumstances in which historical characters found themselves. As your student works through these questions, he might find that Henry was unduly concerned with the Constitution. He might discover that the Articles of Confederation gave too much autonomy to the states and not enough authority to the federal, or central, government. He might discover that the Constitution brought balance between the state and federal governments as well as greater balance between the legislative, executive, and judicial branches of the federal government.

Your student might discover that Patrick Henry was a Christian and opposed the Constitution on theological grounds. He might learn that Henry refused to participate in the convention because he saw it as an illegal convention and that this is why he is known for also having said, "I smell a rat." He might find that James Madison was utterly frustrated with Henry because Madison might spend hours trying to convince delegates to accept a certain aspect of the document, and Henry—Madison claims— could undo all of his efforts with the simple raising of an eyebrow. He might conclude that Henry was overly fearful of the allowance in the Constitution for a standing army and disagree with Henry's belief that the Constitution would make America a more independent federation rather than a God-dependent nation. In the end, your student might find he likes much but not all of who Patrick Henry was. He might find there are aspects of Patrick Henry he wants to emulate, and other aspects he would rather not. That's okay. No mere human has qualified as a hero in every aspect of his life. No mere human has responded perfectly to all of the circumstances in his life.

TESTIMONY

In part because no human is perfect, your student will learn as he asks questions about history that not only are some sources of information more reliable than others but also that all are swayed by certain biases and limited vision. When you study any historical event or person, you will find many claims about the nature of the world and about humanity's rightful place in it. Sometimes historical figures name the source of their authority; sometimes they do not. The common topic of testimony teaches your child how to ask good questions about the kind of testimony we use to judge human actions throughout history. Testimony is a practical line of inquiry because we must decide whether or not to emulate a historical figure's actions. In addition, testimony affects the way your student conducts research. Whenever your student consults a source, ask him why he has chosen to trust that authority. Is the author a historian who has trained in research and analysis? Does the eyewitness stand to gain something from reporting a certain outcome to the battle? Was the writer part of the winning team in a conflict or

When you study any historical event or person, you will find many claims about the nature of the world and about humanity's rightful place in it.

the losing team? What kind of research or evidence does the authority cite to back up his opinions? Are statistics more reliable than testimonials?

The accuracy of authorities is important as we ask questions about history. At first, your student may find it disconcerting to discover that not everyone agrees about who really discovered America or when the Cold War actually ended. If you, however, model curiosity and a spirit of inquiry, you will be able to reassure him that areas of uncertainty do not have to be terrifying. They do not mark the end of his pursuit of knowledge but rather necessitate new caution and thoroughness. This part of studying history can be both exciting and challenging. Start small, by encouraging your student to ask, "Who says?"—politely!—when he encounters a claim about history.

In the first example about the Declaration of Independence, you can practice this dialogue by reading a few early sentences of the declaration and asking what kind of testimony the colonists used to support their ideas.

> We hold these truths to be self-evident, that all men are created equal, that they are endowed by their Creator with certain unalienable Rights, that among these are Life, Liberty and the pursuit of Happiness.

"Who says" all men are created equal? The colonists declared that it was a self-evident truth. Does your student agree?

> —That to secure these rights, Governments are instituted among Men, deriving their just powers from the consent of the governed,

"Who says" that governments have power? The colonists declared that the consent of the governed was the source of their power.

> —That whenever any Form of Government becomes destructive of these ends, it is the Right of the People to alter or to abolish it, and to institute new Government, laying its foundation on such principles and organizing its powers in such form, as to them shall seem most likely to effect their Safety and Happiness.

"Who says" when the people have the right to abolish a form of government? The colonists indicate that when the government becomes destructive to life, liberty, or the pursuit of happiness, the people have a right to alter or abolish it. We could keep going, asking not only where the men who wrote the Declaration got their authority but also what other authorities have said since then about the Declaration and its authors.

In the Patrick Henry example, your student might find a very different picture of Patrick Henry painted by eighteenth-century historians and present-day historians. One book might praise Henry, the hero, while another book might treat him as a calculating manipulator. In the story related by James Madison about Henry's raised eyebrow, was Madison a reliable authority? What did Madison stand to gain from painting this picture of Henry's persuasive powers? Begin to ask your student these questions, and eventually, he will learn to ask them for himself, not only about events in the distant past but also about the testimony he encounters daily in the news, in literature, movies, and television, and in the conversations of his peers.

HISTORY, PERSPECTIVE, AND IDENTITY

"First Principles of History" by Matt Bianco

The power and value of the questions we ask about history can lead to grand places, but they may seem out of reach to the average homeschool parent. Although they are not out of reach, we begin all new endeavors with small steps. Here, I want to provide an example of what a dialectic conversation about history might look like when you are first starting out with your ten- or eleven-year-old.

Present your student with a historical figure such as Christopher Columbus. Ask him to define Christopher Columbus. You might spend the rest of the discussion answering the question, "Who was Christopher Columbus?" He was an explorer who sailed the ocean blue in 1492. He was an Italian. He was commissioned by the Spanish monarch Queen Isabella. He sailed on three ships. He discovered America. You may get no further than that. That's okay; the questions are not a requisite checklist that indicates failure for every missing check.

Maybe a day or two later, you can introduce another historical figure, Leif Eriksson. Who was he? He was Norse, a Viking. He discovered America. What just happened? You created tension, a point of conflict for your student. Your student, recognizing the conflict that they have just been told both Columbus and Leif Eriksson discovered America, will be ripe for a new round of questions. So you ask your student to compare. How are both of these explorers the same, and how are they different? What do they both have that is the same and different? What did they both do that is the same and different?

That may be the end of the conversation you have with your student until much later, maybe as late as the teenage years when he studies world history again. It may not. You may begin asking him, "What were the circumstances of the two men's trips and discoveries? What were the relationships, the causes and effects as well as purposes of their trips? Did Christopher Columbus sail west across the Atlantic to prove the earth was round, to expand the borders of Queen Isabella's empire, to fill the queen's coffers, or to spread Christianity to the peoples of India?"

Engaging in the dialectic is a process. Draw out the grammatical facts your child knows, or can access, using questions. Don't push beyond that for which he is ready. Start with the easier questions: definitions and comparisons. When he is ready, nudge him toward relationships, circumstances, and testimony. You aren't failing; you are progressing.

Recently, I was teaching my children American history. As we considered the South in the War Between the States, we came to some different realizations. We abhor slavery and specifically the oppression of one group of people because of their race, gender, religion, or socioeconomic status. No doubt, some—maybe many or most— Southerners were fighting to protect the institution of, and their dependence on, slavery. What did they say, however? When Northerners, who were primarily fighting to end slavery and protect the Union, asked the Southerners why they were fighting, what did they answer? The average Southern soldier replied that he was fighting simply because they, the Northerners, were acting as an occupying force.

Reading this, we wondered together, in dialectic conversation, what it would mean if this were true. What if the average Southern soldier, who was not a slave owner, was really fighting for that reason? That soldier may have thought back upon history and seen himself in the same situation as the colonists during the American Revolution.

I don't want to qualify this point to death, but let me remind you once again, I oppose slavery. I abhor oppression. I am not defending slavery or racism as institutions. What if, however, the simple Southerner of that day was asking the dialectic questions of history that we should ask? What if he wondered, as we should, what is this war? What if his answer was simply that it was a battle for freedom from a military force seeking to occupy his home?

When the Southerner compared his war with the American Revolution, he may have seen the similarities: soldiers occupying homes, the imposition of laws the occupiers didn't follow themselves, and the violation of political arrangements that had been made between the separate governing authorities.

When he considered the relationships of events surrounding the war, he may have noticed that immediately before the declaration of secession, heavy tariffs were levied that had an inequitable impact on Southern states. He may have noticed that immediately following the declaration, soldiers began occupying their homes and lands, and that their friends, families, and neighbors were being killed. He may have seen the cause as an assault on their culture and way of life (slavery included, no doubt, but not the only aspect of it), and he may have seen the effects as death and destruction. He may have had doubts that the abolition of slavery was the purpose of the war.

When he considered the circumstances of the war, he may have noticed that he was in a fight-or-flight situation, and that not only was war—and victory, he likely believed—possible, but was also probable. Thus, he should fight.

When he considered what the authorities had to say about war, he would have imagined what the colonists would have said, both as eyewitnesses and experts: Freedom is worth fighting for. Liberty is more valuable to a free people than is security. We fight tyranny because it is the right thing to do, because it is our duty.

If this were how he answered the dialectic questions, then we can understand why he would fight the Northern soldiers just because they were there. We can accept that this is not only what he did but also what he believed he should do. Your student might acknowledge, as mine did, that our imagined Southern soldier saw in himself a historical identity that taught him that this is what Americans do: Americans defend against tyranny; Americans fight injustices; Americans risk life, limb, and property for the sake of freedom. They are even willing to give up security for its sake. They are Americans, and that's what Americans do.

We wish that this same Southern soldier would also have recognized that Americans do that because it is right not just for Americans to do, but for all of humanity to do as well. The slaves should have been able to defend themselves against tyranny and injustice, to risk life and limb (they had no property) for the sake of freedom. Alas, the soldier did not. We can, however, guide our students to see this truth for themselves, through the use of these powerful questions.

"Only the careless and unskilled teacher answers questions before they are asked."
—David Hicks, Norms & Nobility, *p. 129*

It is often enough to leave our students right at this point, to think on and contemplate the import of what they have considered through these questions. Some may want to apply these thoughts to their own day immediately. We encourage this. We do want to be careful, however, to discourage ourselves from forcing this next step on them. "Only the careless and unskilled teacher answers questions before they are asked" (Hicks, *Norms & Nobility*, 129). If our students are not ready to ask that question, we waste our answers on an unfertile mind by forcing it upon them at that time.

If they are ready to think about contemporary applications, though, we can encourage them through the process using the same questions. We might bring up the passage of the USA PATRIOT Act of 2001 after 9/11. It may be recent history, but it is still history and is still impacting their lives. What is the definition of the PATRIOT Act? How do the government's actions under the auspices of the act compare to the actions of the Union government around the time of the War Between the States or the colonists during the American Revolution? How are they both the same? How is one different from the other, and vice versa? What happened immediately before and after the passage of the PATRIOT Act? What caused it and what are its effects? What was its purpose? What was happening in America and at the time of its passage? Should it have been passed? What do the experts and witnesses say about it? Remind your student not only to use modern-day experts and witnesses but also to reach into history and literature for authoritative testimony. Are there any maxims, proverbs, or laws that speak to the ideas behind the PATRIOT Act? What do the Constitution and Declaration of Independence say about it and its ideas?

Then take him to the next step—if he is ready. Having connected your student to his historical identity as an American and a free man, ask him how an American should respond to such an act. Do we submit to it? Is it helpful? Is it harmful? Does it promote liberty, security, or both? If it only promotes one or the other, how have Americans felt about the promotion of one of those ideas to the detriment of the other? How have Americans reacted to it in the past?

If your student is really advanced in the dialectic, take him to an even deeper level—but only if he is ready. Does he want to act like an American? Is it good to act like an American? Is it right to act like an American? Is the historical American view that liberty is more valuable than security the right view? Walking your child through these steps is possible precisely because we have the questions available as tools to guide us. We know to ask our students to define the terms. We know to ask our students to compare their terms. We know to ask them to establish the circumstances and relationships of the terms. We know to ask them for authoritative testimony as it regards the terms and the circumstances of the terms. We also know, but need a continual reminder, that our students will eventually make these tools their own in the dialectic (and eventually rhetoric) stage of learning. We ask them these questions not because they will always need someone else to do the asking but because they will eventually be able to imitate us in this and ask the questions themselves.

HISTORY AND HEROES

In closing, I want to give you a glimpse of the ways that a thorough knowledge of history can be put to rhetorical use. Remember, your student may spend years practicing asking questions and researching answers before he is able to use his knowledge to persuade others, but it is helpful to have a vision of where the study of history can lead you.

In one of the great classics of our Western tradition, Homer's *The Iliad*, the warrior Phoenix attempts to move Achilles to accept the apology of King Agamemnon, receive his gifts, and return to battle against the Trojans. Whereas others have pled with Achilles, using gifts as persuasion, or honor as persuasion, or the lives of friends as persuasion, Phoenix uses a different tactic: he reminds Achilles of his history, of the story of Meleager fighting in battle with the Aetolians against the Curetes. Meleager withdrew from battle in anger, as Achilles has done, but Meleager returned to battle and brought victory with him. Meleager, however, returned too late to receive both prizes and glory. Phoenix is trying to persuade Achilles not to make the same mistake.

Phoenix is careful not to describe Meleager as a fool so that Achilles will not think he too is being called a fool. Phoenix describes Meleager as angry, but angry as wise men sometimes will be (*The Iliad*, Book IX). Phoenix is wiser still because he does not just attempt to persuade Achilles to avoid an error but he also attempts to show Achilles that this is who the Greeks are: they are a people who fight for honor, for glory. If Achilles is going to live up to being a Greek, then he is duty-bound to set aside this dispute with Agamemnon, to accept the gifts, and to return to the battle for his sake, for his comrades' sake, and for the sake of being a Greek.

Let me give you another example. In the New Testament, when a follower of Christ named Stephen is about to be martyred, he is brought before a council to answer charges of having spoken out against Jerusalem, the Temple, and the Law of Moses. In his defense, he recites to the council their history. He reminds them of Abraham's call out of Mesopotamia and God's promise that the Jews would inherit that land. He reminds them of their providential descent into Egypt and subsequent deliverance from bondage. He explains to them their historical predilections to despise, to disobey, and to kill the prophets. In reciting this historical record to them, he is proclaiming the same message: the promises of God and their consistent rejection of that message by killing the prophets. He is calling them to honor in practice the prophets they claim to honor, and to not continue in the sins of their fathers. He uses both the good and the bad of their history to call them to a sense of historical purpose. His defense is moving, but his listeners react defensively and, as a result, they martyr him. The disciple Peter, on the other hand, told the same story and it led to the conversion of three thousand men on the Day of Pentecost. People are moved by history and their connection to it, sometimes for good, and sometimes for ill.

> *People are moved by history and their connection to it, sometimes for good, and sometimes for ill.*

The purpose of history, then, is to give us identity, motivation, and meaning for who we are and what we are meant to do and be. This identity and motivation gives us hope and courage in what can sometimes be an overwhelming world to live in. History is necessary, as author Anthony Esolen writes in *Ten Ways to Destroy the Imagination of Your Child*,

> …not least because it cannot go away. It is simply *there*, never to change, and in its constancy it reflects the eternity of God. It presents to the young mind a vast field of fascination, of war and peace, loyalty and treason, invention and folly, bitter twists of fate and sweet poetic justice. When that past is the past of one's people or country or church, then the danger is terrible indeed, because then the past makes claims upon our honor and allegiance. Then it knocks at the door, saying softly, "I am still here." (123)

Without this connection to a past and its people, we are driven not by that identity and motivation but by our own passions and lusts. An ideal as honorable as duty becomes a dirty word. We communicate this purpose to our students in their study of history whether they want to hear it or not, whether they intend to be influenced by it or not. But we serve them all the better when we help them to see the purpose, to identify it, to name it, and to live it well. In this way, cultivating a spirit of inquiry toward history goes beyond the reductionist expectation of higher test scores and the practical application of wisdom learned from the mistakes of others. We reach into history for an identity and a motivation for right and dutiful action.

We don't just want our students to think about history well; we want them to act because of history's purpose in their lives. To do so, we must encourage them to have heroes. The idea of heroes seems so old-fashioned to some, yet so obvious to others. A hero, loosely defined, is someone who extends us—by his example—beyond "the limits of what is human… in the service of something good and noble" (Esolen, 143). Heroes drive us, by their examples, to do what we would not consider possible to do, to be what we would not consider it possible to be, to become what we had not considered it possible to become. In *The Aeneid*, Virgil writes of the dangers at sea that Aeneas and his men were facing. Aeneas appeals to them to be heroic and brave in the face of those dangers by reminding them of their history.

> Friends and companions,
> Have we not known hard hours before this?
> My men, who have endured still greater dangers,
> God will grant us an end to these as well.
> You sailed by Scylla's rage, her booming crags,
> You saw the Cyclops' boulders. Now call back
> Your courage, and have done with fear and sorrow.
> Some day, perhaps, remembering even this
> Will be a pleasure. (Book II, 270–278)

Aeneas appeals to their personal history—their recent history—to remind them to continue with courage and heroism. This is not a time to change who they are and what they do, but to continue facing the dangers they've always been willing to face. Put an end to their fear and continue in courage. And this, too, he tells them, will become a part of the history that will continue to move men and women to valor, remembering that it will be a pleasure to them as well.

In an earlier speech, however, Aeneas includes in his appeal a request for bravery not on the basis of their history alone, but on the basis of the history of their great heroes. He knows that men and women are moved to action by the heroic actions of those who have gone before them.

> Triply lucky, all you men
> To whom death came before your fathers' eyes
> Below the wall at Troy! Bravest Danaan,
> Diomedes, why could I not go down
> When you had wounded me, and lose my life
> On Ilium's battlefield? Our Hector lies there,
> Torn by Achilles' weapon; there Sarpedon,
> Our giant fighter, lies; and there the river
> Simois washes down so many shields
> And helmets, with strong bodies taken under! (Book I, 134–143)

What did these men's heroes do? Their fathers died at the wall of Troy. Their ultimate hero, Hector, lies dead at the hands of Achilles, and their heroic giant, Sarpedon, lies dead. It is not death Virgil is exalting through Aeneas's speech; it is valor. These men died in defense of the people and city of Troy, in defense of Paris and his love for Helen. Their heroic willingness to die for the sake of Troy and love means to Aeneas that his men should be willing to face the dangers of this storm and die in the fight to establish a new Troy, the city that will become the heart of the Roman Empire.

In both appeals, his men are heroic precisely because Aeneas has given them identity, motivation, and models. Your student might not be able to identify immediately the heroic attributes of a model set before him. The solution to this is, I hope, predictable. Guide him through the questions again. Define the model being presented. Compare the model to other heroes. Consider the relationships and circumstances of the model. Finally, ask what the authorities say about the model.

Why is this so difficult for our students? It is difficult because they do not have heroes. Heroes are archaic. When our children meet a hero such as George Washington, they do not recognize him as a hero—they only see a historical figure with certain biographical details: white hair, wooden teeth, chopper of cherry trees, first president, and so on. They need to know the stories to know the man. When a new acquaintance asks you who you are, you do not tell him your height, weight, social security number, and date of birth. You tell him your story: where you were born, to whom you are married, where you have lived, what you work at, what you like (hobbies, television shows, books, and movies). You ask for his story in return. You might even ask him how he plans to let society suck the best of his soul out of his body, just to see how he responds.

When we teach our children the heroes of history, we often limit what they learn to the hero's biographical details. But these should only serve as pegs that anchor a small story into a larger context. We also need to teach them the stories that transcend the simple timeline. Better, we need to guide them into a spirit of inquiry in order to desire discovery of those stories on their own. What better way to incite an unquenchable spirit of inquiry than to give them the questions, or the tools, they need in order to inquire?

What better way to incite an unquenchable spirit of inquiry than to give [students] the questions, or the tools, they need in order to inquire?

Our hope is that these questions will lead our students to discover true heroes. A lack of heroes not only leads to a lack of models to imitate but also to a void in one's life that must be filled. Humans, by definition, are created in the image of God to be imitators. Paul tells the Corinthians to imitate him as he imitates Christ. Nature abhors a vacuum; the very definition of being human means our humanity will abhor a vacuum of heroes. If we do not move our children to discover heroes to imitate, they will invent their own. That is what the cultural icons of our day have become. That is why our children make heroes out of athletes and musicians, actors and artists, politicians and talking heads. They do it because they need someone to look up to, to inspire them. Of course, I'm not saying that the exceptional in any field should not be admired. Watching someone who is the best at what he does can be inspiring, in addition to being entertaining. If, however, I want my child to be pushed beyond the limits of his humanity in the service of something good and noble, then I need my child to have genuine heroes, the real deals.

This is why we ask the questions about history. This is the end of our learning endeavors. Ask the questions, learn history, and be inspired and pushed beyond the limits of one's own humanity in the service of something good and noble, in concert with one's historical identity and place in the story, and with the motivation needed to do so. Fill the void, and imitate humanity well.

CHAPTER TEN

———

SCIENCE

"Those who fall in love with practice without science are like a sailor who enters a ship without a helm or a compass, and who never can be certain whither he is going.

"For nothing can be loved or hated unless it is first known."

—Leonardo da Vinci, *The Da Vinci Notebooks*

On August 2, 1971, *Apollo 15* commander David Scott stood on the surface of the moon in a live television feed and demonstrated an incredible scientific fact that had been described by Galileo more than three hundred years earlier: that two bodies of differing weight will fall at the same rate if they do so in a vacuum. Encased in his cumbersome, protective space suit, Commander Scott held in one hand a hammer and, in the other, a feather. He then said the following:

Well, in my left hand, I have a feather; in my right hand, a hammer. And I guess one of the reasons we got here today was because of a gentleman named Galileo, a long time ago, who made a rather significant discovery about falling objects in gravity fields. And we thought, where would be a better place to confirm his findings than on the moon... And so we thought we'd try it here for you. The feather happens to be, appropriately, a falcon feather for our Falcon [the name of the lunar module]. And I'll drop the two of them here and, hopefully, they'll hit the ground at the same time. ("The Hammer and the Feather" *Lunar Surface Journal* 167:22:06-43)

Then, Scott dropped the hammer and the feather. As predicted, they fell at exactly the same rate and hit the moon's surface simultaneously.

Imagining this astounding scene, we might have the following questions:

- What is gravity and what does it do?
- What is a vacuum?
- What do we mean by falling bodies?
- What is the moon?
- How is the moon similar to Earth?
- How is the moon different from Earth?
- What were astronauts doing on the moon, and how did they get there?
- Is the concept of a vacuum related to the use of space suits?
- What would we observe if we tried the hammer/feather experiment on Earth?

There is something unique about the nature of human beings that drives us to know and understand the natural world.

As you might guess, the questions could keep coming. Do we have to ask these questions? No. But history shows us that human beings are impelled to ask questions about the natural world and man's place in it. There is something unique about the nature of human beings that drives us to know and understand the natural world. Asking questions and seeking answers is the dialectical activity that breathes life into the facts accumulated through the grammar stage.

One does not need to go to the moon to dig into the character of the cosmos (*cosmos* is a word meaning "an orderly and harmonious system"). A child digging in the dirt and feeling the earth between his fingers, a child holding her hands under the faucet in fascination with the running water, and a child noticing how building blocks balance on top of each other and then fall when pushed over, are each engaged in the natural world. They are developing a grammar of nature that will continue to expand for their entire lives. As discussed in an earlier chapter, in our concern for the physical safety of our children, we have forgotten the invisible injuries to the souls of children who no longer play outdoors and understand themselves to be adventurers and discoverers.

As parents, we must return to a way of life in which we direct our children to accumulate scientific grammar. In previous eras, much of this came from life experiences such as tending a garden or boiling eggs or camping under the stars. In some cases, we are more intentional in our direction; we will have our children memorize scientific facts such as the types of volcanoes or the five kingdoms of living things. Dialectic takes over when the questions begin—questions such as "What is it?" "How is it similar to that?" "What caused it?" "What does it do?"

Too often, when we think of science, we have images in our minds of complicated mathematical formulas scrawled on blackboards or professors talking over our heads in a language that sounds as foreign as Sanskrit. If a parent does not step back from these images and explore at a more basic, more fundamental level, then science might seem too daunting to tackle. Much that we learn about advanced scientific discovery can be overwhelming in its complexity and its terminology, but the heart of science is rather straightforward. Science is simply the study of nature, and that can begin simply with wonder and with trying to understand the source of that wonder.

"Wonder in Nature" by Tucker Andrew Teague

When I was about ten years of age, I went with my father and grandfather on a multi-day camping trip by horseback into the Cascade mountains. We rode through forests of giant Douglas fir trees and alpine meadows. When we made camp, instead of using a tent, we put a tarp on the ground and our sleeping bags on the tarp. I fell asleep between my father and grandfather, snug under the darkening sky.

At about 1 a.m. or thereabouts, I suddenly woke, my eyes staring straight into the starry night. At that altitude, where the air is clear and free of pollution, and where there is no competition with the lights of a city, I was overwhelmed by the staggering array of stars. The sky had transformed into unspeakable glory. I could not look away.

I was raised a Christian and had thus read Psalm 19 where it says, "The heavens declare the glory of God; the skies proclaim the work of his hands." Not until that moment did I know what that verse truly meant. Ever since that camping trip, however, I have known. Wonder draws us to nature. Wonder is the beginning of science, which is, simply, the study of nature.

The question is, how do we best study nature? Science takes the facts of the natural world and asks questions about those facts, seeking to understand those facts by defining, comparing, and relating them to each other. Sometimes we act as if scientific thinking only takes the form of doing research and conducting experiments. We forget that the foundation of scientific thought is focused and organized thinking: using one's brain the way it was designed to be used.

DEFINITION

The act of defining continues throughout the scientific journey, beginning with curiosity—the desire to know, to name—and traveling through the process of understanding until one arrives at knowledge about a particular phenomenon or species or rock. The dialectic is a very human process. The engine that drives that process is curiosity. The data that is retrieved and processed comes from observation and has been accumulated as the grammar of science. The processing of that data is thinking, which comes alive in the form of questions—in other words, dialectic. Doing science is to be immersed in dialectic.

Doing science is to be immersed in dialectic.

The inauguration of any scientific process is a question: "What is it?" In the second chapter of Genesis, human beings are, in part, described this way:

> Now the Lord God had formed out of the ground all the beasts of the field and all the birds of the air. He brought them to the man to see what he would name them; and whatever the man called each living creature, that was its name. So the man gave names to all the livestock, the birds of the air and all the beasts of the field. But for Adam no suitable helper was found. (Gen. 2:19–20)

There are three critical elements to this story: The first critical element is that man (Adam) observes nature—the animals God brings him. The second is that Adam gives them names; he fits the right description to each unique beast. The third is that Adam draws conclusions; he recognizes that no animal corresponds to himself, to what he is. What the author of Genesis is telling us is that, from the very beginning of humankind's story, inherent within the human being, is a special relationship between man and nature. In essence, humans relate to the natural world by observing, by naming, and by drawing conclusions. This is the beginning of science—we start by defining the thing before us. We try to name it. And yet, how do we name something unless we know what it is? In a sense, the defining of something is also where we end.

In the grammar stage, we give our children the definitions, and they name lots of things. They learn the three laws of motion and terms like "atmosphere" and "biomes." At best, grammarians may have only the rudest understanding of these definitions. I often remind parents that that's okay; the classical model does not stop with this rude understanding. Instead, these definitions become the pegs on which richer definitions are hung. Later, those definitions will interact to form complex ideas and compelling questions.

Although the brain naturally categorizes everything in order to understand and retain information, science is, in part, the process of formalizing this natural activity through intentionally categorizing things into types (or families) and subtypes. In biology, a student will use the term *genus* to mean "a type," *division* to mean "a subtype," and *differentia* as "the condition(s) that distinguish one division from another." Thus a dog is a division of the genus animal, and a collie is division of genus dog, and a collie is different from a poodle in various ways. Notice how natural this is. If you see a kind of dog that is an unfamiliar breed, you ask what kind (subtype, division) of dog it is. You naturally want to differentiate that dog from other kinds of dogs, just as you want to differentiate oceans from lakes, birches from palms, mountains from hills, or snails from slugs. We help our children become more dialectic by helping them recognize that they are thinking this way all the time. We guide our children in the scientific process by having them organize their thinking specifically in terms of genus, division, and differentia. Definition is thus a natural tool of the mind that we use to begin knowing the world around us. It is also a skill that we develop through application and repetition.

But notice what is at the heart of definition: in order to establish the genus, the division, and the differentia, we must compare things. Fortunately, there is nothing more natural for the brain to do than to compare two things.

COMPARISON

In the eighteenth century, the ancient Roman city of Pompeii was rediscovered under a thick layer of volcanic ash and became the site of archaeological excavations. What was unearthed was an almost perfectly preserved ancient Roman city, a kind of time capsule from the first century AD. A child might find the story of this rediscovery interesting, but he might find even more fascinating the story of Pompeii's demise, namely, its total submersion under twenty feet of volcanic ash from nearby Mount Vesuvius. Volcanoes are inherently wonderful, for they are both beautiful and terrifying. But, "What is a volcano?" the student naturally wants to know. How does an active volcano compare to a dormant volcano? How are they similar and how are they different? And how do volcanic mountains like Vesuvius compare with fault-block mountains like those of the Sierra Nevada range?

Think about what the student is doing here; he is merely comparing. He is simply asking how is this similar to that? And how is it different? And to what degree? Human beings usually learn best by comparison. In fact, we cannot stop our minds from making comparisons. It is part of how the mind engages with the world. Every sense perception immediately stands in comparison with what one already knows. Every idea only has meaning as it relates to other ideas and is judged by those ideas. Comparison is at the heart of dialectic.

Let's say you are guiding a student to a better understanding of Earth and its place in the solar system. How do you do this? Perhaps you will ask how Earth compares with the other planets. What makes it similar? What makes it different? And to what degree? You might then dive into specific details, such as the relative distances of the planets to the sun, or the nature of each planet's atmosphere, or the relative size of each planet. Perhaps you will compare the force of gravity of each planet relative to its size. Then you might focus on Earth itself, asking how it is a unique division of planet, or how the poles relate to each other, or how the continents are similar to and different from each other. Your child will begin to see that there are many similarities and many differences between Earth and the other planets, and seeing a few things leads to more questions, which lead to more seeing. The apparently simple act of definition, of placing things into genus and division, has now blossomed into a robust, mind-engaging, knowledge-expanding activity merely by the means of comparison. Comparisons produce dialectic thinking most naturally, and dialectic is merely thinking come alive.

Comparisons produce dialectic thinking most naturally, and dialectic is merely thinking come alive.

Two things elevate ordinary thinking to the level of scientific thinking: *intention* and *organization*. At all times, our students' minds are working to define things and compare things. But when they think scientifically, they are asking specific questions about specific things. They are then organizing their thoughts in such a way as to make reasonable and coherent statements about those things. For example, in everyday thinking, a child might notice clouds in the sky and assume that rain is coming. In scientific thinking, the student seeks to define the particular clouds he sees, to compare them with other cloud observations, and to ask how they are similar, how they are different, and to what degree. Very soon he realizes that keeping good notes helps him keep his thoughts organized and allows him to later connect previous observations with more recent ones.

As parents, we guide our children in developing proper intentionality and organization so their curiosity can flourish. We help them develop into great thinkers by building on what is most natural. Science is not really a unique approach to the world around us so much as it is taking what is common to us all—to the way we all come to know anything—and applying intentionality and organization. Science is first and foremost dialectical thinking applied to the natural world.

Knowledge is not about understanding things in isolation but in relationship.

Of course, when a student compares, he is relating one thing to another. Knowledge is not about understanding things in isolation but in relationship. Relationships come in different forms, so the apparently simple activity of comparison begins to expand as the student looks at how things relate to each other.

RELATIONSHIP

Scientific discoveries often begin with troubled scientists. Johannes Kepler was troubled by eight minutes. For years, he had made observations of the planet Mars while working within the accepted sixteenth-century model of planetary motion: planets revolve around the sun in perfect circles. But his calculations of Mars' orbit were not fitting *exactly* into the model: the orbit was off by eight minutes. If God is the creator of the universe, as Kepler believed, and if God is the perfect creator of harmony, then eight minutes was too sloppy for God. Eventually, Kepler discovered the true relationship between planetary orbits and his calculations: planets orbit the sun along elliptical paths rather than circular paths. He knew there was a relationship between the sun and its planets. His curiosity made him want to know the true nature of that relationship.

On your wall at home you may have a barometer. Every day, your family can see how the needle changes as the atmospheric pressures change and then observe the weather. As the barometer's needle rises, the weather tends to get better; as it goes down, the weather turns for the worse. How are changes in the weather related to atmospheric pressure? What causes the weather? What is the true nature of the relationship between barometric pressure and weather patterns? The dialectic process of thinking continues as we seek to understand the relationships between things.

In observing the world around him, your student will notice that some things have a causal relationship with other things, that some things precede other things, and that some ideas about the world are demonstrably true or false based on observations in the past. All of these observations have to do with the common topic of relationship. Snow melts in the mountains, and the water flows downhill in rivulets that mingle with streams that flow into rivers and on to the sea. Fruit trees are pruned and then produce more robust fruit. The aerodynamics of a wing creates lift when moving through the air. Apply heat to water, and the water increases in temperature; add enough heat, and the water begins to boil. But apply cold to water, and the water decreases in temperature; add enough cold, and the water turns to ice. In these everyday images, the student can see the idea of relationship. Something produces something else, one event follows another, something is either one thing or another, or maybe it is neither.

When a student begins to dig deeper into defining something in the natural world through comparison, eventually he must ask specific relationship questions. We can divide these questions into the same four basic categories we have used with other subjects: cause and effect, antecedent and consequence, contraries, and contradictions (also known as contradictories).

Let's begin with cause and effect. Causality is simply the relationship between a set of factors (or cause) and a phenomenon (or effect). We might ask questions such as, did X cause Y? Or, was Y the result of X? Sometimes the answer is not so clear. In a scientific experiment, the student will carefully control the factors so as to limit the amount of variability, thus producing results in which the true relationship between cause and effect becomes clear. Here are a few examples:

- Does the crow of the rooster cause the sun to rise each morning?
- Or, does the rotation of the earth on its axis cause the sun to rise in the east and set in the west?

The first question is an example of a relationship that might seem to be causal but is actually just concurrence.

Antecedent and consequence leads a student to ask "if. . . . then" questions when he compares the relationship between things. He might ask if, given a certain situation (the antecedent), what is likely to follow (the consequence)? This is not the same as cause and effect. In everyday life we might observe that if we spend all our money on one thing, then we cannot then buy another. Spending all the money causes the effect of no money, but having no more money does not cause not spending more money; rather, not spending is the consequence of having no more money. In science we use antecedent and consequence to form hypotheses: if X, then Y. A scientific hypothesis begs the question, is it true that if X then Y? Here are a few examples:

- Is it true that if this is an acorn it will grow into an oak tree? Yes.
- If this is a mustard seed, will it grow into an oak tree? No.

As these examples demonstrate, science is as much about disproving false hypotheses as it is about proving true ones.

We can use the third form of relationship, contraries, to eliminate false hypotheses. Remember, in the logic chapter we defined contraries as the relationship between two absolute statements, the A statement ("Every S is P") and the E statement ("No S is P"). If two ideas are opposed to each other, then they cannot both be true. At least one must be false (or both can be false). Frequently, scientific inquiry is fueled by the need to resolve competing ideas. Two contrary propositions will look like this: "Every X is Y," and "No X is Y." A student may simply ask a question of the two propositions: which one is true? Here are some examples:

- The earth is flat. The earth is spherical. (Which one is true?)
- All berries are poisonous. No berries are poisonous. (Which one is true?)

Students may find that both are false, as in the latter question, which leads to more questions. Remember in logic that we had a second set of statements, I and O, which used the word "some." What if there are some poisonous berries? Then you would need to ask, "How do we know which berries are poisonous and which ones are not?" For the pioneers, this kind of question was a matter of survival! With this question, we must start the cycle of definition all over again.

When we have an absolute statement, as in the examples above, we can disprove it by finding exceptions to the rule. Here, we are dealing with the final type of relationship, contradictions. Refresh your memory from the logic chapter by repeating the idea that two statements are contradictory if one of them must be valid and the other must be invalid. The two propositions cannot both be valid, and they leave no third option. Again, we may simply ask the question, "Of two scientific propositions, which one is true?" Here are two examples:

Remember, scientific dialectic is the process of asking questions for the purpose of better understanding the natural world.

- All dogs are animals. Some dogs are not animals. (Which one is true?)
- All planets follow elliptical orbits. Some planets do not follow elliptical orbits. (Which one is true?)

Remember, scientific dialectic is the process of asking questions for the purpose of better understanding the natural world. One question will usually fuel another. Some questions will have to be set to the side and others answered first. As parents, we can bring relationship questions to the table in order to help our children deepen their dialectic skills. Often it is good practice to have discussed definition and comparison first, so that questions of relationship do not become too muddied. At other times, the scientific inquiry may begin with a relationship question that is sparked by the student's interest. In that case, the parent may choose to consider relationship before the other common topics, in order to build on the child's curiosity.

Questions will usually arise out of curiosity, but to be considered scientific they should lead toward a discovery of order.

Questions will usually arise out of curiosity, but to be considered scientific they should lead toward a discovery of order. What makes scientific inquiry different from the everyday way of knowing is that science seeks to organize questions in such a way as to draw specific details from the data. Although scientific questions are naturally based in the way the mind works—we want to know, we seek to define, we compare, we look for relationships—science takes these natural tendencies and pushes them to a higher level of inquiry. We can help build our child's questioning ability the same way an athlete builds muscles—through training; the muscles are already there, but the focused activity of specific training makes the muscles stronger, suppler, and ready to be engaged. Consider how natural it is to ask:

- Did the earthquake cause the avalanche?
- Is it true that if it is cloudy, it will rain?
- Is metal a good conductor of heat, or is it not a good conductor of heat?
- Do all snakes have scales, or do some snakes not have scales?

In science, we help our students build on what is natural. We do this by channeling their natural questioning tendencies in such a way that the questions become increasingly more specific and are applied to increasingly more complex aspects of the natural world. As our children mature, the value of a trained mind—a mind that is more fully capable of understanding the wonders of nature—will become evident.

CIRCUMSTANCE

Seeking definitions, making comparisons, and exploring relationships are ways of guiding our minds to ask specific questions about the natural world such that our observations are rich and rewarding. In short, these questions indicate that we have become deeply attentive to the thing before us. In addition, all things in the natural world inhabit their circumstances, and this leads us to even more questions.

Considering circumstances broadens a student's understanding by asking "what if...?" kinds of questions. Dialectic not only considers the thing at hand but wonders how it could, if possible, be different. A student might ask if, given what she knows of past circumstances, she can predict future results, or given what she knows of current circumstances, what would happen if those circumstances were different? In forming hypotheses, the student not only considers whether certain circumstances are possible but also whether circumstances might, in fact, render something impossible.

Let's say your student is doing a report on tidal activity. She has defined tides as the rise and fall of sea levels. She has also compared measurements (which she gleaned from someone else's research) of tidal activity from different places in the world as well as time intervals between high tides. She has asked questions such as "How is the motion of tides similar to the motion of bodies of water in general?" "How is that motion different?" She has also asked questions about the relationship between tides and coastal areas affected by tides, and about the gravitational pull of the moon and tides. She now has some answers to think about. (This phenomenon, of acquired answers leading to still more questions, is, as discussed throughout this book, a key aspect of dialectic.) Next, she wants to know if it is possible that tides might fluctuate with the seasons. For example, might tidal activity in the summer months occur with greater average rise and fall than in the winter? What kinds of circumstance questions might we ask to determine if she is correct?

- Are seasonal tide fluctuations possible or impossible?
- What qualities, conditions, or circumstances make seasonal tide differences possible or impossible?
- Suppose that seasonal tide fluctuations are possible. Are they feasible? Why?
- When have seasonal tide fluctuations happened previously?
- Who or what has experienced seasonal tide fluctuations?
- If seasonal tide fluctuations start, what makes them end?
- What would it take for seasonal tide fluctuations to happen now?
- What would prevent seasonal tide fluctuations from happening now?

Circumstantial questions open the dialectic to possibility and wonder.

Consider how these questions are similar to Johannes Kepler asking if elliptical orbits might be possible or impossible. If he had never considered that they might be possible, and if he had never considered the possibility that he might be wrong, he would have left the true nature of planetary orbits to be discovered by someone else.

Circumstantial questions open the dialectic to possibility and wonder. We often think of science as being only factual, but notions of circumstance help us ask questions from a different paradigm rather than just the anticipated model. This is where the student's imagination and creativity are important in the realm of science. Think about Louis Pasteur, who realized that germs came from living microorganisms, not from spontaneous generation; or Joseph Lister, who pioneered the use of carbolic acid to prevent gangrene associated with the treatment of broken bones and minor wounds. There is nothing like seeing a potentially new idea for a scientific process to infuse additional excitement into the adventure. However, having sought definitions, done comparison, and examined relationships, we can help keep circumstantial questions from drifting too far afield.

TESTIMONY

Another check on the notion of possibility is testimony or evidence, which takes many forms in the study of science. Testimony is not black and white, as scientists throughout history have discovered. For example, Christopher Columbus understood the earth to be round. What he did not know was how big around it was. That seemingly simple calculation was of enormous personal importance when he contemplated his search for a sea route to the Indies. He needed to know if the Spanish ships of his day could sail the distance needed to make landfall.

The ancient Greek mathematician Eratosthenes had calculated the circumference of the earth to be slightly less than twenty-five thousand miles—a surprisingly accurate estimate. Then, in AD 150, a Greco-Roman astronomer and mathematician named Ptolemy estimated that the circumference of the earth was, instead, about eighteen thousand miles. Unfortunately, it was Ptolemy's work that was rediscovered, translated to Latin, and reprinted widely during the Renaissance. As a result, people came to accept and believe the smaller number. Christopher Columbus faced a dilemma: he had to choose which authority to trust before he could calculate the probability of a successful voyage west. If he accepted the larger value, the trip would be impossible, as the distance to the Indies would be too far for a Spanish ship to sail. If he accepted the smaller value, the trip to the Indies would be possible—approximately six thousand miles, a distance that could be shortened to perhaps three thousand miles, given the likelihood of outlying islands.

Ptolemy's distance was more widely accepted, and it provided the hope Columbus needed to set forth. Ironically, the distance is actually closer to the twenty-five-thousand-mile estimate. Columbus successfully accomplished the journey only because of the unexpected presence of the Americas. Although Columbus did not know that he had discovered a new continent, he accomplished this feat because of his willingness to depend on authority—as it turns out, the wrong one! In this case, an explorer's mistake led to an important discovery; however, other explorers did not fare so well. For example, Henry Hudson led several expeditions in the early 1600s, attempting to find the fabled Northwest Passage that many Europeans believed connected the Atlantic Ocean and the Pacific through North America. When Hudson failed for the last time, his crew mutinied and left him to die in the bay that now bears his name.

As we consider the authorities who inform our opinions, we need to ask many questions. Columbus asked what the experts believed about the circumference of the globe. We might ask what eyewitnesses to certain scientific phenomena have said, or what the experts say. We might ask who the experts are in a particular branch of science. We might ask about experiments or statistics. In answering these questions, we generate a spirit of inquiry that drives us to ask even more questions about the testimony we

As we consider the authorities who inform our opinions, we need to ask many questions.

encounter. Commander David Scott landed on the moon, and with a hammer and a feather in his hands, he proved the testimony of Galileo. We want to encourage our students to do the same. We want them to have the inquisitive desire to confirm or refute testimony—we may even want them to go to the moon to do it.

Authoritative testimony does not always come in the form of expert humans, however. Sometimes, we find testimony in writings, proverbs, laws, or precedents. Columbus's voyage became an authoritative testimony for Amerigo Vespucci because it set precedent that the journey was possible. Inquiry continued into the matter because of Columbus's additional testimony, which transcended and corrected the longstanding errors—over thirteen hundred years old—of Ptolemy.

This, of course, means that we have to ask other questions as a result of the discourse into testimony. Is the authority reliable? Is it biased? What is the bias, and does that bias enhance or discredit the authority? Questions of authority, moreover, may take us back through the dialectic process of definition, comparison, relationship, and circumstances to determine the reliability of the authority. We may need to define who Eratosthenes and Ptolemy are, compare their methods, and consider the relationships and circumstances that surrounded their calculations in order to determine the reliability of their testimonies. Each question answered generates more and more questions. That's what should make science so compelling: the adventure never has to end.

THE SPIRIT OF SCIENCE

The dialectic process, as it applies to scientific discovery, will sometimes lead us to hypotheses that prove correct. Like Commander Scott, we may end up proving a hypothesis and demonstrating what theories have long predicted to be true. However, the dialectic will also lead us to hypotheses that are incorrect. Like Columbus, we may end up disproving a hypothesis that has been widely believed for hundreds of years.

The potential for incorrect conclusions, rather than negating the dialectic process, confirms it. It leads us into further dialogue that continually defines, compares, relates,

Some parents fear that teaching their children to ask questions, particularly about science, will make it difficult for their children to accept anything on faith or to believe with certainty.

and considers circumstances and authority either to build further upon that which we have already discovered or to transcend and correct that which we have hypothesized incorrectly. Good scientists should be humble and open to the idea that they may be wrong. We talked in the writing chapter about the importance of revision, and the same thing applies to science.

Some parents fear that teaching their children to ask questions, particularly about science, will make it difficult for their children to accept anything on faith or to believe with certainty. However, if we are truly engaging in the dialectic, we will not be paralyzed by doubt. Instead, we will be able to accept and act on a dogma without fleeing from all arguments and evidence that seem to challenge it. The dialectic will often lead us through a process that allows us to transcend false or incomplete dogma in order to correct it. This is not a process that should be feared, but embraced. We do science precisely because we believe that truth exists and that it can be known.

Engaging in science dialectically provides us with the necessary humility and dependence upon the past and the authorities that have gone before us as well as the realization that there is still knowledge to know, to learn, and to discover. It is in this spirit that we pursue scientific discovery.

CHAPTER ELEVEN

FINE ARTS

"I think the need to enjoy art and to serve art is inherent in every human being whatever race or class he may belong to, and that this need has its rights and should be satisfied. Taking that position as an axiom, I say that, if the enjoyment and production of art by every one presents inconveniences and inconsistencies, the reason lies in the character and direction art has taken: about which we must be on our guard lest we foist anything false on the rising generation and lest we prevent it from producing something new both in form and matter."

—Leo Tolstoy, *Tolstoy on Art*

In the chapter on history, we talked about why our children need real heroes who can teach them to see beyond their own selves and seek to do good. We might say that the fine arts allow us to express heroism in the media of music, dance, drawing, sports, and other forms. An art is the ability to do something very well, specifically, with the goal of rising above the mundane. We might refer to the *art of sailing*, which includes not just the physical requirements of running up a sail and directing a boat using wind but it also encompasses the coordination of many elements to produce the harmonious movement of a boat through water and wind. It is a result of many hours of practice. In this way, we can see that art is heavily dialectic in that the sailor is combining elements with a practiced understanding of their relationships.

In whatever medium we choose to practice art, we must be dialectic—that is, coordinating and integrating various elements (through diligent practice), which become more than the sum of their parts. The culmination becomes something greater to both

In whatever medium we choose to practice art, we must be dialectic—that is, coordinating and integrating various elements... which become more than the sum of their parts.

the artist and to the consumer. When we are teaching any subject, our goal is to inspire a student to go beyond the plain, crudely made artifact (be it an essay or speech or science research paper) and treat it with such skill that it becomes beautiful and inspirational to the beholder. We want students to create art that inspires wonder in the beholder.

Fine arts is a name for the family of expressive activities like dance, music, and drawing. I would even include sports in this category, as it is possible to reveal a command of the body through football as well as ballet. In order to avoid over-extending this chapter, I will be using the word "art" to talk about drawing, painting, or sculpting, but you can extend the principles to other branches of artistic expression as well. Art defined in this way is a subject that often gets set aside after grammar school. We tend to see art as a luxury to indulge in only after all the other subjects are managed. Is this because art is not on the end-of-the-year test or the SAT? Is it because colleges do not require art test scores for admission? If that is the reason, then what we consider to be valuable is very limited indeed.

Consider that there are approximately three thousand different languages among the cultures that exist or have existed in the history of the world. Of those, less than ten percent have a written language. Every single one of them, however, has some form of music and art. Yet, the one thing common to every civilization is the one thing most likely to be dismissed from modern education. What a paradox! Are fine arts dismissed as a luxury, then, because the student enjoys them? Is that a real reason to remove them from the curriculum? What a bizarre idea, that students would enjoy learning. Someone stop them! It seems to me that any area of study that promotes love of learning should be a top priority, not an afterthought. I propose this reason to preserve fine arts instruction: the study of the arts is one of the most profound ways to protect our humanity.

PRACTICE AND APPRECIATION

As educators and parents, we need to think about art in two ways, and we need to promote the study of both: the practice and performance of art, and the understanding and appreciation of art. Practicing an art (playing an instrument or dancing or painting) is similar to writing, and appreciation of art is similar to reading. Just as we teach both reading and writing (one strengthening the other), we need to teach both the skill of creating art and that of appreciating art. Both offer a wealth of opportunity for developing dialectic skills if you know how to ask the right questions.

Even if we never become a professional artist, we can revel in the sheer love of being an amateur. We can love and study the arts before we master even one note, but we can also approach mastery through diligent practice. Regardless of your level of proficiency, there is joy in the creation of art. I know families who are very musical and who serve as directors of their church choirs or worship teams. Some of these moms and dads work with young children who have autism or Down syndrome. Even if they cannot learn the music as quickly as the other children, they can still learn to approximate notes, and they can stand in front of the congregation with a joyful smile.

Since the beginning of time, humans have created artifacts that clearly reveal thought in the expression of form. It is one of the things that humans have in common with God: we both like to create things. God's creations are purposeful and beautiful. Think of a tree—it is useful to humans as a processor of carbon dioxide and as a home to animals or as a food producer, but its form is also beautiful. It is linear, pointing up toward its creator; it is also balanced and symmetrical. Its trunk has texture; its leaves have color and, often, color that changes with the seasons. It moves in the wind and grows larger over time. When humans create, we find joy in creating useful items with beautiful form. A plain, crudely made bowl is just a tool for mixing. A bowl that was crafted skillfully with a beautiful shape or adorned with decoration is *art*.

Another reason to immerse a student in the practice of fine arts as the student matures is that the practice develops perseverance, and the student is greatly rewarded for her perseverance when she accomplishes her music piece or dance performance or painting. This triumph builds character, which will give the student confidence and the ability to practice and see to completion other academic endeavors. The process of learning an art and practicing it to mastery is only half of the job of the art educator, though; the other half is teaching your student to "read" the arts.

I once had a student tell me that she noticed she got better grades on math and writing assignments as well as demonstrations and presentations when they were neat and visually pleasing. She had received a really good grade on a project, even though she knew she had not done what was asked in the assignment. The instructor seemed to have missed that important detail because the papers turned in were so beautiful. This student felt as though art had tricked the teacher into giving her a better grade. I asked, did she consider that the teacher might have been glad to encourage a gift recognized in a student? Visual literacy and proficiency are, at their most basic, acts of consideration for your neighbor, just as using agreed-upon punctuation rules is a form of kindness. Is it not a common frustration of a reader to be expected to read a completed assignment that is horribly messy? If the content is perfect, but no one can decipher it, have you actually answered a question? Teachers often spend much time digging into the efforts of a student they love when the student has not loved the teacher in return. Maybe the teacher just appreciated someone trying to make her job easier. This is a long way of saying that neatness always counts, even when a student doesn't think so. Physical representations do matter, even in purely cerebral activities.

Physical representations do matter, even in purely cerebral activities.

American society is largely visually and musically illiterate because art literacy has been neglected. I have a friend who is a graphic designer, and she is very often frustrated when she has to educate the CEO of a company in the basics of visual literacy so that he can make a wise decision about the logo for his company or the layout of his catalog. Even if your child is bound for a career in engineering, she needs to be equipped to make decisions involving visual communication, known as graphic design. Donis Dondis writes in *A Primer of Visual Literacy*, "Visual expression is the product of highly complex intelligence, of which we have pitifully little understanding. What you see is a major part of what you know, and visual literacy can help us to see what we see and know what we know" (19). In our increasingly visual society, we all need at least a vocabulary of visual literacy.

DEFINITION

The vocabulary of visual literacy begins with questions of definition. The first question, of course, is, "What is art?" This may be the most dialectic and complicated of all questions. It has been asked for ages and is still up for discussion, so it should be a frequent question you pose to your student. Ask it often, but do not expect a definitive answer. Just ask it in order to have a discussion. Whenever you or your student comes across an artifact or is immersed in creating art, ask, "What makes this art?"

It is easier to talk about divisions within art than it is to define art. Painting, drawing, and sculpture certainly come to mind first, but throughout history, art has also included pottery, jewelry making, dance, sports, theatre, and architecture. Even burial necessities, such as coffins and graves in ancient Egypt, can be considered art. Modern technology has added photography, filmmaking, book design, posters, billboards, performance art, and, most recently, digital art on websites and electronic games. The grammar of an art is the separate elements that make up the art form. In drawing, the grammar begins with dot, line, shape, texture, pencil, and paper. The grammar of painting includes color, brush stroke, lightness and saturation, brush types, canvas, and painting techniques. The grammar of dance includes body positions, individual steps or movements, music, and perhaps special shoes or clothing. The grammar of architecture includes foundation, entryway, floor, space, window, light, structure, and roof. Perhaps there are other divisions you will discover, and perhaps you will identify other activities as arts as technology develops. Keep asking, "Could this activity or artifact be considered part of the arts?"

In order to understand and discuss specific works of art, we need to be sure our students have an adequate vocabulary. Many of the words will be applicable to both music and visual arts. Once we have the basic vocabulary, we can discuss and begin to understand and interpret art and our visual culture. Begin with these words for visual art: *dot, line, shape, direction, color, texture, scale* (relative size), *motion, contrast,* and *harmony.* Write these on an index card, have the student look them up if they need to, then sit down with an art book from the library and ask the child to look for examples of each. Then, have the student discuss what she sees. At this point, the only question she needs to ask is, "Do you see _____?" (Fill in the blank with the words above: *line, texture, motion,* etc.)

In order to understand and discuss specific works of art, we need to be sure our students have an adequate vocabulary.

If you can, take the note card to an art museum and ask your student to find more examples. Seeking and finding the elements is more fun than listening to an expert point it out, so be sure to use questions, not statements, in this activity. Ask, "What feature is this?" or "Where do you see the artist using this technique?" Questions will generate definitions and bring out the grammatical knowledge your student has already acquired. If you are visiting a museum and are beginning to train your brain to appreciate art, ask for the children's version of the self-guided audio tour. Museums go out of their way to be clear and concise when reaching a younger mind. I like learning the unusual things in an artist's life, as it makes me appreciate their humanity and struggles in creating a masterpiece. Information provided on the children's tour often allows us to realize that artists struggle just like the rest of us.

COMPARISON

To ask good questions about works of art, your student should take the definitions he has studied and use comparison to generate more questions.

To ask good questions about works of art, your student should take the definitions he has studied and use comparison to generate more questions. The dialectic of art begins to take shape when you compare and combine the elements of drawing, dance, or music. Comparing two works of art is a great way to train your student's eye and elicit good conversation. For example, you could compare Donatello's and Michelangelo's sculptures of David. "How are they similar?" They are both sculptures of David from the biblical account of David and Goliath. Both are men. Both are strong and handsome. "How are they different?" One is wearing a hat and boots, the other one has no hat or boots. One is holding a sword; one is not. One is captured at the moment just before killing Goliath; one has just killed Goliath. These may seem like simple questions, but they begin a good dialogue and get your student thinking. Go one step further and ask the questions, "Why might the artists have created these two sculptures differently?" "What is the effect of the different techniques?" "How do the different details of these two sculptures affect the way we 'read' each one?"

To pose questions about music, ask, "How are pianos and violins similar?" "How are they different?" "How does time affect a melody?" "To what degree does tempo affect the melody?" These thoughtful comparisons help the student consider the artful arrangement of elements in relationship to each other, which we call composition. Just as you took the list of art terms to the art museum, use a list of music terms when you listen to classical music, and try to identify examples of each. Listening guides are available, too, if you want a modeling of listening. You do not, however, have to be guided by an expert; the joy of listening to or looking at art is in discovering it for yourself.

Allow your student to experience that joy by not telling them what they should notice; instead, ask them what they do notice.

Another way to generate dialogue is to ask questions that compare and contrast different media. Ask, for example, "Can you find an example of motion expressed in a painting and motion expressed in a sculpture?" You can see motion in the shimmering of light on water in Monet's *Water Lilies* and in the implied movement of David in the act of throwing the stone in Bernini's sculpture *David* (1623–1624). You may be surprised at the connections even a young student will make once you model this type of questioning. It is rewarding to make an observation and share it with others, so this has to be a shared visual and auditory experience. Getting dialectic in an art museum or over an art book is very enjoyable for children and adults. Make sure you communicate that there are no right or wrong answers, just simple questions and thoughtful observations.

"Contrast in Art" by Courtney Sanford

Contrast is a profound tool used by artists, and we should train our students to seek contrast and use it effectively in their own creations. Following the model given in this chapter, use questions of definition to develop a working understanding of each term in the following pairs of words. Then, take the list to the symphony or art museum and look for and discuss examples of each. Use both definition and comparison. Can you see (or create) these contrasts in visual arts?

- Balance / instability
- Symmetry / asymmetry
- Simplicity / complexity
- Pattern / randomness
- Lightness / darkness

Can you hear (or create) these contrasts in music?

- Consonance / dissonance
- *Forte* (loudly) / *piano* (softly)
- *Allegro* (lively and quickly) / *adagio* (slowly)
- *Staccato* (with short, detached notes) / *legato* (smoothly strung together)

RELATIONSHIP

The next level of art study is to look for the relationships between elements within a composition. To understand relationship, you can ask questions about elements of art such as "What happens when you combine a dot and a circle?" "What happens to a particular shade of blue when it appears next to a particular shade of yellow?" and "Which notes sound nice together, and which ones don't?" For example, in a painting, a small figure is placed next to a large figure to create an illusion of depth. Our brain naturally and effortlessly interprets the depth, but your student will delight in knowing how the artist can create illusions using simple techniques. The repetition of elements creates pattern, which is pleasing to our brain. We like to know what comes next, so patterns are comforting. Listen to Haydn's *Surprise Symphony* for a great example of the power of creating and then breaking a pattern. He sets up a predictable pattern, the listener becomes comfortable with the pattern, and then, Haydn intentionally breaks the pattern with a loud note that is unexpected. It is surprising and delightful. American conductor Benjamin Zander points out in a talk for a TED conference that the C note makes a B note sad when one is played right after the other. This is a relationship between notes, which Zander discovered by playing and discussing music.

You can also ask questions about specific performances or artworks. For example, "Why do people say da Vinci's *Mona Lisa* appears mysterious? What techniques did the artist use to create this effect?" Or, you might go to a Christmas performance of *The Nutcracker* ballet and ask your child why the dance sequences in Act II occur in the order that they do. "Why do the Spanish Hot Chocolate performers appear just before the Arabian Coffee performers and the Chinese Tea performers?" "How would the flow of the performance change if the Waltz of the Flowers were placed between the Coffee and Tea dances?" This kind of dialogue gives you the chance to relate art to other subjects such as writing. We call pieces of music "compositions" for a reason; each movement in a symphony is similar to a paragraph in an essay. The composer must consider how the movements relate to each other and how to transition between them. A recording artist creating an album or a deejay playing music for the enjoyment of guests at a wedding reception is also a composer: his work is all about creating smooth transitions from one musical concept to the next. You can extend this lesson to any style of music that your child enjoys by asking questions about the relationship between the music and the lyrics of a particular song, or by asking him to explain why he likes to listen to loud music in the car and instrumental music while solving math equations.

CIRCUMSTANCE

Too often, art and music form the backdrop of our lives—the painting on our kitchen wall and the background music in our headphones—yet we never study them in earnest. Another reason our modern education system fails to teach art well is that we think of it as a separate subject, and if we do not have a time slot for a separate class called "Art," we do not study it at all. This practice teaches students that art exists outside of history, which is a false supposition. Artists lived in a specific time period and geographical location, within the specific circumstances of a culture or time period. Although viewers and listeners today may still appreciate and learn from art that was created in a different time, exploring art within the artists' circumstances will generate valuable historical, scientific, and sociological questions,

Another reason our modern education system fails to teach art well is that we think of it as a separate subject...

which will, in turn, help students understand historical cultures in terms of art. Art is often considered a mirror of what the artist sees. Its purpose is—as Hamlet avers—"to hold as 'twere the mirror up to nature" (*Hamlet*, act 3 scene 2). A simple Internet search can give you examples of the art of the culture you are studying in history. Use the visual vocabulary you have developed to discuss the art. Ask your student, "What visual elements were the ancient Greek artists using?" "What elements can you find in Aztec art?" "What can the art tell us about these people?" "Why do you think they created that?" "How did their circumstances affect their art?" Notice that you are using definition and comparison as well as relationship and circumstance. The five common topics always build on one another to enrich our questions and understanding.

When my boys study history, they memorize a timeline of events that includes artwork of or from each era in human history. In the grammar stage, we just look briefly at the artwork and associate it with the event. In the dialectic stage, we take time to look more closely at the artwork and discuss the elements of composition and the style in which it is represented. Your child can keep a history sketchbook, which can become his own timeline. Ask your student to draw his own versions of the artwork you study in your history timeline. You can even ask your student to draw maps showing where historical or current events have taken place. As a result, your student will spend more time looking closely at the elements and will learn how they relate to each other. He will pause long enough to see how color is used and to ponder the details. To begin, have your student choose some artifacts to sketch from each culture and time period you study; have him include drawings of maps in his history sketchbook as well. Choose all kinds of artifacts, from pottery to jewelry to buildings. Your student's drawing skills will develop as he imitates compositions of the masters and dwells in scientific diagrams.

We also include famous musicians in our study of history. When you delve into a period of history, do not forget to search out and listen to the music of the period. Search on the Internet to find out what the people of the time would have heard. Include in your research what other sounds existed in their soundscape. For example, in my childhood, the soundscape included the sound of a phone when you dialed the number on a rotating wheel as it went around and back and an actual ring when someone called. A young student today hears the tones and tunes of cell phones. What other sounds might have been present in different cultures at different times? Think about the relationship between technologies and sounds: the new clicking sound of a telegraph, for example, or the sound of a train. Think about the way poets describe the sounds of war: from hooves, to cannons, to planes, to bombs.

As you study art and music as a part of history, you will discover that not only is art a reflection of culture but art also reacts to and influences events. You will want to ask yourself and your student, "What happened in art or music just before this piece was created?" "What happened just after the work of art was created?" "Did this piece of art trigger any kind of reaction or social change?" Research art just as you would research a science or history topic. Ask your student to gather information and write a short paper on a work of art from the time period you are studying or even from the time period in which your literature studies are based. Your student may surprise you by how quickly he learns to "read" the circumstances surrounding art.

TESTIMONY

When you reach the point where you feel like there is more to a piece of art than you can see on your own, you may need to encourage your student to do some research to find out what experts have to say about it. So, you will need to ask what kinds of authorities are relevant when you study art. You might attend a lecture by an expert performer, composer, or director of music, or by a respected artist or teacher of art. Listening to the audio tours in museums can provide testimony from music and art historians. Sometimes you can find audio clips or essays by the original artist, talking about the goals and methods he used to create his art. Encourage your students to ask questions such as, "Whose interpretation of a painting is more important—the artist's or the viewer's?" It is fascinating to learn how one artist developed a style in reaction to the previous style.

The common topic of testimony is relevant to the "writing" as well as the "reading" of art. Nature might be one of the authorities you consult when learning to draw. Leonardo da Vinci famously instructed an aspiring painter to

> ... have his Mind continually at work, and to make Remarks on every Object worthy of notice, that he meets. He ought even to stand still in order to view them with the greater attention; and afterwards to Form rules on what he has observ'd, with regard to Lights, Shadows, Place and other Circumstances. Let him make himself a Master of the Theory, before he meddle with the Practice, and be very curious in comparing the Limbs and J[u]nctures of different Animals with one another: taking Minutes of every thing he learns, the better to fix them in his Memory. (*A Treatise on Painting*, 32)

Many young artists delight in keeping a nature sketchbook, recording the details of flowers and trees in their own backyard.

To practice artistic technique, you might also have your student draw or paint a re-creation of a master's work. The idea of copying a painting is decidedly classical, not modern. A modernist would call this "copying" or "cheating." The classical educator would call it "learning from the master." In re-creating a masterpiece, the student must slow down and look very carefully at the elements and then try to re-create them. This gives the student time to think about the art and the context in which it was originally created. The challenge with students over the age of eleven or twelve is allowing them to enjoy the process without focusing too heavily on the product. A simple line drawing of a masterpiece, or just capturing its colors or shapes, is enough to experience the art more deeply. Make the assignment an attainable one relative to the ability of the student. You could ask your child to draw the shapes she sees in a painting. Or you could ask her to sketch out the major color blocks, or just do thumbnail sketches of artwork in a museum.

The challenge with students over the age of eleven or twelve is allowing them to enjoy the process without focusing too heavily on the product.

Learning artistic techniques from other masters does not squelch the young artist's creativity; instead, it frees your child to choose from a wide range of techniques and styles when he is ready to present his own message to the world, just as learning to write in a range of forms gives your child many templates with which to convey his ideas. Invite your child to consider when it is good to break away from traditional forms of art, and when artists are being different for the sake of getting attention. Ask, "Can art be a kind of testimony?" The idea of artists as revolutionaries may capture the imaginations of your boys. Talk about photographs taken in the aftermath of war, or the tapestries that tell us about medieval history, or the statues that monarchs commissioned to preserve their faces for posterity. When you begin to see art as a means of communication, you may see more ways to integrate art into your current studies as a way of helping your student process ideas.

ADDING ART TO YOUR LIFE

As parents, we should encourage our students to continue to draw even as they enter the teen years. There is no need to treat art studies as a separate subject. As I have already argued, art can be integrated into other subjects, ranging from history to science and literature. For example, I have students keep a science notebook in which they record their research and drawings of the subject. If we study dolphins, they research a specific type of dolphin, write a brief paper, and draw the dolphin in their notebook. Their scientific observation skills are strengthened during the drawing process, and drawing skills can be further developed. Your student should lightly sketch the basic shapes she sees in the animal's form. In a dolphin, for example, she would sketch an oval for the body, a triangle in shape and direction of the head, and triangles in the shapes of the lower body and tail. (This is described as "blobbing" in *The Core*.) She would then take a softer (darker) pencil and sketch in the contour of the dolphin's body, adding details such as the eye shape and fins. She would then turn her attention to shading the underside and edges that are turned away from the light. A study of texture of the body follows, and texture is added to the dolphin. The environment of the dolphin is also included when the student adds the background—in this case, the water and water plants or other fish. Incorporating art into science benefits both the study of science and the development of the student's art skills.

The sketchbook is a tool you can use in any subject; a literature sketchbook might include the cover of the books read or drawings of items that were significant in the book. For example, after reading *Amos Fortune, Free Man*, your child might want to draw the chains and shackles that bound Amos in contrast to the wedding ring that freed his wife or draw maps of where Amos was born in Africa and where he was sold in the United States after his capture. A student I know created a large painting in response to his reading of *The Phantom Tollbooth*. He painted mountains and numbers and chaos and fire and what each represented. He spent more time wrestling with the ideas as he planned and executed his painting. He worked in layers, laying down a layer of symbols and then another layer of symbols over the first, and created a beautiful work of art. You could also have a student draw sketches based on stories from an illustrated children's Bible, Aesop's Fables, or Greek mythology, creating a personal visual record of favorite verses or passages.

Both visual and auditory arts should be a part of your child's art education. If you haven't already made classical music a part of your life, begin to listen to music at home or in the car. A great starting point is a set of CDs called *Beethoven's Wig: Sing Along Symphonies*. I have a student who can whistle Mozart's *Nachtmusik* because he and his family listened to these CDs often. *Classical Music for Dummies* also has a CD and a written listening guide. In addition, you can find local symphonies that offer programs for children. The conductor usually explains musical concepts during these performances and helps the students appreciate the music. Seek opportunities to hear symphonies for free in your area, or, if the budget allows, buy season tickets to all the performances for children. As you find classical music you like, add it to your household soundscape and play classical music as background music while your student is doing homework or drawing or doing dishes.

Expose your children to lots of different kinds of music, and expose yourself to new things at the same time. Classical educators do not go to presentations for youth just because they are taking a young person; they go because youth productions done well can edify all of us. To my contemporaries, I may seem too old to go to a children's performance of *Peter and the Wolf* by myself. I go nonetheless, because I want to learn something new, and if the piece of music is too hard, I will not appreciate the art as much. All students enjoy attending live musicals, such as *The Sound of Music, The Lion King*, or *Mary Poppins*, in which the music is an integral part of storytelling and is accompanied by dance and visual arts. If you purchase the soundtrack and listen to the music separately later, you will have the opportunity to ask some focused listening questions at that time. Do not be afraid to introduce dialectic-age students to live opera, either. If you have a reputable company in your area, choose an opera that would appeal to a younger audience and give it a try. Start with light-hearted operas such as *The Barber of Seville, The Mikado*, or *The Pirates of Penzance*, which have funny stories that teens can appreciate. Do not worry if the opera is not performed in English; most now project subtitles, and your middle school students will not even remember afterward that they were reading along.

Listening to the work of great musicians is like studying the work of great painters: it can inspire your children to create their own art. Many classical educators include the

Just as the creative writer needs to learn grammatical rules so that he can decide wisely when to break them, the music student must learn musical forms so that he can choose wisely when to bend or break them in his own music.

playing of an instrument as fundamental to their student's education. They begin with the grammar of individual notes, correct handling of the instrument, correct posture, and counting time. They progress naturally to the dialectic phase of combining notes, handling increasingly complex music, and perhaps learning to play with others in a symphony orchestra or band. During this phase, the student practices the elements over and over until they become natural extensions of himself. Just as the creative writer needs to learn grammatical rules so that he can decide wisely when to break them, the music student must learn musical forms so that he can choose wisely when to bend or break them in his own music.

Students must master their craft so that they can progress to the stage in which they can express themselves through their instrument. This is also the phase where the practice is demanding and difficult; many students are apt to give up. The parents' role is to help the student know that perseverance is its own reward while encouraging the student to continue practicing the art. The practice involved in the dialectic stage of performing music develops the brain like no other activity.

The cost of art instruction should not be a deterrent to a developing musician. As long as there are libraries, and now YouTube, students can learn the craft (or instrument) themselves. I know a young woman who taught herself to draw entirely from library books and is now an accomplished artist and art teacher. I know three brothers who fell in love with Irish music, taught themselves to play traditional Irish instruments, and are now accomplished musicians (and missionaries) in Cork, Ireland. The oldest brother loved music enough to find a violinmaker and ask for a job sweeping the floor. After he proved himself faithful in sweeping the floor, he was allowed to polish the violins. One thing led to another, and the young man became an apprentice. Eventually, he was given the violin shop, and he is now a renowned, world-class violin crafter. His parents never paid for a single lesson. Where there is a will, there is a way. Being a master just begins by being willing to sweep floors.

Participating in artistic endeavors does not have to be a solitary pursuit. Another way to add art to your child's education is to have him participate in physical arts.

Sports offer a dialectic experience similar to the arts. The grammar stage of basketball, for example, includes dribbling, passing, and shooting. The dialectic stage of basketball means coordinating those elements with teammates in order to achieve a goal (literally). Like the artist, the athlete practices many combinations of elements, forming plays until he can execute the plays with precision. If you remember Michael Jordan's precisely timed jump shots, you know that there is an art to basketball. Ballet and other performance dances offer a combination of music and movement across time, demanding expression through a different language. Likewise, theatre combines music, movement, speaking, acting, and visual (stage and costume) design, all arranged in time and space. Encourage your child to join an existing drama club or youth theatre company, or start one of your own with other like-minded families so that you can choose your own performance pieces, suitable for your children's maturity level. The experience of participating in drama usually improves the student's self-confidence, public speaking skills, and memorization skills, which will spill over into many other subjects.

After all, your goal for your child is not to be able to say of him as an adult that he achieved a perfect score on the SAT. A robot could do that.

The inclusion of arts in education does require some additional effort and some time on your part, and you must become comfortable with the knowledge that little or none of the art you study will appear directly on the SAT. But do not be discouraged. Perhaps the fact that it will not be on the test will allow you to enjoy the study of arts with your children. Just keep asking questions about what you see and hear, and enjoy the dialectic discussions the questions initiate. After all, your goal for your child is not to be able to say of him as an adult that he achieved a perfect score on the SAT. A robot could do that. Rather, we want our children to become full, free humans with the ability to rise above the mundane. Studying art with a spirit of curiosity and questioning will go a long way toward achieving that goal.

EPILOGUE

RHETORICAL THOUGHTS ON THE PROCESS OF WRITING A BOOK

In my first book, *Echo in Celebration*, written years ago, I tried to answer the personal questions people across the nation were asking me about our family's journey in home-centered education. The first edition was rough and unedited, but it made people laugh and continues to sell well (in spite of the grammatical errors) because it made people think about their children's education in new ways and with a new sense of possibility. You would think that it would be embarrassing to call yourself a classical educator and then to release a book with so many errors, but I agree with C. S. Lewis, who said that if you wait for things to be perfect, you will never get anything done. I had a couple of young sons to care for at the time, and the book served its purpose.

My next book, *The Core: Teaching Your Child the Foundations of Classical Education*, was published by Palgrave MacMillan and had a team of editors. That book addressed the grammar stage of the trivium, the first of the seven liberal arts. I was much more aware of my audience and purpose as I wrote that book, mostly because I had an excellent editor who kept me on task.

While *The Core* was being produced, my team of writers was working on a collection of my previous writings and many of their own in order to produce a response to the question, "What is a classical education?" The resulting book, *Classical Christian Education Made Approachable*, is a well-written explanation that will help even those who will never homeschool or think about education theory to appreciate a classical, Christian education.

Now you have finished reading *The Question: Teaching Your Child the Essentials of Classical Education*. This book addresses the second of the seven liberal arts, the dialectic.

Questions force a stronger vocabulary, build an arsenal of ideas, and launch us to the next thought. Once again, I worked with a team of classically educated students and parents to write this book. Along the way, we rediscovered that the questions derived in light of the five common topics strengthen a writer's grammatical skills. Questions force a stronger vocabulary, build an arsenal of ideas, and launch us to the next thought.

My next book will be called *The Conversation: Teaching Your Child the Challenges of Classical Education*. It will address the challenge of transforming a young adult into a good rhetorician using the five canons of rhetoric. Rhetoric is the third of the seven liberal arts. Just as we have used the five common topics to provide insight into the questions that make any subject interesting, there are five devices that a wise person considers before communicating.

As I wrote each of these books—alone with *Echo in Celebration* and *The Core* or as a team leader with the books that followed—it became newly obvious to me that writing is thinking on paper. Writing forces us to employ the arts of grammar, dialectic, and rhetoric. In fact, a book is an artifact of one who studies the trivium arts.

DEFINITION

When you write anything—but especially a book—you must first define the audience, the message, and the format. Then, as you write, you must grapple with word choices. For this book, we argued over definitions for the five common topics, not just how they were used historically but also how they have been defined for modern educators. We agreed to stretch the meaning of the common topics so parents would have only five ideas to think about in their dialectical discussion. In some cases, there may have been better words, but a consistent outline has its own rhetorical value. So we re-defined.

I just used the word "argued" and realized that an angry brawl is normally associated with that word. In this case, however, the writing team argued in the sense that we used syllogisms and proofs and historical context as we wrestled with words and ideas. We defined the terms "numbers" versus "numerals" and terms in logic. We frequently asked, "What do you mean when you say . . .?" In each situation, we tried to assess what effect our choices would have on our audience. As we defined words and then argued over them, we were comparing their meanings to one another in order to determine which definition to use and in what context.

COMPARISON

Once we determined our parameters—what we wanted to say—we had to discuss the logical order in which to present our arguments, definitions, stories, and examples. As we compared the format of each chapter, the consistent use of terms, the design of the cover, redundancies, gaps, and practical examples, we had to decide what to keep, what to edit, and what was just perfect. (Recall the notion in the math chapter about some word problems having not enough information to be solved and some problems having too much information. We found the same analytical skills to be necessary in this situation.) We went into the project knowing we would write and rewrite. We compared the rewrites to the originals. As we wrote, we compared literary examples from books, blogs, movies, and songs. Someone would say something, and the comment would make another thought appear, and then someone would say, "Oh, that's a good idea. What chapter should we put it in?" The word "good" inherently implies that a comparison is taking place.

We joked about calling an inset story "Three Easy Steps and One Hard Step," because we knew that "easy" sells better in comparison to "hard." But you will find no such chapter title in this book, because we believe in honesty over salesmanship, which, of course, is another comparison.

RELATIONSHIP

When the writing team first met, I gave everyone an outline with key words to incorporate. But as we wrote, we discovered that some of the initial ideas did not relate very well to certain chapters. Then we would go to the whiteboard to brainstorm. How do you express the ideas specific to each chapter while maintaining the coherent feel of a two-hundred-page book? It is difficult to keep the same theme throughout an essay, let alone a whole book. Did we lose a train of thought? Did we jump in, thinking we had already explained an idea, only to discover that we had talked about it among ourselves, but that no one had owned the idea enough to put it in writing?

Ideas are real things, which are embodied in words and actions. When the first draft was written, we took a four-month break to let the ideas sit and sift on their own. Ideas are real things, which are embodied in words and actions. They need to rest. Words on the page often need a Sabbath, as do the authors. When we finally met again, we could see the book as a whole and knew which chapters needed to be totally rewritten and which could be salvaged.

After defining more terms and making more comparisons to find better examples and more logical explanations, we had to read each paragraph and think about how it related to everything else. Since no one person wrote any chapter, we had to understand what the original author was thinking and then relate our corrections to the thoughts we were keeping. For example, what is the difference between being spontaneous and being serendipitous? Which word relates better to the idea of teachable moments?

The next step involved writing transitions between paragraphs, then sections, then finally between chapters. In each case, we had to consider the needs of our readers, who would not know the logic behind our decisions and would need additional guidance to follow our trains of thought. We needed to reiterate key ideas without being repetitive, particularly for readers who had already finished *The Core*, the first book in the series.

CIRCUMSTANCE

The circumstances surrounding this book's publication also affected our decision-making process. This book is meant to be one of three books. The first book, *The Core*, explains grammar. So, just as grammar provides the content to analyze and weigh against new ideas in the dialectic, thoughts expressed in *The Core* affected ideas in *The*

Question. In addition, we were already looking ahead to the rhetoric stage and to *The Conversation,* imagining how our format and writing methods would translate to this third book of the series.

Another circumstance influencing *The Question* was my decision to self-publish this book. I wanted to be able to honor God more than the previous publisher allowed. I could have gone with a Christian publisher, but since the book was meant to be one of a set of three, I did not want to risk having three publishers telling me what to do. I am thankful to Palgrave MacMillan for publishing the first book and teaching me so much, but I am grateful they turned me down on the contractual first right of refusal, so that I could have more editing control than before. What if the second or even the third publisher wanted the books' covers to look different? Then, the three books would not be much of a set.

Another circumstance to consider was writing conditions. I am too busy to write a whole book alone; I need a team to help. By self-publishing, I can fully acknowledge their efforts, rather than treating them as ghostwriters. Some people may enjoy writing alone, but I do not. I get inspired by other people's ideas. Most of the examples in this book were written as the result of a lot of laughter; however, we did not make the content particularly funny, because this book is not a comedic endeavor. Instead, we tried to make the ideas that engaged us relevant to the book's purpose, rather than to the people seated around the table.

TESTIMONY

Any time you work with multiple authors, you must ask many questions to clarify and weigh competing ideas. As we wrote this book, we also needed to incorporate the testimony of experts in education and authors of literature. We had to come from a place of doubt in our own memories and actually find the resource and check what was said. Again, we argued over definitions and the use of other authors' terms while considering our own authorship. Did they mean what we think they meant? Were we taking their words out of context? How much of an author's text could we use without requiring copyright permission or robbing them of the opportunity to earn from their talents? We wanted to give them full credit for their ideas, so we had to consider how to cite our sources. We also made every effort to verify our quotations—a process made both easier and more difficult in the age of the Internet, when misinformation, as well as information, readily circulates.

The authorities or experts we chose needed to provide appropriate encouragement to our audience of mostly young parents. We tried to select words that would inspire an adult dedicated to love children, while giving examples appropriate for a young teenager. In addition, as homeschoolers, we are naturally skeptical of professional educators. We are amateurs who are trying to teach our children the art of living, rather than the necessity of pleasing others to get ahead. So, we discussed what to glean from which experts and when to defer to others' opinions. A classical education teaches you to hold man's ideas lightly until they have been proven, no matter whence they come. Our ultimate test was to confirm thoughts in light of Scripture, toward the goal of classically educating homeschoolers and families who are doing their best to reflect God's image to a suffering world.

"My Classical Journey with the Magi" by Jen Greenholt

Last year, I had the opportunity to study T. S. Eliot's poem "The Journey of the Magi" (1927) with a high school student whom I was tutoring. My plan was neat, impersonal, and clinical; however, as so often happens when you study great literature, my agenda moved quietly to the backseat when I embarked on my personal journey with the magi.

The first week, we began with the *grammar* of literary analysis. We reviewed the definitions of rhyme and meter, alliteration and consonance, end-stopped lines and enjambment, blank verse and free verse. Then we looked at examples of these literary devices and styles in famous poems by Shakespeare, Keats, and Dickinson. We practiced reading the poems aloud and counting out the number of stressed syllables in each line until my student could tell the difference between iambic pentameter and iambic tetrameter. Then, we turned to Eliot. After a brief discussion of Eliot's background and historical context, I sent my student home with a list of rhetorical techniques that he might find in Eliot's poem.

My student returned for the second week with a printed copy of the poem, which was covered in highlighting and penciled notes. So far, everything was going according to my lesson plan. We began a *dialectic* discussion using questions to generate and organize my student's ideas about the poem.

In the final set of questions, we reached the dreaded "so what?" and for a moment, the rapid-fire responses decelerated. My student had identified major devices in the poem. He knew part of *what* Eliot was doing, but he had yet to figure out *why* or *to what end.* Why write this poem in this particular way? With our discussion hanging from this pivotal point, we reached the end of our second session. For the last few questions, the ones that mattered, I had no answers. We would have to wrestle our way through them together.

The third week, when we met again, the "so what?" question hovered over both of us, but this time, I let him take the lead; he had done the groundwork, and now I was the student as much as he was.

At first, our conversation circled around the concepts of birth and death, gentle and sharp alliterative sounds, unity and fragmentation. Then, ever so slowly, his thoughts began to catch fire, igniting his words. Here was a familiar story, the Christmas story, that modernists might find increasingly difficult to believe in light of the horrors of war experienced by the world. What could a baby's birth possibly offer to a world ravaged by poisoned gas and exploding planes? That tension between softness and harshness, beauty and ugliness, was everywhere in Eliot's poem.

But, my student mused, what if a seeming contradiction were the solution as well as the problem? He focused on one line of the poem: the magi had "seen birth and death, / But had thought they were different." How could birth and death be the same thing?

I did not have a list of questions to guide this discussion. All I could do was to ask questions such as, "What do you mean by that?" or "Can you unpack that idea?" or "Can you clarify that point?" These questions enabled him to think through a tough idea and formulate a tentative response.

This birth carried in it the promise of a death that would change everything, and the magi instinctively knew it. Faced with the reality of the Savior's birth, the magi understood that their comfortable world could never be the same, nor would they want it to. "I should be glad of another death," the narrator concludes—a death to self, a death of the old ways of life, a death that destroyed the divide between God and man. Christ's birth could not be separated from His death, and that tension, so eloquently expressed in Eliot's poem, was precisely what allowed the Christmas story to speak to a hurting world.

When my student paused for breath and looked to me for feedback, I was silent, still mesmerized by the journey we had just taken. There is nothing quite like the experience of sitting across from a young rhetorician. It is like teaching a camper how to build a fire: gathering kindling alongside him, training him to arrange it in an orderly fashion, and then handing him tinder and a flint, all the while moving gradually from an active to a passive role, until finally it is your turn to be warmed by his fire.

Thanks to my student's hard work, the resulting blaze was magnificent indeed.

HOMESCHOOLING THROUGH HIGH SCHOOL

Now that so many students are homeschooled through middle school, parents are considering homeschooling at the high school level. And when the parents are not, often the students are. More high school students are requesting to be homeschooled. Many young adults are making YouTube videos on why they dropped out to homeschool themselves since their parents were not interested. Online global education is changing the academic paradigm for everyone, and in some cases, students notice the advantages of self-education before their parents do.

Even though homeschooled students have been successfully attending college and raising families for twenty years, many parents question the feasibility of homeschooling through high school. Even though I espouse a very hands-on form of parent-student academics, I realize that high school subjects can seem daunting. I would challenge that fear by asking more questions: Didn't you go through high school? So now you want your children to go through high school and not be able to teach their children in twenty years just like you have? When will someone break that cycle for your family? Is learning a lifelong endeavor requiring discipleship and conversations or questions, or is it something we can knock off a checklist of credits?

Lots of parents tell me their students don't want to be home for high school. Do the students have a good reason? As a parent, have you made them feel like an inconvenience? Are you not your child's hero? Is there a reason your children don't want to be with you? Are you tired of parenting and want someone else to do it? Have you told them the world is their classroom and then made them sit at a desk and call it school? I think it is unnatural for a young adult to want to sit in a building all day. I don't know why a student would want to be so limited just when she is mature enough to really explore the world. Is the reason, perhaps, that she doesn't get to do real things with people that share her interests?

Homeschooling high school students becomes a partnership as your student transitions from being your child to becoming your brother or sister in Christ. In course requirements as well as in personal choices, he should do more on his own, relying on his parents only for wisdom and direction. Even more important, parents should be training the young adult to serve others instead of himself. I don't have my children study math because they need it (although they do); I have them study math because the community needs to know the truth about God's creation. Their curriculum has some personal choices, but I need to direct them in God's purposeful choices.

Homeschooling high school students becomes a partnership as your student transitions from being your child to becoming your brother or sister in Christ.

I have now graduated three sons from Classical Conversations. For my first two, it was a typical graduation from high school and a commencement into college. Our third son is eager to go to college some day, but just not yet. For now, he is still pursuing his academic interests from home. He has earned his scuba certification and is working on his pilot's license as he considers how to pay for his love of being forty feet underwater or four thousand feet in the air. He is well grounded in politics, history, and classical literature from being in Classical Conversations for twelve years. He wants to strengthen his theoretical mathematical skills, so he will participate in the Mandala Fellowship, a quadrivium program, for a year. He has spent the spring building an addition onto our house with his older brother, learning about business finances with his parents, and combatting "senioritis" as he says goodbye to childhood friends. He plays rugby and shoots guns and plays video games. He is spending May in Alaska, where he will help build a friend's house and will work on plane repairs in exchange for flying lessons. He told me yesterday that he is going to keep working on his *Aeneid* translation, even though high school is over, because he feels like he should conquer the task he started. He likes to learn and seeks out his own teachers, who include his older brothers, parents, and church members as well as peers. He surrounds himself with interesting people.

Classical Conversations is a great academic compromise between staying accountable to a community of students interested in academics and having the time to pursue personal interests and service work. One day a week, a tutor works alongside the parent to provide academic accountability while developing a community of learners for the student. William's tutor took his class to Washington, DC; another parent took them camping; and another parent took them to Carowinds Amusement Park. My boys attended Protocol, a formal spring concert, with a program in another state. A set of parents put together a beautiful graduation ceremony for the local Challenge IV (high school senior) students. Another parent made sure the students went to Teen Pact and that driver's education was made available to the students. They went to concerts, parties, and movies together. Since Classical Conversations meets only once a week, older students have time to work, hire other expert tutors as needed, and delve into different subjects. I had one student work on physical science with my Challenge I (high school freshman) class and also complete a course in marine biology on his own. His marine studies added greatly to our physical science studies because he studied both sciences and led the other students in additional conversations, demonstrating the integration of subjects. And of course, they all come to my house to swim at the lake. Two students from William's program took additional classes each week to strengthen skills hindered by some severe learning disabilities. Two students worked part-time throughout the year in the service industry. A few of our students went to Germany together for ten days. These students like homeschooling because the world really is their classroom.

If you can catch the vision that high school students can contribute to their community while engaging in rigorous classical academics, you will love homeschooling through high school. If you make this commitment, I encourage you to continue the practice of asking questions as you dig deeper into the skills of presenting answers in the rhetoric stage.

ON TOWARD THE RHETORICAL ARTS

The fundamental skills practiced in the high school years in a classical education are the rhetorical arts. All accomplished leaders possess these arts. Just as we have seen how dialectical analysis strengthens grammatical knowledge, in my next book we will investigate the way rhetorical wisdom strengthens both the grammatical and dialectic arts. The study of rhetoric is traditionally divided into five parts, also known as *canons* (only one "n," unlike the cannons of the American Revolution!). The five canons of rhetoric are as follows:

- Invention (*inventio*)

  Some disputes revolve around matters of fact, like a police officer informing you of the speed limit. Others require invention in order to persuade someone of your point of view. Rational appeal (*logos*), emotional appeal (*pathos*), and ethical appeal (*ethos*) are three aspects of invention that we will cover. I believe that *logos* often applies to our thoughts, *pathos* to the person we are trying to reach, and *ethos* to the balance between *logos* and *pathos*, on one hand, and truth, on the other.

- Arrangement (*dispositio*)

  We will discuss the traditional forms of arranging an essay, speech, or presentation, including introduction, statement of fact, confirmation, refutation, and conclusion.

- Style (*elocutio*)

  We will discuss the appropriate use of language for specific forms of communication as we persuade others to accept our point of view.

- Memory (*memoria*)

  Once ideas have been invented, arranged, and elocuted, they need to be practiced and incorporated into the speaker's memory, whenever possible, so they can be used at the right time and so that the listener, rather than the speaker's notes, is the focal point.

- Delivery (*pronuntiatio*)

  Will we write a speech, poem, song, essay, lab report, mathematical proof, symphony, or dance? Where will we deliver the argument? How will the form of delivery structure the words we choose?

In *The Conversation*, I will define these terms within the context of each of the major academic subjects as well as offer a more thorough discussion about the integration of subjects. After all, conversations are where we practice the integration of our ideas. They are the test in which we discover errors in logic, the need for clearer definitions, and the joy of a well-received idea. Conversations are places to wrestle with ideas before we put them down on paper or in another permanent form.

Just as it has taken modern classical educators thirty years to recover the lost tools of the trivium while educating young children, I expect that it will take a while to recover the lost arts of learning for our older students. It is difficult to be a pioneer in most things. I am challenging you to not only homeschool but also to develop a fully Christian and classical mode of education. As Mr. Tumnus urged the Pevensie children in *The Last Battle*, "Further up and further in." Will you join me?

APPENDIX ONE
MODEL QUESTIONS

I have said it before, but it bears repeating: this is not a checklist. Because every child learns at a different speed, and because dialectical thinking takes time to master, your younger children may not be able to ask questions related to all five common topics right away. At first, they might just ask questions of definition. Later, as they become more comfortable with definition, they might focus on comparison. Even after they master all five topics, they may not apply all of them to every situation.

BASIC QUESTIONS

Start with whatever you can draw from your child's existing knowledge. Ask:
- What do you know?
- How do you know it?
- What do you not know?
- How can you find out?

DEFINITION

- What is _____?
- What is _____ not?
- Is this _____ a _____?
- To what group does _____ belong?
- How can _____ be broken down into parts?
- What are the essential qualities of _____?
- What are the characteristics of _____?
- What are the stages of _____?

COMPARISON

- How is _____ similar to _____?
- How is _____ different from _____? (Term A from B?)
- How is _____ different from _____? (Term B from A?)
- To what degree is _____ similar to/different from _____?
- How are _____ and _____ both similar to/different from _____?
- Is _____ better/worse than _____?
- Is a _____ more or less _____ than _____?

RELATIONSHIP

- Did _____ cause _____?
- What will happen if _____?
- If _____ is true, what cannot be true?
- Are _____ and _____ mutually exclusive, or can they coexist?

CIRCUMSTANCE

- Is it possible or impossible to _____?
- What might prevent us from _____?
- Do we know for sure that _____?
- If we _____, can we be certain that _____?
- What else is going on at the same time?

TESTIMONY

- On what type of testimony does this argument rely?
- What types of testimony are available on this topic? What are they?
- Should a _____ be considered an authority?
- What are this authority's biases? Do they invalidate his testimony?
- What does this testimony assume about the world? Is the assumption valid?
- How were these statistics gathered? Who gathered them?
- How recent are these statistics? How many cases were included?
- Should we trust majority opinion about _____?
- Do we know for sure that _____ is true?
- Is this example universally true, or are there counter-examples?

Now, using this list as a model, create your own questions, and let the conversation begin!

APPENDIX TWO
RESOURCES

CHAPTER ONE: WHY WE STILL NEED CLASSICAL EDUCATION

Bortins, Leigh. *The Core: Teaching your Child the Foundations of Classical Education.* New York: Palgrave, 2010.

Capon, Robert Farrar. *The Supper of the Lamb: A Culinary Reflection.* New York: Macmillan, 1989.

Chesterton, G. K. *Orthodoxy.* Chicago: Moody Publishers, 2009.

Classical Christian Education Made Approachable. West End, NC: Classical Conversations MultiMedia, 2011.

Garelick, Barry. "An A-Maze-ing Approach to Math: A Mathematician with a Child Learns Some Politics." *Education Next* 5.2 (spring 2005): 29–36.

Sayers, Dorothy. "The Lost Tools of Learning." Lecture. Oxford University, 1947.

Wilson, Douglas J., and N.D. Wilson. *The Rhetoric Companion: A Student's Guide to Power in Persuasion.* Moscow, ID: Canon Press, 2011.

CHAPTER TWO: HOW THE DIALECTIC TEACHES FAMILIES TO WRESTLE

Aristotle. *Rhetoric.* [c. 350 BC] Trans. W. Rhys Roberts. 2nd ed. Oxford, UK: Oxford UP, 1954. Web. Accessed 07/09/12 from http://classics.mit.edu/Aristotle/rhetoric.html.

Austen, Jane. *Pride and Prejudice.* New York: Dover Publications, Inc., 1995.

Bortins, Leigh. *The Core: Teaching Your Child the Foundations of Classical Education.* New York: Palgrave, 2010.

Chaucer, Geoffrey. *Selected Canterbury Tales.* New York: Dover Publications, Inc., 1994.

Cicero, Marcus Tullius. *The Academic Questions, Treatise De Finibus, and Tusculan Disputations.* Trans. C.D. Yonge. London: George Bell & Sons, 1875. Project Gutenberg. Web. Accessed 07/13/12 from http://www.gutenberg.org/files/29247/29247-h/29247-h.html.

---. *Topics.* Trans. C.D. Yonge. Web. Accessed 07/13/12 from http://www.classicpersuasion.org/pw/cicero/cicero-topics.htm.

Classical Christian Education Made Approachable. West End, NC: Classical Conversations MultiMedia, 2011.

Dill, Bert. "Rhetoric from a Classical Perspective." El Cajon, CA: Grossmont-Cuyamaca Community College, 2011. Web. Accessed 07/09/12 from http://www.grossmont.edu/bertdill/rhet/Rhetoric.pdf.

Elder, Linda, and Richard Paul. *The Miniature Guide to the Art of Asking Essential Questions.* Tomales, CA: The Foundation for Critical Thinking, 2004.

Hiller, Mark. "A Brief Summary of Classical Rhetoric." Harvard Rhetorical Society. Web. Accessed 07/09/12 from www.hcs.harvard.edu/~rhetoric/summary.doc.

---. "The Reference Guide to Classical Rhetoric." Harvard Rhetorical Society. Web. Accessed 07/09/12 from http://www.hcs.harvard.edu/~rhetoric/reference.doc.

John of Salisbury. *The Metalogicon of John of Salisbury: A Twelfth-Century Defense of the Verbal and Logical Arts of the Trivium.* Trans. Daniel D. McGarry. Berkeley: U. of California Press, 1955.

Miller, Carolyn R. "Aristotle's 'Special Topics' in Rhetorical Practice and Pedagogy." *Rhetoric Society Quarterly* 17 (Winter 1987): 61–70.

Plato. *Meno* [c. 380 BC]. Trans. Benjamin Jowett. Project Gutenberg. Web. Accessed 07/09/12 from http://www.gutenberg.org/files/1643/1643-h/1643-h.htm.

---. *The Republic* [c. 360 BC]. Trans. Benjamin Jowett. Project Gutenberg. Web. Accessed 07/13/12 from http://www.gutenberg.org/files/1497/1497-h/1497-h.htm.

Potok, Chaim. *The Chosen.* New York: Random House, 1967.

Thoreau, Henry David. "Walking" [1862]. Project Gutenberg. Web. Accessed 07/10/12 from http://www.gutenberg.org/files/1022/1022-h/1022-h.htm.

Wilson, Douglas. *Recovering the Lost Tools of Learning: An Approach to Distinctively Christian Education.* Wheaton, IL: Crossway Books, 1991.

CHAPTER THREE: FREQUENTLY ASKED QUESTIONS

Aristotle. *Nichomachean Ethics.* 2nd ed. Trans. Terence Irwin. Indianapolis, IN: Hackett Publishing, 1999.

Gatto, John Taylor. *Dumbing Us Down: The Hidden Curriculum of Compulsory Schooling.* 10th anniversary ed. Gabriola Island, B.C.: New Society Publishing, 2005.

Simmons, Tracy Lee. *Climbing Parnassus: A New Apologia for Greek and Latin.* Wilmington, DE: Intercollegiate Studies Institute, 2002.

CHAPTER FOUR: READING

Bortins, Leigh. *The Core: Teaching Your Child the Foundations of Classical Education.* New York: Palgrave, 2010.

Greenholt, Jen. *Words Aptly Spoken: Children's Literature.* 2nd ed. West End, NC: Classical Conversations MultiMedia, 2010.

---. *Words Aptly Spoken: Short Stories.* 2nd ed. West End, NC: Classical Conversations MultiMedia, 2010.

Veith, Gene Edward, Jr. *Reading Between the Lines: A Christian Guide to Literature.* Wheaton, IL: Crossway Books, 1990.

Great Books for Junior High Students

Alcott, Louisa May. *Good Wives.* New York: Puffin Books, 1995.

---. *Jo's Boys.* New York: Bantam Classics, 1995.

---. *Little Men.* New York: Signet Classics, 2012.

---. *Little Women.* New York: Signet Classics, 2012.

Angeli, Marguerite de. *The Door in the Wall.* New York: Bantam Doubleday Dell Books for Young Readers, 1990.

Avi. *Crispin: The Cross of Lead.* New York: Hyperion Books, 2004.

Blos, Joan W. *A Gathering of Days: A New England Girl's Journal,* 1830–32. 2nd ed. New York: Aladdin Books, 1990.

Burnett, Frances Hodgson. *The Secret Garden.* Illustr. Tasha Tudor. New York: HarperCollins, 1962.

Fitzgerald, John D. *The Great Brain* series (8 vols.). Illustr. Mercer Mayer. New York: Puffin Books, 2004.

Juster, Norton. *The Phantom Tollbooth.* 35th Anniversary Edition. Illustr. Jules Feiffer. New York: Random House, 1996.

Latham, Jean Lee. *Carry On, Mr. Bowditch.* Illustr. John O'Hara Cosgrave, II. New York: Houghton Mifflin, 1955.

L'Engle, Madeleine. *The Austin Family Chronicles* (5 vols.). Reprint ed. New York: Square Fish, 2008.

---*The Time Quintet* series (5 vols.). Reprint ed. New York: Square Fish, 2007.

Lewis, C. S. *The Chronicles of Narnia.* Illustr. Pauline Baynes. New York: HarperCollins, 2001.

Lowry, Lois. *Number the Stars.* New York: Bantam Doubleday, 1989.

Montgomery, L. M. *Anne of Green Gables* series (8 vols.). Reprint ed. London: Starfire, 1998.

Moody, Ralph. *Little Britches* series (8 vols.) Lincoln, NE: Bison Books, 1991–1994.

Rawls, Wilson. *Where the Red Fern Grows*. New York: Dell Laurel-Leaf, 1989.

Speare, Elizabeth George. *The Bronze Bow*. New York: Houghton Mifflin, 1989.

Ten Boom, Corrie, John Sherrill, and Elizabeth Sherrill. *The Hiding Place*. Minneapolis, MN: World Wide Publications, 1971.

Tolkien, J. R. R. *The Hobbit*. Boston: Houghton Mifflin, 1997.

---. *The Lord of the Rings* trilogy (3 vols.). Boston: Houghton Mifflin, 1993.

Yates, Elizabeth. *Amos Fortune, Free Man*. Illustr. Nora S. Unwin. New York: Puffin Books, 1989.

CHAPTER FIVE: WRITING

Bain, Joseph. *What the Best College Teachers Do*. Cambridge, MA: Harvard University Press, 2004.

Bortins, Leigh. *The Essentials of the English Language*. 4th ed. West End: Classical Conversations MultiMedia, 2010.

Corbett, Edward P. J., and Robert J. Connors. *Classical Rhetoric for the Modern Student*. 4th ed. New York: Oxford UP, 1998.

Crider, Scott F. *The Office of Assertion: An Art of Rhetoric for Academic Essay*. Wilmington, DE: Intercollegiate Studies Institute, 2005.

Fish, Stanley. *How to Write a Sentence: And How to Read One*. New York: HarperCollins, 2011.

Foucachon, Daniel, dir. *Grammar of Poetry* (4-disc set). Feat. Matt Whitling. Moscow, ID: Roman Roads Media, 2012.

Hicks, David. *Norms & Nobility: A Treatise on Education*. New York: Praeger Publishing, 1981.

Kern, Andrew. *The Lost Tools of Writing*. 3rd ed. Concord, NC: CiRCE Institute, 2007.

Littlejohn, Robert, and Charles T. Evans. *Wisdom & Eloquence*. 4th ed. Wheaton, IL: Crossway, 2010.

Payne, Lucile Vaughan. *The Lively Art of Writing*. New York: New American Library, 1969.

Pudewa, Andrew. *Teaching Writing: Structure & Style*. Locust Grove, OK: The Institute for Excellence in Writing, n.d.

Rhodes, Suzanne. *The Roar on the Other Side: A Guide for Student Poets*. Moscow, ID: Canon Press, 2000.

Simmons, Tracy Lee. *Climbing Parnassus: A New Apologia for Greek and Latin*. Wilmington, DE: Intercollegiate Studies Institute, 2002.

Strunk, William, and E. B. White. *The Elements of Style*. 4th ed. London: Longman, 1999.

Truss, Lynne. *Eats, Shoots & Leaves: Why, Commas Really Do Make a Difference!* New York: Putnam, 2006.

Tyre, Peg. "The Writing Revolution." *The Atlantic Magazine.* Online edition. October 2012. Accessed from http://www.theatlantic.com/magazine/toc/2012/10.

Williams, Joseph M. *Style: Ten Lessons in Clarity and Grace.* 7th ed. London: Longman, 2002.

CHAPTER SIX: MATH

Bortins, Leigh. *The Core: Teaching Your Child the Foundations of Classical Education.* New York: Palgrave, 2010.

Corbett, Edward P. J., and Robert J. Connors. *Classical Rhetoric for the Modern Student.* 4th ed. New York: Oxford UP, 1998.

Crider, Scott F. *The Office of Assertion: An Art Of Rhetoric For Academic Essay.* Wilmington, DE: Intercollegiate Studies Institute, 2005.

Crilly, A. J. *50 Mathematical Ideas You Really Need to Know.* London: Quercus, 2008.

Galilei, Galileo. *The Assayer.* [1623, *Il Saggiatore*] Discoveries and Opinions of Galileo. Trans. Stillman Drake. New York: Doubleday, 1957.

Kern, Andrew. *The Lost Tools of Writing*, Level 1. 4th ed. Concord, NC: The CiRCE Institute, 2007.

Leonard, George. *Primary Arithmetic for Children.* 2nd ed. Boston: Otis, Broaders, and Co., 1843.

Pappas, Theoni. *The Joy of Mathematics: Discovering Mathematics All Around You.* 2nd ed. San Carlos, CA: Wide World Publishing/Tetra, 1993.

CHAPTER SEVEN: GEOGRAPHY AND CURRENT EVENTS

Aristotle. *Politics: A Treatise on Government* [c. 350 BC]. Trans. William Ellis. London: J. M. Dent, 1912. Project Gutenberg. Web. Accessed 07/13/12 from http://www.gutenberg.org/files/6762/6762-h/6762-h.htm.

Bortins, Leigh. *The Core: Teaching Your Child the Foundations of Classical Education.* New York: Palgrave, 2010.

Classical Christian Education Made Approachable. West End, NC: Classical Conversations MultiMedia, 2011.

DK Compact Atlas of the World. 5th ed. New York: DK Publishing, 2012.

Esolen, Anthony. *Ten Ways to Destroy the Imagination of Your Child.* Wilmington, DE: Intercollegiate Studies Institute, 2010.

Hicks, David. *Norms & Nobility: A Treatise on Education*. New York: Praeger Publishing, 1981.

Plato. *The Republic* [c. 360 BC]. Trans. Benjamin Jowett. Project Gutenberg. Web. Accessed 07/13/12 from http://www.gutenberg.org/files/1497/1497-h/1497-h.htm.

Richter, Sara J. *The Oklahoma Panhandle*. Mount Pleasant, SC: Arcadia Publishing, 2011.

Shakespeare, William. *Henry V*. Dover Thrift Edition. Mineola, NY: Dover Publications, 2003.

---. *Julius Caesar*. Dover Thrift Edition. Mineola, NY: Dover Publications, 1991.

Tolkien, J. R. R. *The Hobbit*. Boston: Houghton Mifflin, 1997.

CHAPTER EIGHT: LOGIC

Bortins, Leigh. *Tour Guide: Logic* (DVD, CD). West End, NC: Classical Conversations MultiMedia, 2011.

Cothran, Martin. *Traditional Logic I: Introduction to Formal Logic*. Louisville, KY: Memoria Press, 2000.

Kreeft, Peter, and Trent Dougherty. *Socratic Logic*. 3.1 ed. South Bend, IN: St. Augustine's Press, 2010.

Lee, Harper. *To Kill a Mockingbird*. New York: Warner Books, 1982.

Nance, James B., and Douglas J. Wilson. *Introductory Logic*. 4th ed. Moscow, ID: Canon Press, 2006.

Parsons, Terence. "The Traditional Square of Opposition." *The Stanford Encyclopedia of Philosophy* (Fall 2012 Edition). Ed. Edward N. Zalta. <http://plato.stanford.edu/archives/fall2012/entries/square/>.

Quintilian. *The Institutio Oratoria of Quintilian*. Trans. H. E. Butler. Cambridge, MA: Harvard University Press, 1980.

CHAPTER NINE: HISTORY

The Declaration of Independence
The Anti-Federalist Papers
The Federalist Papers
The U.S. Constitution
Bortins, Leigh. *The Core: Teaching Your Child the Foundations of Classical Education*. New York: Palgrave, 2010.
Classical Christian Education Made Approachable. West End, NC: Classical Conversations MultiMedia, 2011.

Esolen, Anthony. *Ten Ways to Destroy the Imagination of Your Child*. Wilmington, DE: Intercollegiate Studies Institute, 2010.

Guroian, Vigen. *Rallying the Really Human Things: Moral Imagination in Politics, Literature, and Everyday Life*. Wilmington, DE: Intercollegiate Studies Institute, 2005.

Hicks, David. *Norms & Nobility: A Treatise on Education*. New York: Praeger Publishers, 1981.

Homer. *The Iliad*. Tran. Robert Fagles. New York: Viking Press, 1990.

Moes, Garry J., and Eric Bristley. *Streams of Civilization. Vol. 2: Cultures in Conflict Since the Reformation*. 2nd ed. Peabody, MA: Christian Liberty Press, 1995.

Peacock, Anthony A. *How to Read The Federalist Papers*. Washington, DC: The Heritage Foundation, 2010.

Schweikart, Larry, and Michael Allen. *A Patriot's History to the United States: From Columbus's Great Discovery to the War on Terror*. New York: Penguin, 2004.

Stanton, Mary, Michael McHugh, and Albert Hyma. *Streams of Civilization. Vol. 1: Earliest Times to the Discovery of the New World*. 2nd ed. Peabody, MA: Christian Liberty Press, 1992.

Virgil. *The Aeneid*. Trans. Robert Fitzgerald. New York: Vintage/Anchor, 1990.

Wise Bauer, Susan. *The Story of the World*. 4 vols. Charles City, VA: Peace Hill Press, 2003–2007.

CHAPTER TEN: SCIENCE

Boorstin, Daniel J. *The Discoverers*. New York: Random House, 1983.

Discovering Atomos: A Grammatical Introduction to Atomic Processes in Chemistry. 2nd ed. West End: Classical Conversations MultiMedia, 2011.

DiStasio, Joan. *Biology, Grades 9–12. The 100+ Series*. Greensboro, NC: Carson-Dellosa Publishing, 1999.

"The Hammer and the Feather." Apollo 15 Lunar Surface Journal. Trans. Eric M. Jones. http://history.nasa.gov, 1996.

Latham, Jean Lee. *Carry On, Mr. Bowditch*. Illustr. John O'Hara Cosgrave, II. New York: Houghton Mifflin, 1955.

Lee, Laura. *Blame It on the Rain: How the Weather Has Changed History*. New York: HarperCollins, 2006.

Leonardo da Vinci. *The Da Vinci Notebooks*. New York: Profile Books, 2005.

Mays, John D. *Teaching Science so that Students Learn Science: A Paradigm for Christian Schools*. Austin, TX: Novare Science and Math, 2010.

Pearcey, Nancy R., and Charles B. Thaxton. *The Soul of Science: Christian Faith and Natural Philosophy*. Wheaton, IL: Crossway Books, 1994.

Tiner, John Hudson. *Exploring Planet Earth: The Journey of Discovery from Early Civilization to Future Exploration.* Green Forest, AZ: Master Books, 1997.

CHAPTER ELEVEN: FINE ARTS

Casey, William C. *Masterpieces in Art.* Ed. Michael J. McHugh. Arlington Heights, IL: Christian Liberty Press, 1992.

Dickins, Rosie, and Mari Griffith. *The Usborne Introduction to Art: Internet-Linked.* New York: Scholastic, 2005.

Dondis, Donis A. *A Primer of Visual Literacy.* Boston: MIT, 1973.

Leonardo da Vinci. *A Treatise of Painting.* Trans. J. Senex. London: Senex and Taylor, 1721. Accessed 01/11/13 from http://www.treatiseonpainting.org.

Maude, Aylmer. *Tolstoy on Art.* London: Oxford UP, 1902. Open Library. Web. Accessed 07/13/12 from http://www.archive.org/stream/tolstoyonart00tolsuoft.

Myers, Kenneth A. *All God's Children and Blue Suede Shoes: Christians and Popular Culture.* Wheaton, IL: Crossway Books, 1989.

Pearcey, Nancy. *Saving Leonardo: A Call to Resist the Secular Assault on Mind, Morals, & Meaning.* Nashville, B&H Publishing, 2010.

Perlmutter, Richard. *Beethoven's Wig: Sing Along Symphonies* (CD). Burlington, MA: Rounder Records, 2002.

Pogue, David, and Scott Speck. *Classical Music for Dummies.* Hoboken, NJ: John Wiley & Sons, 1997.

PreScripts. (All vols.) West End: Classical Conversations MultiMedia, 2013.

Strickland, Carol. *The Annotated Mona Lisa.* 2nd ed. Riverside, NJ: Andrews McMeel, 2007.

"TED Talks: Ideas Worth Spreading." Technology, Entertainment, Design. http://www.ted.com/pages/about.

Veith, Gene Edward, Jr. *State of the Arts: From Bezalel to Mapplethorpe.* Wheaton, IL: Crossway Books, 1991.

Zander, Benjamin. "Benjamin Zander on music and passion." TED Talks. February 2008. Web. Accessed 07/13/12 from http://www.ted.com/talks/lang/en/benjamin_zander_on_music_and_passion.html.

EPILOGUE: RHETORICAL THOUGHTS ON THE PROCESS OF WRITING A BOOK

Eliot, T. S. "The Journey of the Magi." *Selected Poems.* New York: Houghton Mifflin Harcourt, 1964. Print. 97-98.

Lewis, C. S. *The Last Battle.* New York: HarperCollins, 2000. Print.

INDEX

repetition 7, 9, 84, 119, 143, 165, 182
report card(s) 47, 56
Republic, The 20, 21–23, 24. *See also* Plato
rhetoric
  five canons of 192, **200**–201
  in classical education **12**–14
Rivendell Sanctuary 56
Robinson Crusoe 66
rote memorization. *See* memorization

Sanford, Courtney
  "Brainstorming" 80–81
  "Contrast in Art" 181
  "The 'Who-What-How-What'" 68–69
Santayana, George 143
SAT (Standardized Achievement Test) 189
Sayers, Dorothy 8, 93
  "The Lost Tools of Learning" 19, 25, 33–34
Scarlet Letter, The 81
science. *See also* physics
  anatomy 14
  astronomy 6
  biology 139, 165, 200
  earth 45, 125, 162, 166, 168
  engineering 50, 178
  experiment(s) 24, 28, 32, 46, 140, 162, 163, 168, 173
  hypothesis / hypotheses 168, 169, 171, 174
Scott, Commander David 161–162, 173
Secret Garden, The 65
self-control 38
self-esteem 10
Seneca Falls Declaration 136
sentence structure 54, 136
Shakespeare, William 84
  Hamlet 183
  Henry V 123
  Julius Caesar 123
"should" questions 83, 120
similarity. *See also* common topics, five
  as category of comparison 29, 73
simile **85**

Simmons, Tracy Lee
  Climbing Parnassus 20, 35, 91
Sinclair, Upton
  The Jungle 74
social media 121
social networking 61
social skills 51
Society for Classical Learning 53
Socrates 78, 91
  dialogues 20–27
  logic 130
  Plato
    Meno 17, 25, 28–32
    Socratic method 20, 25, 26, 113
    The Republic 20–27
Socratic method **20**, 25, 26, 113
Something Beautiful for God 66
soul 17, 27, 37, 47, 99, 159, 162
sources
  authority of 44–49, 88, 150–151
specialization 12
species. *See also* common topics, five
  as category of definition **28**, 131, 164
spirit of inquiry 40, 124–126, 151, 157, 159, 173
square of opposition **133**–136
standardized testing. *See* testing
statistics. *See also* common topics, five
  as category of testimony **32**, 88, 121, 151
"stick in the sand" 49
Stowe, Harriet Beecher
  Uncle Tom's Cabin 74
style
  in artwork 183, 185
  of music 182
  of writing 79, 84, 85, 87, 89, 90, 196
style (elocution) **201**. *See also* canons of rhetoric, five
subaltern statements 135
subcontrary statements 135
Supper of the Lamb, The 9, 36
supplement **100**. *See also* math: geometry
syllogism(s) 128, **130**, 141, 193